GNVQ Core Skills Level 3

Information Technology

Core text

David Turner

STANLEY
THORNES

Contents

Introduction

This book has been written to cover the 1995 specification of the Information Technology Core Skills up to Level 3 from NCVQ. These skills may be used as part of a GNVQ programme at Intermediate or Advanced level, an 'A' level programme, or an NVQ-based Modern Apprenticeship. In each case, the Core Skills in Information Technology are best developed in the vocational context of the main programme, if possible.

The book can be used for students as part of an IT course, or for self-directed study. The comprehensive coverage of the IT concepts is supported by over 70 graded exercises and 25 assignments. These provide plenty of opportunities for students to collect evidence of competence in their IT skills. The Unit can also be accredited as a stand-alone unit by City and Guilds of London Institute, for those who simply want an IT qualification.

Students

This book has been written to help you become competent users of information technology and help you apply it to the other subjects you are studying. Whatever career you undertake, it is likely that in future you will be expected to be able to use a computer to undertake a variety of tasks.

This book aims to give you the following skills:
- An understanding of the language of information technology
- Knowledge of how to undertake basic tasks
- The ability to decide which is the best way to tackle a problem
- The ability to choose the most appropriate type of computer software in a given situation
- Knowledge of how to use IT facilities safely

You are expected, as part of your studies, to demonstrate that you have acquired skills in IT by collecting suitable evidence in a portfolio. This evidence may be collected as part of projects or assignments which also provide evidence for other parts of your course. For example, if you do an assignment on the cash flow in a business you may use a spreadsheet and demonstrate skills in IT at the same time. This will be the usual way to collect most of the evidence for the Core Skills.

You can also use other evidence to demonstrate your skills. By undertaking some of the exercises and assignments in this book you can also show that you have acquired IT skills. A cross-reference chart has been provided for you to show which exercises and assignments can provide evidence for each part of the range of the Core Skills units. The Performance Criteria that can be demonstrated are also listed with each assignment.

How to use this book

You can work through this book at your own pace. Study the first two chapters first, because they provide the background to much of what follows. After that the order is not important, although it is best to study the introductory chapters before the advanced ones. If you wish to study databases before word processing, start at Chapter 5. As you come to each Progress Check, try to answer the questions honestly to find out how much you have learned.

Each chapter contains a series of exercises. These are short tasks to help you develop the basic skills in operating whatever type of software you have available. Work through these until you feel confident in using your software. Your teacher or lecturer may also provide additional exercises to help you.

When you are reasonably confident with the software, try the assignments in each chapter. These will take longer to complete, but will give you the opportunity to provide evidence to add to your portfolio if you wish. The cross-reference chart in Appendix C shows which assignments can provide evidence for each element of the Core Skills unit.

Collecting evidence for your portfolio to cover the IT core skills requirements

Many of the assignments, projects and other activities you have undertaken during your GNVQ programme will have contributed evidence to meet the requirements of the Core Skills units. However, additional evidence may also be provided by undertaking the exercises and assignments in this book.

If you need to find evidence for a particular Performance Criterion or Element, first check the exact requirements in the GNVQ Units (Appendix B). These give the description of the Range for each of the PCs. Then, when you understand the requirements of the Unit, look at the chart to find out which Assignment could be used to provide the evidence. Make sure when you do the assignment that you cover the requirements of the PC by adding your own interpretation to the assignment if necessary. For example, you may wish to 'explain the reasons for using IT' to cover Element 3.4, PC 1 in an assignment which asks for a 'comment on the work you have completed'.

Additional evidence may be gathered by completing the exercises in each chapter, although these have not specifically been mapped.

Teachers and lecturers

The Core Skills units in a GNVQ are far more complex than the introductory IT courses of a few years ago. They demand an understanding of the use and application of IT skills to many different aspects of business and commerce. Ideally, students need to gain the basic skills early in a course so that they can use them with increasing confidence throughout their programme. It is important that students know more than which keys to press on a keyboard.

Unfortunately, many students have little time to acquire such skills in a formal IT course, and they have to be left to study on their own once the basics have been taught. This book can be used as both a source of background information in a formal IT course and for further directed study.

Different students will use different software packages for their training. As software changes, the student may need to learn to use new systems. This emphasises the importance of learning transferable skills.

How to use this book

As part of an IT course, the book can be used as a normal textbook to provide background information and avoid the need to issue notes. The exercises are not software specific, so they can be used with whatever software package you wish to use. They will, however, need to be supplemented with instructions specific for each type of software. If a Windows operating system is being used, these instructions may be minimal.

The exercises provide a good source of material that can be completed by students either under supervision or as directed work. They are intended to cover all of the basic operations that will be required by students who wish to use IT later as part of assignments or projects.

Core Skills are intended to be assessed as part of the portfolio of evidence collected by each student. Different assignments may contribute to this evidence in different ways. The assignments can be used as they are to help gather evidence for the Core Skills elements; however, they can also be 'customised' by putting them into a vocational context, if required.

The assignments from this book may be used to provide supplementary evidence to help assess aspects of the Core Skills which have not been assessed. For example, if a student has had no opportunity to create labels from a software package, assignment 2 from Chapter 6 can provide this. There are over 25 assignments to choose from to ensure that all aspects of the unit are covered.

The Core Skills units contain 'Evidence Indicators'. These are one way in which the evidence for a portfolio may be gathered, but they are not the only way! The assignments included in this book more than adequately cover the Evidence Indicators and provide other assessment opportunities if required.

Some students may wish to provide evidence of higher achievement in IT than the level for which they are being assessed. They can use the assignments to provide this kind of evidence.

Students who have a copy of the book at the start of the course will have a ready source of reference when they need to use their IT skills later in their programme.

D. Turner
October 1995

CHAPTER 1

Introduction to information technology

Objectives

When you have finished this chapter you should be able to:
- Recognise the types of computer commonly available and their main functions
- Appreciate the function of each part of a computer system
- Recognise the parts of a keyboard
- Use a mouse
- Understand the types of computer disk
- Recognise common computer peripherals
- Understand the terms 'serial' and 'parallel'
- Appreciate the benefits of a computer network
- Understand the health and safety requirements for IT users

This chapter covers the Performance Criteria and Range from the IT Core Skills Elements 2.4 and 3.4 related to the reasons for using IT, evaluation of systems, the effects of problems in the use of IT and safe working practices.

Types of computer

Information technology (IT) is all about computers, and the way in which they store, process and transfer information. It is difficult to imagine what it would be like to live without the influence of computers because they now control so many parts of our lives. They control most of the appliances in our homes, our telephone systems, our bank accounts, our watches, much of our entertainment and virtually any other part of our lives that we can think of.

Computers come in all shapes and sizes. Some are so small that they can fit inside a wrist watch, others need a very large room to accommodate them. Computers also vary in their capabilities. Some of the smallest are able to perform only one set of operations and they do this continuously as long as they have power. Others can perform many different functions depending upon the program, or software, that they are running at the time. (In computer terminology, the American spelling of 'program' is used rather than the English 'programme'.) These are the general purpose machines that most people regard as 'real' computers. The largest of these can perform millions of operations every second and communicate with hundreds of people at the same time.

The way in which computers work is controlled by a program. Computer programs may also be called 'Applications' or 'Software', both throughout this book and in general use.

The most common type of computer has a keyboard, a screen and often has a mouse connected to its main system box. This is usually called a personal computer, or PC. Personal computers were first produced in about 1980 and have steadily become more powerful as technology has advanced. The speed of each new generation of computers has increased, so that modern computers run at least ten times faster than those designed a few years ago. They also contain about ten times more memory than the early computers. This means that they are capable of performing much more complex tasks.

People who use computers as part of their normal work can now choose the type of computer that suits them best.

A secretary

People who work in an office generally need a computer that is capable of running some basic programs or applications. The most common are **word processors**, **databases** and **spreadsheets**. Word processors are essential in an office because they can be used to do most of the typing. Databases are used for storage and analysis of lists of information, and spreadsheets can replace calculators for complicated business calculations.

An office computer would probably have a colour screen to take full advantage of the latest programs, a solid and robust keyboard and enough memory for the main programs. It also needs a disk drive system so that it can store both the programs and the information created in the office. Speed is not critical, but the faster the better, especially if it has to do a lot of calculating or searching for data in a database.

Figure 1.1 Typical PC

An architect

A modern architect is more likely to do drawings on a computer than on a drawing board. The reason for this is that a number of computer programs have been produced for 'Computer Aided Design' (CAD), which make it very easy to create a computer-based drawing. These programs work to a very high accuracy and the drawings can be modified later with very little extra work. This speeds up the design process considerably.

A typical computer for an architect would have to be as fast as possible so that the more complicated drawings could be handled as quickly as the small ones. It would also need a very large memory since most of the programs take up a lot of space. The computer screen needs to be large and have a very high resolution so that the smallest lines can be seen in detail even when a complete drawing is being displayed. Some architects prefer a monochrome screen that gives a very high resolution, others prefer to use a colour picture.

People who work on the move

People who travel a lot to do business often find that they need to have a computer with them wherever they are so that they can make notes and keep records. Some of the latest portable computers are designed for such people because they can fold into a case not much bigger than an A4 folder.

Portable computers are often called 'notebooks', but they can be as powerful as some of the bigger office machines. Some types are battery powered so that they can be taken on trains or into meetings and still function normally. They can also be plugged into the mains supply either for use or for recharging the batteries. The most recent portables have colour screens so that they are almost identical to the larger models found in most businesses.

Computer terminology

Many of the difficulties that people have with computers stem from the fact that they do not understand the terms being used or the meaning of the computer jargon. Once you understand the basic terms and have some idea of how the computer works, a lot of the mystery will be removed.

A **computer system** refers to everything which is needed to make a computer work. However, there are only three main parts to any computer system – the hardware, the software and the peripherals.

Hardware

The hardware is the part of the computer you can touch. It is a term generally applied to any physical part of a system, but it is frequently used to mean the internal electronic components. These include the microprocessor, which is the 'brain' of the system, and the memory, which stores the computer programs.

Software

The software is another term for a computer program. Software contains instructions in electronic codes which tell the computer how to operate at any moment. Traditional programs are very detailed, since the computer has to be instructed about every possible action it must take. The software is stored on a computer disk until it is needed and is then transferred to the computer's memory. The more complex the program, the more memory will be required. Memory is measured in bytes or, for larger sizes, kilobytes (KBytes) or megabytes (MBytes). A byte is the memory space needed for one character, such as the letter a.

There are two main types of software:
• the operating system and
• applications programs.

The **operating system** is the set of programs the computer needs to run itself. For example, the operating system controls the transfer of data between the computer's internal memory and the disks, and how information is displayed on the screen.

Applications programs determine the main function of the computer. Applications include word processors, which are loaded whenever there is some typing to do, graphics software, which may be used for drawing pictures, and spreadsheets, which are used for doing calculations.

Peripherals

Peripherals can also be regarded as computer hardware, but they do not have to form part of the basic system. They are the parts which allow human interaction with the computer. The most common peripherals are keyboards, screens or visual display units (VDUs), printers, mice and disk drives. There are many other specialist devices which are required for special purposes. These include light pens, graphics tablets, optical scanners, plotters and many other industrial devices.

Information is passed between the computer hardware and the peripherals through devices known as **ports**. These are electronic circuits found inside the computer, but the connections to them are normally made using the sockets at the back of the computer box.

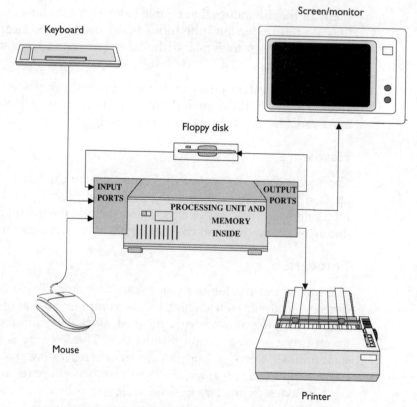

Figure 1.2 A typical computer system

How computers work

All computers work in much the same way. They deal with information and commands which are in the form of electrical signals. Information enters the computer from one of the peripheral devices, such as the keyboard or mouse, via a port. These are normally connected to the sockets on the back of the computer case. The microprocessor inside (the computer's 'brain') receives the information from the port and performs some operation that results in an **output signal** being created and passed via another port to a peripheral such as a screen or printer. The microprocessor then waits for its next instruction. Exactly what the computer does with every piece of information or command depends upon the program running at the time.

The same basic process of receiving information, acting upon it, then waiting for more information is followed for every action, however small. For example, one tiny movement of the mouse will result in the pointer on the screen being moved slightly. Words typed on the keyboard will normally appear on the computer screen or will start off another operation such as a calculation or a search through a database. Each command can result in different actions, depending upon the software program.

The computer is always controlled by its software. The instructions contained in the program tell the computer what to do when it receives each command and how to react if the mouse is moved or if more information is needed from the disk. It works through its program in a continuous 'fetch–execute' cycle, fetching one instruction and executing it before fetching and executing another. This happens millions of times per second. The computer continues the same process with its operating system programs even when an application is not being used.

Parts of the computer system

All human communication with the computer takes place using one or more of the peripherals. It is therefore important to understand what can be done with each one of them.

Keyboards

Keyboards are by far the most widely used and important computer peripherals. If you want to operate a computer you will probably need to be able to type. The days of direct voice entry are not yet with us, even though limited systems do exist, such as with telephone banking.

The computer keyboard still has the same arrangement of keys as the original typewriter keyboard, known as the QWERTY layout. These are the letters on the top row. France and Belgium have some keyboards with an AZERTY layout, but apart from the A, Z, Q and W, these are otherwise the same as the UK keyboard layout, which is shown in Figure 1.3.

Most keyboards have four sections:
- the function keys
- the numeric keys
- the control keys
- the alphanumeric keys.

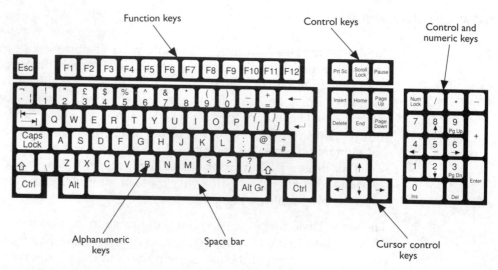

Figure 1.3 The standard UK keyboard layout

Some keyboards do not have the separate control keys. Look at the keyboard you normally use and identify the different parts of it.

Function keys

There are 10 or 12 function keys on most keyboards, labelled F1, F2, etc. Each one is given a special function by the software running at any moment. These keys provide 'short-cuts' to some of the more common operations in programs such as word processors and databases.

Numeric keys

The numeric keypad is very useful when a lot of numbers have to be entered. It also doubles as a set of cursor or arrow keys when required. People who do many calculations, or deal with financial transactions on the computer, tend to use them most.

Control keys

The control keys each have a special function. They include the cursor control keys and others that affect the position of the cursor on screen. They also include keys that insert and delete letters and which produce a copy of the computer screen on a printer.

Alphanumeric keys

The alphanumeric keys are by far the most important. Each one has at least two functions, printing lower case and capital letters. In addition, most keys have special functions when a letter is pressed at the same time as the Control key or the Alt key. For example, when using Microsoft Windows, pressing Alt and a letter at the same time usually activates a menu. In a word processor, pressing Control and the letter B may make a word **bold**.

Surrounding the alphanumeric keys are the keys for punctuation marks or special operations such as the **backspace** and **tab** keys. All keyboards contain these keys somewhere, but they can often be in different places.

Typing

It is worth your while to learn to type correctly. Many IT users wish that they had done so when they were beginning to use computers since it would have saved them many hours later in their work. Most people can manage with one finger at a time while looking at the keyboard, but this is a very slow method of typing. A lot of practice is needed at first, but it is a very good investment if every document you type can be done in half the time it would have taken.

Many methods exist to help you learn to type. One of the most basic is to use a special typing tutor program on the computer. However, you will need an iron discipline if you are to stop yourself looking at the keyboard while you type. It is surprising what a difference simply using the correct fingers for each key makes to your speed.

The cursor or insertion point

Whenever a keyboard is being used, the letters pressed appear on the computer screen. They appear at a place on the screen known as the **cursor** or the **insertion point**. This is generally a flashing vertical line that moves to the right as letters are typed. Its position on screen can be controlled with the cursor (arrow) keys or the mouse.

The mouse

The mouse is a relatively new device, but most modern computer programs seem to need one. It provides an easy way of moving the cursor or insertion point around the screen. It also allows selections to be made from menus, sections of the screen to be highlighted and drawings to be done, so it is a very useful device. A mouse may have one, two or three buttons. On a mouse with more than one, the left-hand button is the most important since it is usually the 'pick' button.

The mouse is used to select objects or to start certain functions, as follows:
Point   Move the pointer to a place on screen
Click   Press and release a mouse button without moving the mouse
Double click   Press and release the button twice in quick succession
Drag   Hold down the mouse button while moving the mouse

Normally, the mouse first points at the required object on the screen then one of the other actions takes place.

Computer screens

A computer screen is by far the most useful output device used by computers. It allows the user to 'look' inside the machine. As computers have developed, so have the screens used. Those used with modern computers are generally colour, and have better resolution than a television picture. This gives a very sharp image, and it helps prevent eye strain for people who have to use them for many hours each day. Some of the older screens were so blurred that they were very hard to look at for long periods of time. There are now regulations about the working conditions of people who have to work at computer screens. These are dealt with later in the chapter.

The colours on a computer screen are made of 'picture elements', or **pixels**, in red, blue and green. The more pixels on a screen, the better the resolution and the sharper the picture. A typical computer screen has over a million pixels. All of the colours are made by combining different intensities of the three primary colours.

Generally, the more pixels the better, but the more work the computer has to do to keep the picture updated. This may mean that the screen sometimes appears to flicker a little as information is updated. Modern computers use a Super VGA standard, which means that there can be 1024 pixels by 768 pixels with 256 colours on screen at once. With a slightly lower resolution of 800×600 pixels, there can be up to 65,535 colours on screen at once.

Computer disks

Computer disks are used to store the programs or software that makes the system work. Like most things in computing, the physical size of disks is reducing, but the amount of data that can be stored on them appears to be increasing at a faster rate. There are three main types:
- floppy disks
- hard disks
- optical disks.

Floppy disks

Floppy disks are by far the most common, and for historical reasons these come in two sizes, $5\frac{1}{4}''$ and $3\frac{1}{2}''$. Each one can store different amounts of information depending upon how it is prepared, or formatted. The $5\frac{1}{4}''$ disks are gradually dying out in favour of the $3\frac{1}{2}''$ versions.

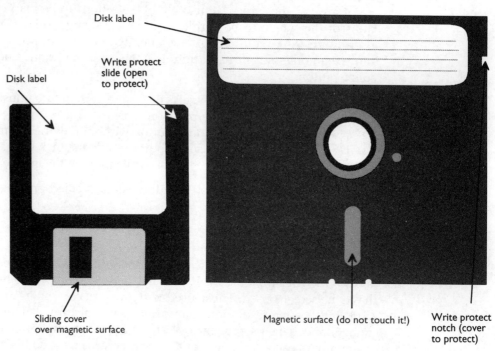

Figure 1.4 Floppy disks – $3\frac{1}{2}''$ and $5\frac{1}{4}''$

A $5\frac{1}{4}''$ floppy disk can normally store up to 1.2 MBytes (1.2 million characters) of information. This book contains about 300,000 characters, so four complete copies could be stored on one disk. A $3\frac{1}{2}''$ disk can store slightly more, about 1.4 MBytes.

Floppy disks are made of a plastic material covered in a magnetic coating that can have the data written onto it. Music is stored on cassette tape in a similar way. Floppy disks store data on tracks that have to be put on the disk first. This is done by 'formatting' the disk. If a disk is not formatted, nothing can be stored on it, and the computer will give an error message if an unformatted disk is used. Formatting takes about a minute and can be done in the computer disk drive by running a special program.

Write protection

Floppy disks are known as 'read/write devices' because their information can easily be changed by overwriting. Sometimes it is vital that the data is protected from accidental changes and this can be achieved with the disk 'write protect' notch. Move the plastic slide to the edge of the disk or cover the notch to prevent data being written on the disk. The computer will send you an error message if you try to write anything on a disk that is write-protected.

Hard disks

Hard disks are made of metal rather than plastic and they are generally fixed inside the computer. They work in a similar way to floppy disks but have a much greater storage capacity. Typical disks store about 200 MBytes and some are available that can store over 4 GBytes (4,000,000,000 characters). They are much faster than floppy disks so they are mainly used to store computer software. Most computers have a hard disk which holds the application programs, such as a word processor or a database. The data these programs generate, such as letters or reports, are often kept on floppy disks so that they can be taken away and kept in a safe place. This also stops the hard disk from getting filled up with unwanted information.

Without the hard disk most modern computers are virtually useless. It is almost impossible to run most modern software with only a floppy disk drive. Some computers, particularly in companies, can be connected to a computer **network** instead of the hard disk to store all of the programs that the computer needs. This also allows all the computer users to share data.

Computer networks are groups of computers that are connected together electronically so that they can share programs stored on a 'file server'.

Directories

> Remember the terms **directory** and **sub-directory**: they are the parts of a computer disk used to store related programs or information.

Hard disks have such a large capacity that if all of their programs were loaded randomly on them it would be very difficult to find the right ones for each purpose. It would be a little like storing all of the documents required in an office in one large box. Therefore the disk is normally divided into different sections, called **directories**, to store all of the programs or data for each application in the same area. For example, one directory may contain all the spreadsheet programs and the spreadsheets themselves. Another directory may contain the word processor programs and the letters or other documents produced by it.

Each directory can be further divided into sub-directories if necessary.

Optical disks

There are two types of optical disk. One type is like a CD and its data can be read but not changed. This type is the most common and many computer systems are now equipped with CD drives to allow them to be read. They are dealt with in more detail later in the chapter.

Another type of optical disk can be used for both reading and writing. These tend to be used for large data storage systems where the information does not need to be changed very often.

Progress check

The information covered so far is largely intended to help you understand the basic terminology of IT. Check that you have understood the main ideas and how they apply to you by answering the following questions.

1. What are the special features you would expect to find in a computer used by:
   (a) an architect?
   (b) a travelling salesman?

2. What features and what type of software might you find in a computer used by:
   (a) a garage owner?
   (b) the manager of a large company?
   (c) a graphic designer?
   (d) a travel agent?

3. What is the function of a computer operating system?

4. For each of the following computer terms, write down whether they are hardware, software or peripherals
   (a) database
   (b) port
   (c) microprocessor
   (d) operating system
   (e) mouse
   (f) floppy disk
   (g) spreadsheet
   (h) keyboard
   (i) application
   (j) printer.

5. How many function keys are present on the computer keyboard you normally use? What is their purpose?

6. Find out how much memory is inside the computer you normally use. How much can be stored on its hard disk (if it has one), and how much on its floppy disk(s)?

If you would like to do some further investigations into your computer system, and collect evidence which may be able to be used in your GNVQ assessment, try Assignment 1 at the end of this chapter.

Other peripherals

There are many different types of peripheral, but the most common are the keyboard, the mouse and the computer screen, which we have already discussed. The keyboard and mouse convert the actions of a computer operator into the types of electrical signal that the computer can use. The screen does the opposite, converting the computer signals into written or visual form so that users can understand them.

Peripherals each have a specific function, all based on some form of conversion process. Disk drives convert magnetic data into electrical form and vice versa, while printers convert the electrical signals into printed form. Apart from those already discussed above, the peripherals you are most likely to come across include plotters, digitisers, light pens, modems, scanners and tape systems.

Connecting peripherals

Some peripherals work quite slowly, so they are connected to the computer with a single set of wires called a **serial connection**. Other peripherals require large amounts of data to be passed between them and the computer because they work very quickly. These require a **parallel connection**.

Serial connections

In a serial connection between the peripheral and computer, one wire passes data to the peripheral and another passes data back if necessary. Passing data in this way is slow, but it can be sent over long distances and even transmitted via telephone lines or satellites all over the world.

The connections for these peripherals are known as 'communication ports' or 'COM' ports. Most computers have at least one and some have up to four. They are known as COM1, COM2, etc. The computer end of the link must be matched with the peripheral end of the link so that data can be passed successfully. This is done as part of the process of setting up the operating system.

Peripherals which are likely to be connected serially are the mouse, printers more than about 10 m away from the computer, modems and plotters. They can often be recognised because they have a nine-pin or 25-pin socket on the end of their leads which connect to the computer. These types of connection are quite difficult to set up correctly, so you should seek the help of a computer technician.

Note that the difference between plugs and sockets on computer leads is that the plugs have the pins visible, whereas the sockets have holes for the pins to go in.

Parallel connections

High speed transmission of data is achieved by sending it over eight wires at the same time. The speed of transfer is very much higher than for serial transmission not only because of the extra wires, but also because the data is sent much more quickly. The only disadvantage of parallel transmission is that it cannot be used over distances of more than about 10 m.

Most printers that are near the computer can use parallel connections to ensure that the printing takes place as quickly as possible. For historical reasons, the parallel ports are known as 'line printer ports' or 'LPT' connections. Most computers have at least one LPT port, and some have two, known as LPT1 and LPT2. They can be recognised by the fact that their leads will probably have a 25-pin plug on the computer end and either a 25-pin or a 36-pin plug on the other.

Printers

There are many different kinds of printer, and their performance has been steadily improved to keep pace with the developments in computers themselves. The main types are dot matrix, laser and ink jet printers. Each of these types is available in black and white or colour-printing versions, and they each have characteristics that make them suitable for certain types of printing. It is very important to make sure that the software being used is set up correctly for the type of printer which is connected to the computer. If not, some very unpredictable results will occur! More details on printing are given in the next chapter.

Dot matrix printers

Dot matrix printers were the most widely used computer printers until recently, but they are becoming less popular because of the availability of good quality alternatives. However, there are still very many dot matrix printers in use because of their versatility and low cost. With the right software, they can produce good quality text together with pictures and graphics. They are capable of producing an A4 page of text in about a minute.

The ink from a printer ribbon is transferred to the paper by a row of nine or 24 needles in the print head. As the print head moves across each line on the page, different needles are pushed out momentarily and make dots on the paper to form letters or pictures. The quality of the printing depends upon the size of the dots and how close together they are. Modern printers can produce 'letter quality' printing in a range of different styles.

Paper for dot matrix printers

One of the reasons for choosing a dot matrix printer is the variety of types of paper it can print on. Most printers come with a tractor feed mechanism which permits them to use paper with sprocket holes such as the wide 'music-score paper'. If a single sheet feeder is attached, they can also print directly onto normal A4 paper.

Because they use an impact printing method, dot matrix printers can also print on NCR ('no carbon required') paper. This type of paper has two or more sheets fastened together and is sometimes called multi-part stationery. It is often pre-printed with a form or company documentation. Printing on the top sheet produces a copy on each sheet underneath. These can then be separated and sent to different people.

Sheets of sticky labels can also be printed easily using the tractor feed mechanism. The labels come on backing sheets so they can be fed through the printer, then separated and stuck on envelopes or other places.

Dot matrix printers cannot be used for transparencies or for very high quality work. However, some versions print in colour using a three-coloured ribbon by printing each line three times.

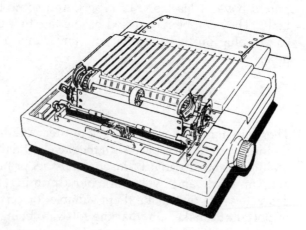

Figure 1.5 A typical dot matrix printer

Ink jet printers

Ink jet printers also work on the dot matrix principle to form the letters, but they do not have a ribbon. Instead they squirt a series of small dots of ink at the paper in the right positions to make the letters or pictures. These ink dots are so small that there can be up to 300 per inch, giving the printer a very high resolution. Their quality is almost as good as a laser printer.

The print head with its ink cartridge moves across the page one line at a time and is positioned very close to the paper. Each ink jet is controlled separately so that many different types of letters or graphic images can be produced.

Ink jet printers have to use ink that is very thin to prevent the nozzles getting clogged up. They therefore have regular head cleaning built in, which takes place automatically every few minutes. Occasionally the thinness of the ink can lead to it smudging slightly or creeping away from the letters if the right type of paper is not used.

Paper for ink jet printers

Most ink jet printers can only print on A4 or smaller sized paper. This is because they are designed for office use where this format is the most popular. Larger printers are available, but they can be expensive. However, they do have one advantage over dot matrix printers – they can print on transparency film. Normally a special film has to be used which will allow the ink to dry very quickly without smudging or running. The ink density is good enough to give a dark image when used with most overhead projectors.

Special gloss papers can also be used successfully with an ink jet printer. For example, they can be used to print names on special paper for certificates or plaques. The quality and resolution of an ink jet printer are almost as good as a laser printer with the right type of paper.

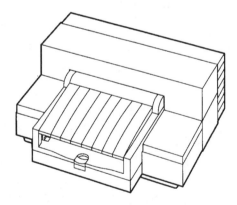

Figure 1.6 Ink jet printer

Colour ink jet printers

The most popular type of colour printer is probably the colour ink jet. Instead of a single black ink cartridge, the colour printer contains two cartridges, one for black ink and the other for three colours – cyan, yellow and magenta. These three colours, when mixed together, can create all the others. The intensity of each colour is carefully controlled by the computer software and the printer electronics so that the inks are mixed together accurately. Each ink colour can have up to 256 different intensities, giving up to $256 \times 256 \times 256$ (16,777,216) colour combinations.

Colour ink jet printers can also be used to make overhead projector transparencies so they are of a great help in creating material for a professional looking presentation. Not all computer programs support colour printers, so it is only possible to make full use of them in certain cases. Most recent word processing and spreadsheet software can print in colour, together with most of the graphics packages. Most colour printers can only print on paper which is A4 size or smaller.

Laser printers

For the highest quality printing available, most people turn to a laser printer, which will produce documents that look as though they have been professionally produced at a printers. Many printing companies use laser printers to make their proofs and can print books directly from them. They produce a very dense black image, usually 300 or 600 dots per inch and are equally happy with text or pictures. One important feature, particularly for an office, is that they are almost silent. However, they can give off ozone gas, and should be fitted with special filters which have to be regularly replaced.

Laser printers work by building up an image of each page in a large memory inside the machine. This is then used to attract an ink or toner onto the surface of a drum using a laser beam, where it is held electrostatically. The toner is then fused onto the surface of the paper as it passes through the printer and comes into contact with the drum.

A lot of time is needed to build up the image in the printer memory, especially for some complex pictures, so the printing can appear to be slow. However, when printing text, a laser printer is normally capable of printing about eight pages per minute.

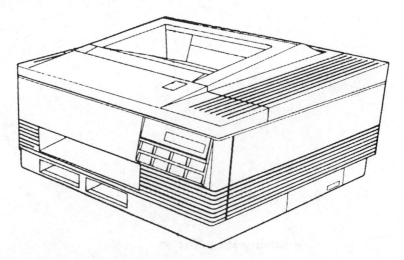

Figure 1.7 A laser printer

Paper types

Laser printers, like ink jet printers, are mainly designed to use A4 paper. Versions do exist which take bigger sheets, but they tend to be very expensive. Some laser printers have twin sheet feeders so that two types of paper, such as plain and headed, can be used without the need to insert each type when needed. Most of them can print to within a few millimetres of the edge of the paper.

Special sheets of sticky labels are available for laser printers. Unfortunately, not all label printing software can make use of them. Some printers can also be used to print directly on envelopes.

Laser printers can also produce transparencies for overhead projectors. These have to be special sheets that are resistant to high temperatures so that they will not buckle up when they go through the printer.

Colour laser printers

Colour laser printers will probably take over colour printing from colour ink jet printers in the same way that monochrome laser printers have taken over most standard printing. Until recently, colour lasers have only been available in specialist versions but some commercial printers are now available which promise to make high quality colour printing available in any office. Prices are relatively high but these are likely to fall as demand increases.

The printing process is much the same as a monochrome laser printer except that three different coloured toners are used as well as black – cyan, magenta and yellow. Printing resolution is up to 300 dots per inch. This means that the quality of printing is almost as good as a photograph onto standard A4 paper, but the speed is relatively slow, about 3 pages per minute. They can print directly onto normal paper, onto envelopes or onto transparencies used in presentations.

Scanners

Scanners are devices which can transfer an image from a sheet of paper into a computer both quickly and easily. The most common scanners are small hand held types or desktop versions capable of scanning an A4 sheet. Images can be captured in both colour or black and white depending upon the design of the scanner. Like printers, they are capable of resolutions of 300 dots per inch in their basic versions and higher in the more advanced versions.

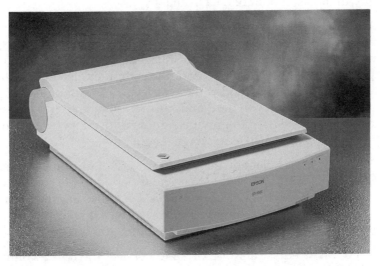

Figure 1.8 A desktop scanner

Scanners are basically simple devices which can be made very much more useful if they are supported by sophisticated software. Light reflected from the image is picked up on a photosensitive device similar to that inside a modern video camera. This converts the image to an electrical signal which is interpreted by the computer. The software can treat the image as a simple picture and as such it can be manipulated with a graphics package. Some of the best software allows all sorts of modifications to be done so that the end product can be totally transformed.

One of the most useful features of an optical scanner is that it can be used to capture pictures which can later be incorporated in documents or reports created on a word processor. Whenever a picture is needed for an illustration, it can be scanned from something similar rather than having to draw it again. This can then be modified either with the drawing facilities built into the word processor or with a separate graphics package.

Optical character recognition

If the right software is available for a scanner, it can be made to convert a scanned image into characters. This is known as 'optical character recognition' or 'OCR'. The quality of the results depends upon the quality of the text being scanned. If typed text is scanned from a book or magazine, most of it will be recognised with very few errors. However, if an old photocopy of poor quality is used, then the OCR software is likely to make many errors. Even if this occurs, a word processor with a built-in spelling checker should be able to put the errors right. The scanning speed is bound to be much faster than most typists can key in the text. Some OCR software also ensures that the same font (the shape of the letters) and character size is used by the word processor that was used in the original.

CD-ROMs

CD-ROM stands for 'Compact disc-Read Only Memory'. A CD-ROM is an optical disk which looks the same as a music compact disc but which can contain hundreds of pages of information. The information can be in many forms: text, pictures, diagrams, software programs, video clips and music. Since they can store such a variety of data and so much of it, there has been a tremendous growth in the amount of data available.

Different publishers are beginning to produce their information on CD-ROM because it can be mass produced very easily and it is simple to distribute. It is much easier to send a copy of a compact disc by post than thousands of pages of A4 paper in a book. The power of the computer also makes the compact disc a very sophisticated method of data retrieval. The computer can perform searches for the information you need and can cross-reference it if necessary. The built-in software may be used to provide a guide to the data or may form part of a self-teaching package such as a foreign language.

CD-ROMs are available with a wide variety of information, ranging from complete sets of newspapers for a particular period to the complete set of postcodes and addresses for the UK. There are lists of books in print, hundreds of graphics images, computer system manuals and technical information, language courses, encyclopaedias, maps – just about anything you can think of.

CD-ROMs need a CD-ROM drive to connect them to a computer system. The drive can be connected individually to a computer and the various CD-ROMs

Figure 1.9 CD-ROM and drive

can be inserted when required, or it can be connected to a computer network so that all the network users can gain access to them. In this case, a number of CD-ROMs may be put into a CD-ROM tower so that they can all be accessed at the same time.

Modems

A modem is a peripheral which is used to connect a computer to the telephone system. Modem comes from '**mo**dulator/**dem**odulator'. Modems allow computers all over the world to communicate with each other. The computer works with electrical signals at very high speed, which are not in the right form to be

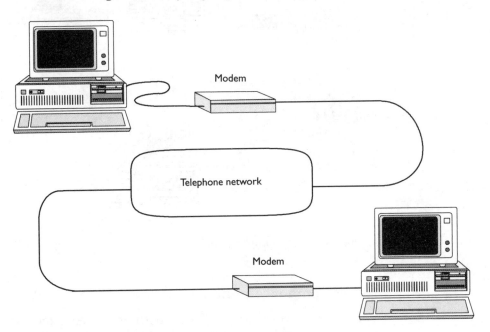

Figure 1.10 Computers connected by modems

transmitted along telephone cables. The modem converts the signals, and slows them down to make it possible to transmit them over long distances. The signals from one computer are fed into a modem, where they are converted and sent to another computer by telephone. The second modem converts the signals back to computer signals before sending them to the computer at the other end.

The process makes it possible for two computer operators miles apart to have a conversation using their computer keyboards.

Computer networks

Most companies have now replaced their large computer systems with much smaller computers connected together in a network. This means that the computers are each fitted with a special adapter so that they can share a common cable and pass data between them. The whole system is controlled by a computer known as a **file server**, which runs special programs to manage the system.

The file server's job is to provide a means of storing the programs needed by all of the users. It is therefore fitted with one or more large capacity hard disks typically over 1 GByte (1,000,000,000 bytes). Its operating software manages the whole system so that whenever data is requested by one of the computers in the network it is provided as quickly as possible. The network can also provide access to other shared facilities such as high speed printers, plotters, scanners and modems which may be too expensive to provide for each user. Each user often has the ability to communicate with all the other users via an electronic mail system.

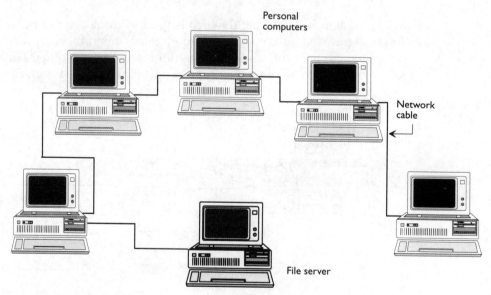

Figure 1.11 A computer network

Network management

Computer networks have to be properly managed if they are to be a valuable resource in a company or institution. For example, a network supervisor has to ensure that the contents of the hard disks are regularly backed up. This ensures that the system is secure and any disk or computer failure will not result in loss of vital information. In addition, whenever new software has to be installed, it has to be done very carefully so that all the users can gain the right access to it. There are frequent demands from users because of systems faults or special requirements which the network supervisor must resolve.

Advantages of networks
The advantages of networks over stand-alone computers are:
- Large storage capacity for software
- A wide range of software can be made available
- Regular backup by the network supervisor
- Access to special resources such as printers
- Connections to other computer systems
- Electronic mail between users
- Regular updating of software is achieved centrally.

Disadvantages of networks
However, there are some disadvantages, including:
- Other users may get access to personal files if security is not good
- Network failures may be more frequent than stand-alone computer failures
- Some networks may be slowed down by a lot of users
- Extra equipment is needed, which can be expensive.

Safe use of IT equipment

Working with computers is generally quite safe but there can be a number of hazards which you must be aware of to avoid any dangers. These may be in the layout and positioning of equipment and in the way in which it is used.

If you think that the equipment being used is in a dangerous condition or that accidents may occur, it is your responsibility to tell someone in authority. The safe use of IT equipment is the subject of the *Health and Safety (Display Screen Equipment) Regulations 1992*. General safety is also covered by the *Health and Safety at Work Act 1974*.

The safety regulations apply to people who are classified as 'display screen users'. These are people who generally spend a long time working at a screen or who have to concentrate on it very hard for shorter periods. However, most of the advice applies to anyone who uses a screen even for quite a short time.

What are the problems?

There are three main problems:
- pain and discomfort in the arms and hands
- fatigue and stress
- eyesight-related disorders.

A number of possible conditions can result from poor workplace design. These include soreness in the limbs, soft tissue disorders and back or neck problems. They can be made worse by increased stress due to short deadlines and high volumes of work. With careful design of the workplace they can be reduced significantly.

Some people may experience eye problems that are temporary but can include impaired vision, red or sore eyes and can result in headaches. These problems may be due to poor lighting, insufficiently clear characters on screen, reflections and glare or poor screen positioning. There is no medical evidence to suggest that the use of computer screens causes any damage to the eyes, but it may make people who have these conditions more aware of them.

Workplace organisation

The layout of a workplace should minimise all of the potential hazards as far as possible.

Points to note are:
- The lighting must be sufficient for the task and there must be sufficient contrast between the screen and the background.
- Distracting noises (such as from printers) should be minimised.
- There must be sufficient leg room to allow the operators to change positions easily.
- Windows should have blinds or curtains.
- The software should be appropriate for the task.
- The screen must have a stable image, without glitter, glare or reflections.
- The keyboard must be usable, adjustable, detachable and legible.
- The work surface must allow a flexible arrangement of objects, with sufficient space for documentation, keyboard, etc.
- The chair should be adjustable in height and have an adjustable backrest in both height and tilt, (see below).
- A footrest should be provided for those people who need one.

Seating position for office tasks
It is important to have a good seat if back problems and aching limbs are to be avoided. This means that the seat must provide:
1. An adjustable back support
2. Good lumbar support

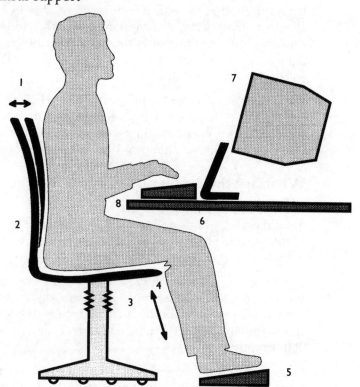

Figure 1.12 Correct seating posture for IT work

3. Adjustable seat height
4. No excess pressure under the thighs or back of the knees
5. Foot support if needed
6. Space to change position when needed
7. Adjustable screen position in height and angle to allow a comfortable head position
8. Space in front of the keyboard to support the hands and wrists during pauses in work.

Other hazards

All electrical equipment should be treated with respect because it can cause serious injury, or even death, if it is not used correctly. Problems can arise with the physical size of equipment if it has to be moved, its installation or the high electrical voltages or temperatures inside.

Cables trailing from the back of computers are quite common – they should be avoided at all costs. Proper installation ensures that the loose cables are kept as short as possible and that they are fastened in place. Ideally, cables should be routed inside cable ducts provided in most computer furniture. It is a good idea to check the system that you normally work on to make sure it is safe before switching it on.

All electrical equipment must pass regular safety checks. You must make sure that no drinks or other liquids go anywhere near the equipment so that there is no possibility of getting an electric shock. This will also help to ensure that you keep drinks well away from your disks, so there is no chance of them getting contaminated. It is a very difficult task to clean orange juice out of a keyboard – and almost impossible to get it off a floppy disk!

Take special care when cleaning printers or changing their ribbons. Some print heads and the inside of laser printers can get very hot, so it is a good idea to let them cool down before opening them. Always seek advice if you find faults with any part of your system. Tell the computer technician or another responsible person straight away. It can be very dangerous to poke around inside equipment and may cause serious damage to both you and it. Some parts, such as the small wires inside a laser printer, are very easily damaged by clumsy handling.

Take care of your disks

A floppy disk is one of the most important parts of the computer system because it is normally where all of the valuable work is kept. Unfortunately, floppy disks are also very easily damaged, so extra care needs to be taken to make sure that they are kept safe. The $5\frac{1}{4}''$ disks are the most vulnerable because they can easily be bent if they are handled roughly. The $3\frac{1}{2}''$ inch disks are better protected but they can also be damaged with poor treatment.

Never touch the magnetic surface of a floppy disk. The grease from a fingerprint can make it unreadable. Keep disks well away from extremes of temperature. If they are left in bright sunshine the heat can cause them to warp. Placing floppy disks on or near magnetic surfaces can also cause problems because the data on them can be corrupted. This means they *must not* be left on top of the computer screen.

$5\frac{1}{4}''$ disks are best stored in their sleeves, in the disk boxes they come in. This keeps them flat and protects them from contamination. They also should be properly labelled, but make sure that the disk name is written in the label *before* it is stuck on the disk so that the pen does not dent the disk. With a little common sense, most computer disks can be used for a number of years with very few problems.

The effects of IT on employment

The development of IT in business has changed both the nature of the work people do and the number of people needed to do it. For example, the introduction of electronic banking, with cash machines, telephone banking, automatic cheque processing and debit cards has meant that the number of jobs in the banking industry has been dramatically cut over the past few years.

The effects on organisations

From a business point of view, computers offer cheaper ways of processing information and the ability to access types of data previously thought impossible. Databases can be analysed to provide market information; communications are now global so the world can be the marketplace; computers are relatively cheap and reliable and are able to operate at very high speed so business decisions can be made much more rapidly.

Computers require significant financial investment, and users need training to make the best use of them. Once a company becomes dependent upon their computer system, they can be very vulnerable to any computer failure. This means that more investment is needed in newer systems which are said to be more reliable and capable of much more that the previous generations. Companies have to stay ahead of the competition.

The effects on individuals

Although there are fewer jobs in some industries as a result of computer technology, this is not universal. In some places, staff are retrained to use IT skills in the jobs they still do. However, more work is often expected since working with a word processor or a spreadsheet, for example, means that more can be accomplished in a shorter time.

Some companies have recognised the changing nature of work and pay staff more if they achieve higher productivity. However, in general, working with computers is now the norm so it is a skill expected of a far greater range of people that ever before. Some of the routine tasks can now be carried out automatically, but some people find that working with a computer system can be just as routine as working with a typewriter or calculator.

Review questions

Try these questions when you have read through the whole chapter or when you are confident that you understand the topics covered. If you can answer the questions you can attempt the assignment after them.

1. A hotel has installed a computer system with machines in the manager's office, reception desk, bar, and restaurant. Describe the applications for the computers in each location and the types of peripherals they would each need.

2. What is the function of the hard disk in a computer? Is it necessary for every computer to have a hard disk?

3. Computers can be connected to peripherals with two types of connection. What are the types of connection and what are the differences between them?

4. Some computers are part of a computer network. List some of the advantages and disadvantages of networks.

5. How is it possible to connect a computer in America with a computer in the UK and pass data between them?

6. Describe three types of printer and explain the reason for choosing each one of them for particular tasks, or in particular circumstances.

7. What is the function of a scanner? How could a scanner be useful in the production of a report?

Exercises

These exercises will help you to become familiar with the computer system you use and its main parts. You may have to ask other people to help you with the answers.

1. For one computer system to which you have access, find out the following:
   (a) How many function keys are there on the keyboard?
   (b) How many floppy disk drives does it have?
   (c) What is its screen type – CGA, EGA, VGA, Super VGA or something different?

2. Look at a computer printer.
   (a) What type of printer is it?
   (b) What are the names and functions of its operating controls?
   (c) What types of paper can it print on?

3. Write a paragraph explaining how to reload your usual printer with paper as a set of instructions for someone having to do it for the first time.

4. Draw a diagram of all the connections on the back of your computer and label it with the function of each one.

5. If your computer is connected to a network, find out the name of the network software.

6. Write down a list of the precautions which must be taken to ensure that the data on a floppy disk is not corrupted.

Assignment 1 starts on the next page

Assignment I
Types of computer and software

This assignment can be used to provide evidence for the following Performance Criteria:

Element 2.4   PCs I and 3

Element 3.4   PCs I and 4

Introduction

This assignment is designed to test your understanding of some of the concepts covered in the first part of the chapter and how they apply to the GNVQ you are studying. It may be used as part of your study to help you relate the work covered in IT to the rest of your qualification.

Your task

Use your own experience, or information you can find by looking around your school or college, to do the following.

1. Produce a list of the main types of computer which are in use in your school or college. List the makes, whether they have monochrome or colour screens, the types of floppy disks and whether or not they have hard disks or are connected to a network. If there are too many in the whole building, choose a restricted area.

2. Report on the main types of software in use and, in particular, list the names of the main programs and their function. Give examples of the applications of each one.

3. Report on the name and version number of the operating system.

4. Find out how many of the main programs you have identified above can be operated by using a mouse.

Compile your results into a short report, indicating the reasons why the computers in use were chosen for the task. In each case say how the use of the computer may improve the working efficiency of the people who use it. Compare the speed, effort, ease of use and accuracy of using a computer against the manual methods of performing the same task. Include at least three computer applications.

Assignment 2
Safe use of computer equipment

This assignment can be used to provide evidence for the following Performance Criteria:

Element 2.4   PC 5

Element 3.4   PC 6

Introduction

All computers need to be used safely. The working environment must also comply with certain regulations if the computers are used by 'display screen users'. This assignment will help you to take a critical look at the computers you are using and suggest ways in which their environment may be improved. It could equally apply to any computer you may use as part of any work experience or other work you do.

Your task

1. Look carefully at the computer you normally use, the seating position, the lighting and the type of software available and the rest of the working environment. Write a short report on whether or not the environment would be suitable for long term computer users.

2. If there are points raised which appear to fall short of the requirements for 'display screen users', decide whether they are acceptable for occasional users and why.

3. Draw up a list of Dos and Don'ts for new computer users so they will be aware of some of the possible hazards of computer use.

4. Make recommendations regarding any improvements which could be made to the computer workplace and so help to safeguard the health of the computer users.

5. Are there any potential electrical hazards in the workplace? Make some notes on areas which could be improved or comment on the ways in which these hazards have been eliminated.

CHAPTER 2

Operating and storage systems

Objectives

When you have finished this chapter you should be able to:
- Understand why computers need an operating system
- Appreciate the main functions of an operating system
- Know the conventions about file names
- Understand why disk storage is organised in tree structured directories
- Configure parts of an operating system to suit your requirements
- Set up a printer correctly and ensure that the right printer driver is used
- Back up important files from a disk
- Copy files between directories and disks
- Delete unwanted files from a disk
- Run programs from the operating system
- Deal with simple faults

This chapter covers the Performance Criteria and Range from the IT Core Skills Elements 2.1, 2.2, 2.4, 3.1, 3.2 and 3.4 related to the preparation, configuration and use of storage systems, the use of backup systems, the evaluation of alternative operating systems, and the methods of dealing with simple problems.

Making a computer work

One of the facts most people know about computers is that they work very fast. They carry out millions of instructions every second, from the moment they are first switched on each day. The first instructions they get come from programs built into the computer itself which form part of its **operating system**. The operating system is a vital part of the computer which tells it how to run itself. Its instructions tell the computer how to get information from the keyboard and what to do with it, how to send information to the screen, how to send and receive information from printers and other peripherals.

The most important instructions in the operating system tell the computer how to store information on the computer disks and how to retrieve it later. The disks, whether floppy or hard disks, form the main storage devices for programs and data. This is why some operating systems are called 'disk operating systems'. It is very important for computer systems to have an efficient operating system since most other programs which the computer runs rely upon the operating system to pass data to and from the disks.

Different operating systems

When personal computers were first developed each manufacturer designed their own operating system to suit their own computer. This gave rise to many systems which were incompatible. The less popular systems have now given way to a smaller number of systems which are used by most modern computers. These are the Microsoft disk operating system (MS-DOS), the Apple Macintosh system, a universal system called Unix, the Digital Equipment Corporation system VMS, and the Microsoft Windows operating system.

The Unix and VMS systems are mainly used on multi-user computers but it is possible that you will come across them. The most popular systems for personal computers are MS-DOS, the Macintosh and the Windows system. These can also be used with a network operating system, the most popular of which is Novell Netware.

MS-DOS

The first PC developed by IBM had an operating system written by a company called Microsoft – this was the first version of MS-DOS. Since then, many versions have been produced, each with additional features. The basic system, however, has remained the same.

MS-DOS is a 'character based operating system', which means that the instructions generally have to be entered from the keyboard as sets of characters. It is still the basic operating system used in most IBM compatible computers since it has to be loaded before some versions of the Windows operating system is started or before a PC is connected to a network.

Commands are shortened forms of English language instructions, such as DIR for 'Directory' and REN for 'Rename'. Although they are quite easy to understand once they have been learned, the basic instructions are not always obvious. The format required for some commands may need to be entered precisely if the instruction is to be carried out as required. With the DOS commands it is possible to control most of the major functions of the computer from the keyboard. Some commands can be made to occur automatically one after another, which helps to speed up certain operations.

The screen of a computer using the MS-DOS operating system normally looks like that shown in Figure 2.1. This shows the listing of the files on a floppy disk and the line known as the 'system prompt'.

It is a good idea to learn the basic commands of the MS-DOS operating system if you normally use an IBM-compatible computer. Even though other operating systems, such as Windows or Netware, may be used in addition there are often occasions when it is more useful to be able to use a DOS command for a particular operation. For example, if you need to make a copy of some of the information on a disk, it is sometimes quicker to use the DOS command than to have to load the Windows software and use that.

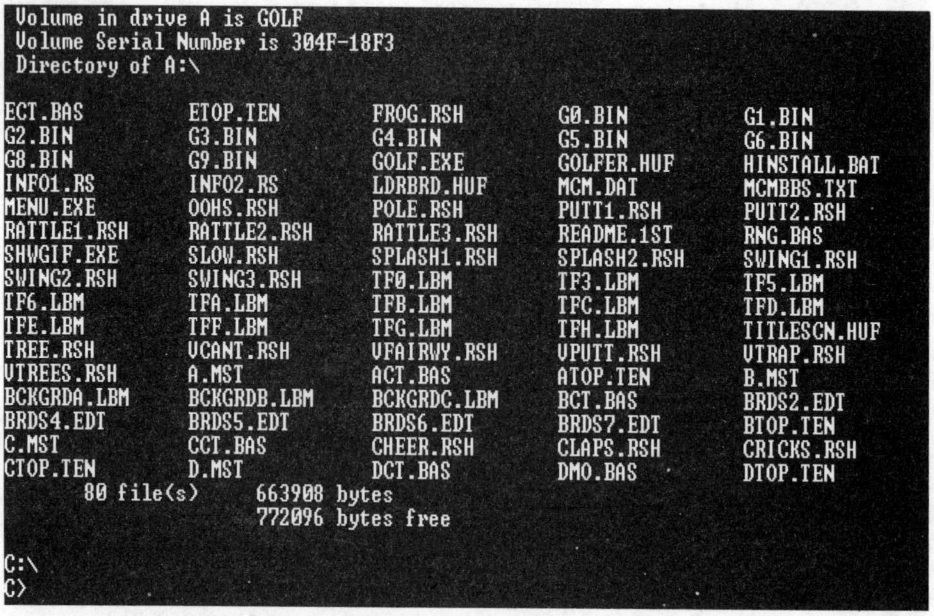

```
Volume in drive A is GOLF
Volume Serial Number is 304F-18F3
Directory of A:\

ECT.BAS          ETOP.TEN         FROG.RSH         G0.BIN           G1.BIN
G2.BIN           G3.BIN           G4.BIN           G5.BIN           G6.BIN
G8.BIN           G9.BIN           GOLF.EXE         GOLFER.HUF       HINSTALL.BAT
INFO1.RS         INFO2.RS         LDRBRD.HUF       MCM.DAT          MCMBBS.TXT
MENU.EXE         OOHS.RSH         POLE.RSH         PUTT1.RSH        PUTT2.RSH
RATTLE1.RSH      RATTLE2.RSH      RATTLE3.RSH      README.1ST       RNG.BAS
SHWGIF.EXE       SLOW.RSH         SPLASH1.RSH      SPLASH2.RSH      SWING1.RSH
SWING2.RSH       SWING3.RSH       TF0.LBM          TF3.LBM          TF5.LBM
TF6.LBM          TFA.LBM          TFB.LBM          TFC.LBM          TFD.LBM
TFE.LBM          TFF.LBM          TFG.LBM          TFH.LBM          TITLESCN.HUF
TREE.RSH         VCANT.RSH        VFAIRWY.RSH      VPUTT.RSH        VTRAP.RSH
VTREES.RSH       A.MST            ACT.BAS          ATOP.TEN         B.MST
BCKGRDA.LBM      BCKGRDB.LBM      BCKGRDC.LBM      BCT.BAS          BRDS2.EDT
BRDS4.EDT        BRDS5.EDT        BRDS6.EDT        BRDS7.EDT        BTOP.TEN
C.MST            CCT.BAS          CHEER.RSH        CLAPS.RSH        CRICKS.RSH
CTOP.TEN         D.MST            DCT.BAS          DMO.BAS          DTOP.TEN
        80 file(s)       663908 bytes
                         772096 bytes free

C:\
C>
```

Figure 2.1 *Typical MS-DOS screen display*

Windows

One of the drawbacks of the MS-DOS operating system is that all of the commands have to be learned before they can be used. Windows is an alternative operating system that makes a personal computer much easier to use. It is simple to learn because it is based on pictures instead of a set of commands. This development from Microsoft followed the success of the system pioneered by Apple Computers in their own machines. The pictures are known as 'icons' and each one represents a program, a data file or an operation which the software can perform. Future versions of this type of graphical system may look even more like a real office as the pictures become much more lifelike.

Remember:
'Application' or 'Application program' is the name given to a program such as a word processor, graphics package, database or spreadsheet, used on a computer.

Windows is a 'graphical user interface' or 'GUI', which uses a mouse and screen to perform all of its basic functions. However, its great advantage is that these operations are the same for all of the applications that work with Windows. Therefore, similar operations are carried out in a Windows-based word processor as in a Windows-based spreadsheet, which makes it very efficient to learn. Its built-in help facility means that even if you cannot remember exactly how to perform a certain operation, you can look it up without leaving the computer.

Many companies are now changing over to this type of operating system because their staff find it much easier to work with than DOS. Most software manufacturers are also introducing Windows versions of their products to keep up with the demand from customers. Very soon, it is likely to be standard on most personal computers.

Running Windows is a little like working at a desk because it is possible to be working on several tasks at the same time. This feature is known in computer

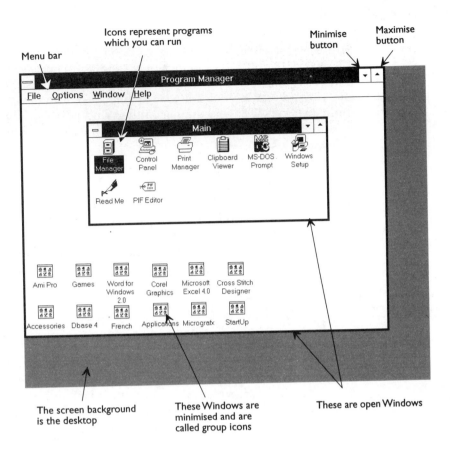

Figure 2.2 A typical Windows screen

jargon as 'multi-tasking'. One task is active at any moment, but the others can still be functioning in the background.

Program Manager

The icons (small pictures) representing programs are grouped in Windows so that related functions are kept together. The programs in each window can be chosen by the user, which means that no two computer screens will look exactly alike although they operate in the same way.

All of the programs in a system are controlled by the 'Program Manager' which is shown in Figure 2.2. This shows one Window enlarged, or 'maximised' to show all of the programs in it. The 'Main' window has been enlarged and has the programs File Manager, Control Panel, Print Manager, etc. in it. Other Windows are 'minimised' at the bottom of the screen. This means that they contain programs but they are kept out of the way until they are needed.

Windows or programs are selected with the mouse. Pointing at an icon and double clicking the left mouse button selects an operation or makes a program operate.

Apple Macintosh

Apple's Macintosh computer was one of the first computers to use a graphical method of operation. Each part of the system is represented on screen by icons, which are selected with a mouse pointer. The system has a pull down menu system and a system of 'folders' to hold the computer programs and data files. In many ways it is very similar to the Windows operating system although the terminology is slightly different. For example, instead of deleting files, the Macintosh user drops them into a waste bin.

Another useful feature of the Macintosh is its ability to use a system known as 'hypertext'. This permits links to be made between different parts of the system. By clicking with the mouse on different words or pictures the system can immediately jump to the related or linked information in the system. A similar idea is used as part of the 'Help' facilities in Microsoft Windows. Most software companies now produce virtually the same software for both the Macintosh and the PC market, so it is less important which computer you work on.

Novell Netware

There are a number of different network operating systems on the market, such as Microsoft LAN Manager and Windows for Workgroups. Novell Netware is by far the most popular and widely used network system. Each computer starts up using MS-DOS, which runs programs to connect it to the network. This then displays a simple menu system. The menu allows programs to be selected by highlighting them with the cursor keys or by typing their first letter on the keyboard. Once selected, the programs run normally and return the user to the menu when they are completed.

Networks are ideal for many organisations because they allow access to a range of programs under careful control. For example, if a company decides to standardise their word processing by using only one system, they can install it on a network and make sure that everyone uses it. This also makes maintenance easier because the package can easily be updated and all users will immediately benefit.

With many networks it is possible to exit from the menu system. When this happens, the operating system may be almost identical to MS-DOS with the addition of a few extra commands to carry out network operations.

It is also possible to use Windows with networks. This means that the operating system will be the same regardless of whether the computer is connected to a network or not.

Some of the reasons for an organisation choosing a networked computer system are:
- Software only has to be installed once for all users to benefit.
- All the main software can be shared if it is stored on a file server, which is accessed by all users.
- Large computer disks are relatively expensive. If only a small number have to be fitted to the network file servers the costs can be minimised.
- The cost of network connections is much smaller than the equivalent hard disks would be.
- Expensive peripheral devices such as plotters, printers and modems can be shared.
- Additional services can be supplied such as connections to mainframe computers or the telephone network.

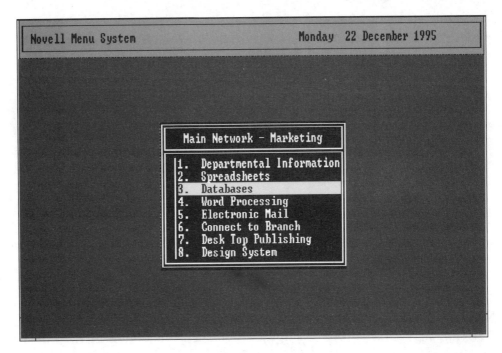

```
┌──────────────────────────────────────────────────────────┐
│ Novell Menu System                 Monday  22 December 1995│
├──────────────────────────────────────────────────────────┤
│                                                            │
│                                                            │
│              ┌────────────────────────────────┐            │
│              │   Main Network - Marketing      │            │
│              ├────────────────────────────────┤            │
│              │ 1.  Departmental Information     │            │
│              │ 2.  Spreadsheets                 │            │
│              │ 3.  Databases                    │            │
│              │ 4.  Word Processing              │            │
│              │ 5.  Electronic Mail              │            │
│              │ 6.  Connect to Branch            │            │
│              │ 7.  Desk Top Publishing          │            │
│              │ 8.  Design System                │            │
│              └────────────────────────────────┘            │
│                                                            │
└──────────────────────────────────────────────────────────┘
```

Figure 2.3 A network menu

- Electronic mail between users may be available.
- Regular backup facilities are normally provided onto high density tapes.

Files and file names in MS-DOS and Windows

Whatever the operating system, the information stored on a computer disk is known as a 'file'. The files can be used to store programs, documents, pictures, data or other reference information for the computer. Each file has to be given a unique name so that the computer can find it when necessary. It is a similar idea to that used in any office filing system.

File names are made up of two parts, the name itself and an extension. These parts are separated with a full stop. The file name itself can be up to eight characters long, and the extension can be up to three characters. Some very recent systems are attempting to overcome this restriction but it is likely to continue in most systems for many years to come.

README.LST and MENU.EXE are examples of typical file names. Many more can be found in Figure 2.1, which shows the files on a typical computer disk. The first part of the name gives you an idea of the contents of the file. This has to be chosen quite carefully so that it can be recognised perhaps months later. The second part of the name indicates the type of file it is.

File names are normally chosen by you. They can be anything as long as they do not contain spaces, full stops, and punctuation marks such as " , \ / : ;. Also, they cannot be any of the special names such as COM1 or LPT1.

File types

The file type or extension has similar restrictions but is only three characters long and has a meaning not only to the user but also to the computer. Certain file extensions indicate special types of file, for example:

31

.EXE   an executable file or program
.COM   a machine code file or program
.BAK   a backup file
.DOC   a document file (normally from Microsoft Word)
.WKS   a worksheet file from the Lotus 1-2-3 spreadsheet
.DBF   a database file
.XLS   a spreadsheet from Microsoft Excel

Often the computer program will add an extension of its own to a file name automatically.

Choosing file names

Remember that it is generally your responsibility to name each of your files. It is very easy to give a file the first name that comes into your head! That is also the way to guarantee that you will not be able to remember what the file contains a few months later when it may be required again. It is a good idea to develop a system so that files can be identified quickly.

> **Hint:** Try to make sure that the file name appears somewhere on each printed copy of a document so that you will always be able to refer back to it.

Choose a file name which is related to the file contents, and not simply your name. For example, a document about tourism in the UK may be called UKTOURSM.DOC or TOURUK.DOC. If a few versions were produced as the document is developed, they may be TOURUK1.DOC, TOURUK2.DOC, TOURUK3.DOC, and so on. Saving files regularly should become a habit as you work with computers. By saving a file with a different file name, you automatically create a backup at the same time.

Try to develop a systematic approach, so you will save yourself a lot of time in future. Otherwise you will waste time checking the contents of many files trying to find the one you want.

File sizes and attributes

Computers store more information about a file than just the file name. They also store information about its size in bytes (characters), the date and time it was last changed and whether it has any special characteristics. These special characteristics are known as **file attributes**.

Look at the list of files in Figure 2.4. Each file is listed with its name and extension, followed by its size, the date and time it was last changed, and in some cases by a group of letters showing its attributes. These can be:

a archive, to indicate that the file has not been backed up
r read only, to prevent the file being changed
h hidden, to prevent the name appearing in file listings
s system, to indicate special system files.

The file attributes help with the security of the computer data. For example, if certain files are erased from a disk the computer will not work. Erasure can be prevented either by hiding the file name or by making it 'read only'. Any attempt to erase the file will then be unsuccessful.

Normally you need not worry about file attributes. The computer takes care of them automatically so that anything you create, such as a document or a spreadsheet, can be changed or copied. If you do need to make sure that a file cannot be changed, then use the operating system commands to make the file 'read only'.

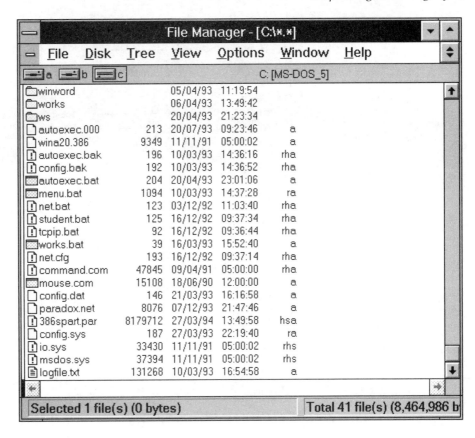

Figure 2.4 File list, showing sizes and attributes

Active disk and directory

The disk drives in MS-DOS and Windows-based computers are traditionally identified by the letters A:, B:, C:, etc. The drive letter is followed by a colon. Since most computers can have up to two floppy disks these are normally drives A: and B:. The first hard disk drive is normally drive C:. Computers attached to a network may have additional drives labelled alphabetically up to Z:. In an Apple Macintosh system the disks can have whatever name you choose.

The files on a disk are normally grouped together into **directories**. Some computer systems refer to these as **folders**. They allow related files to be kept together so that they can be found easily. The computer usually deals with only one disk drive and one directory at a time. These are known as the 'active disk drive and directory'.

In the MS-DOS operating system, the active directory is shown as the system 'prompt'. This appears on screen whenever the computer is ready to accept a new command. An example is shown at the bottom of Figure 2.1, which shows that the active disk drive is C:. In the Windows operating system, the active directory is shown whenever a file has to be opened or saved.

Directories

The directories on a disk are arranged in a tree structure which has a root and branches. It is often drawn with the 'root' at the top or at the side of the picture, as in Figure 2.5

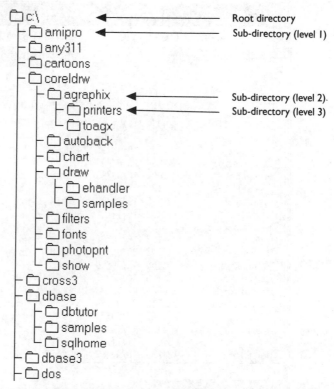

Figure 2.5 Part of a tree structured directory

The first directory in the list is called the 'root' directory and is indicated with the \ (backslash) symbol. The root directory contains a number of sub-directories that are used to store the various programs needed by the computer user. Each sub-directory may contain a word processor program, a database program, some games programs or something similar. If a program needs extra space to keep its own files, these are often grouped in further sub-directories.

For example, in Figure 2.5, the directory containing the Corel Draw graphics program, coreldrw, has two further levels of sub-directories. The first of these is agraphix which has two further sub-directories, printers and toagx. Not all software requires such a complex directory structure, but two levels of sub-directories is very common.

Finding out the disk contents

It is likely that there are hundreds of files on a hard disk, but it is not usually necessary to find out the names of all of them. Instead, you can see the contents of the 'active directory' in a computer with an MS-DOS operating system as follows. The files in a directory are easily discovered with the 'Directory' command, 'DIR'. At the prompt, whether it is A:>_ or C:>_, type:

A:>**DIR**   and press Return, or type

A:>**DIR/W**   for a wide listing in five columns.

The computer reads the contents of the disk directory and gives a complete listing, which will be similar to that shown in Figure 2.1. Any sub-directories are shown in square brackets – e.g. [SAMPLES].

Changing directories

Changing to a different directory requires the 'Change directory' command, 'CD'. Type CD followed by the directory name together with is full location in the tree structure. For example:

C:>**CD**   Returns to the 'root' directory

C:>**CD\CORELDRW\DRAW\SAMPLES**   changes to the SAMPLES sub-directory within the coreldrw tree structure

C:>**CD..**   goes back one level in the directory tree.

In a Windows-based system, you will need to use the 'File Manager' program. In the 'Main' window, double click the 'File Manager' icon to obtain a picture like that shown in Figure 2.4. Select the 'Tree and Directory' option from the 'Tree' pull-down menu. Then select the required disk by clicking the icon on the third line. The screen will show a list of files and the directory tree for the disk.

Select the required directory by clicking on it, and its list of files will be displayed. Changing from one directory to another is simply a matter of clicking on the required directory. It is a good idea to practice selecting a few different directories until you are familiar with its operation.

Making and removing directories

Sometimes new directories have to be created either on a hard disk or on a floppy disk. This is a very easy operation as long as a few simple precautions are taken. The point to remember is that the new directory created will be a sub-directory of the current directory.

With MS-DOS, to make a sub-directory called LETTERS, in the current directory, type:

C:\>**MD LETTERS**

With Windows, the operation is carried out with the File Manager program as follows:

In File Manager, select 'File', 'Create directory', then type LETTERS when the dialog box appears.

Removing directories is done in a similar operation. In MS-DOS directories can be removed only if all of the files are erased from them first. To remove the empty directory, change to the directory level above the one to be removed, then type:

C:\>**RD LETTERS**   to remove the LETTERS directory.

With Windows, choose 'File Manager', then select the directory to be removed by clicking on it. Then choose 'File', 'Delete' from the menu and click 'OK'.

Wild cards

Wild cards are characters which operating systems interpret in a special way.

* replaces any number of letters

? replaces a single character

Using a wild card, it is possible, for example, to list all the files beginning with B, or all the .DOC files, as shown below:

```
A:>DIR B*.*   the first * replaces the last seven letters of the file name
              and the second * replaces the three letters of the extension
A:>DIR *.DOC  the * replaces the whole file name for anything with a
              .DOC extension
```

Wild cards are very important in system commands and can be used in many of the others to help simplify or speed up the typing.

The same effect can be used in Windows 'File Manager' if only files from a certain group are needed. In the 'View' pull-down menu, click 'By file type'. Instead of the *.* which appears in the box that opens, type *.DOC, to list only the .DOC files for example.

Worked example

Disk contents

A friend has asked you to find out the names of all of the files on a floppy disk. When you enter the 'DIR/W' command, the screen shows

```
Volume in drive A is TEXT
Volume Serial Number is 3044-2017
Directory of A:\
[LETTERS ]   [POSTERS]   STOCK.DOC   SALE.DOC
```

What commands would you enter to discover all of the file names on the disk, assuming none are hidden?

SOLUTION
There are two sub-directories, [LETTERS] and [POSTERS] on the disk, as well as the two files in the root directory. The following commands would be required:

```
A:\>CD LETTERS        change to the LETTERS sub-directory
A:\LETTERS>DIR/W      list the files in LETTERS sub-directory
A:\LETTERS>CD..\POSTERS   change to POSTERS sub-directory
A:\POSTERS>DIR/W      list the files in POSTERS sub-directory
```

Paths

A **path** is the route to a file in the tree-structured directory. However, it can also be used as a special operating system command. When the computer operating system needs to find a file, it first looks in the active directory. If the file is not there, it looks in other directories along a fixed path in an attempt to find it. The 'path' is simply a group of directories which it searches in order until the file is located. If the file is not in any of the directories, the message 'File not found' will be produced.

Setting the path helps to improve efficiency because it allows the computer files to be stored logically in directories, and also makes them available quickly whenever they are needed. It saves the computer a lot of time searching for each file it needs throughout the whole disk.

In the DOS operating system the 'Path' command can be entered from the prompt and contains a list of directories in the tree separated by semicolons. For example, the command

```
C:>PATH C:\;C:\DOS;C:\WINDOWS;C:\WORD
```

would make the computer search the root directory, then the DOS, WINDOWS and WORD directories for any files it needed.

The path to each file is kept automatically in the Windows operating system so this problem does not usually arise.

Formatting a disk

Before a floppy disk can be used it needs to have a set of tracks written onto its magnetic surface. These are all numbered and are arranged in sectors so that all the information can be easily retrieved. Disks are prepared for use in a process known as **formatting** the disk.

If MS-DOS is being used, the process is simply
* Insert a new disk in drive A:
* Type at the prompt **FORMAT A:**

With Windows, choose the File Manager program, then
* Select 'Disk', 'Format disk' from the menu
* If the data in the selection box is correct, select 'OK'.

When the process is complete, the disk is ready for use.

Copying files

The quickest way to copy printed information is to use a photocopier. If the information is on a computer disk, it is much easier to copy it with a simple command.

The MS-DOS command is in the form
    C:>COPY source destination   where source and destination are file names, and they are separated by spaces in the command.

For example, to copy the file FIGURE1.DOC on drive C: to FIGURE2.DOC on drive A:, the command is
    C:>COPY C:FIGURE1.DOC A:FIGURE2.DOC

When a number of files have to be copied at the same time, the 'wild card' symbols can be used, so to copy all the files which have .DOC extensions from drive C: to drive A:, the command would be
    C:>COPY C:*.DOC A:

Windows makes the task of copying files a very easy, and uses the 'File Manager' program. Open two windows – one showing the directory the files come from, and another showing the destination directory. An example of this is shown in Figure 2.6.

The two Windows show the directory containing the file, AMORTIZE.XLS, which is to be copied, and the destination – in this case, drive A:.

To copy the file simply highlight it by clicking on it with the mouse, then use the mouse to drag it to the destination directory.

Groups of files can be copied in the same way as a single file if you first highlight them by clicking them with the mouse while holding down the Control key on the keyboard. Hold down the Control key to copy between directories on the same hard disk or the files will be moved instead of copied.

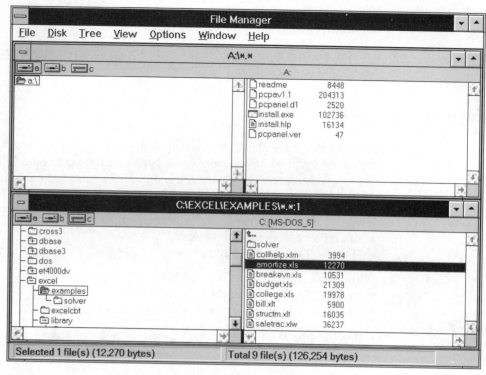

Figure 2.6 Copying files using Windows

Worked example

Copying files

You have just created three files – CHAP1.DOC, CHAP2.DOC, and CHAP3.DOC – with a word processor, and think it would be useful to create a backup copy in another directory called BACKUP, on the same disk. What commands would be required using the Windows File Manager?

SOLUTION

1. First, create the BACKUP directory. Using the File Manager Program, click on the directory containing the files, then select 'File', 'Create directory', then enter the name BACKUP.

2. Hold down the Control key and click each file in turn and ensure that they are highlighted.

3. Drag the files onto the new directory on the left side of the display, then confirm the action when the dialog box appears.

Progress check

These questions are designed to check your understanding of the ideas covered so far in this chapter. They will also enable you to think about how some of the topics may apply to you in the GNVQ you are studying. Try to answer them without looking back at the previous pages unless you really get stuck.

1. Why do computers need an operating system? Briefly describe three of the functions an operating system performs.

2. What are the restrictions which apply to file names in the MS-DOS and Windows operating systems?

3. Why do file names in MS-DOS and Windows-based computers have two parts?

4. How does a directory structure on a computer disk improve the efficiency of its operation?

5. If you buy a new floppy disk, what do you need to do to it before it can be used?

6. Why would you need to create a directory on one of your own disks?

7. A file called REPORT.HDR is stored on the hard disk drive C: of your computer. Briefly describe how you would copy it onto a floppy disk.

8. Why is Windows a popular operating system?

9. What applications programs are you likely to use in the course of your studies?

10. What is a file attribute, and what is its purpose?

11. In the operating system you normally use, how do you perform the following operations:
    (a) Rename a file, say from CHAP1.DOC to CHAP2.DOC?
    (b) Erase or delete a file?
    (c) Make a new directory called TEMP on a floppy disk?
    (d) Copy file CHAP2.DOC to the TEMP directory on a floppy disk?
    (e) Display the time on the screen? (You may need to look this up)

To help you to find out more about your own computer system, try Assignment 1 now, which is at the end of this chapter.

Setting up the operating system

Different people like their computers to work in different ways. For example, an accountant may always want to start a session on the computer by using a spreadsheet program. A receptionist in a dentist's surgery may immediately want to load the appointments database when the computer is switched on. A sales representative may wish to start every day with an electronic diary of the appointments for the day.

Each person has different requirements, not only for the way in which the computer starts up but also for how it performs. Some people like bright colours on the screen while others prefer a more subdued colour scheme. Some people like the mouse to move fast but others like it to go slowly.

Fortunately, most of these preferences can be accommodated because the computer operating system can be set up for each individual so that it performs in the way they prefer. Of course, if you share a computer with other users and the computer is set up for you any changes you make to the way in which it operates will affect other people. It would be a good idea to agree any changes with the other users before making them.

Automatic starting procedure

When most computers are started, they perform an automatic starting routine. In DOS-based machines this routine is stored in a program called AUTOEXEC.BAT, which is found either on a floppy disk or on the hard disk of the computer in the root directory. AUTOEXEC.BAT is a list of operating system commands which the computer performs before letting the user enter any commands. The commands in the file can be changed to make the computer do different things when it is switched on. However, it would be very unwise to make any changes to this file unless you have a clear understanding of the effects the changes will have. If you do not own the computer, you should get permission from the owner first.

```
@Echo off
path c:\windows;c:\dos;c:\dbase
c:\windows\smartdrv/q a- b-
set mouse=MICROSOFT
set display=ET4000
loadhi c:\dos\keyb uk,,c:\dos\keyboard.sys
prompt $p$_$n$g
set temp=c:\temp
win
```

Figure 2.7 A typical AUTOEXEC.BAT file

The file shown in Figure 2.7 contains nine different commands, each of which sets up certain operating system functions. The first line, `@Echo off`, stops the commands form being shown on the screen as they are being executed. This is followed by lines which set up the path so that all the files can be found easily, then a series of commands to set up the smart drive, the mouse, the display and the keyboard. The prompt is defined on the third last line, then a temporary directory is set up, and finally the program starts the Windows software. This means that every time this computer is switched on, it will automatically start up the Windows software.

Starting Windows

If you choose to run Windows as soon as the computer is switched on, or if you start it from the keyboard, it can also be made to run one of the other programs on disk automatically. To make this happen, open the 'Startup' window and drag the icon of the programs you wish to start first into this window. The next time Windows runs, it will automatically run the programs in the 'Startup' window first. With Windows you can have a number of different programs running at the same time.

Controlling the peripherals

When a computer is operating, there are times when you may wish to change the way it behaves. For example, the screen colours may not be what you want, the cursor may blink too fast or the mouse may move too slowly. These

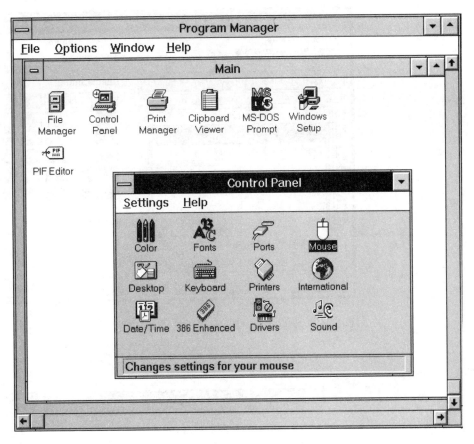

Figure 2.8 The Windows Control Panel

functions can be controlled from the MS-DOS operating system, but they are much easier to control using Windows.

The Windows Control Panel can be activated from the 'Main' window by double clicking the 'Control Panel' icon. This will give you a window like that in Figure 2.8.

The Control Panel allows the main functions of the computer to be set according to the user's wishes. In particular, the settings for the screen colours, the mouse, the desktop, the date and time, the keyboard and printers can all be set up from this window.

Screen colours
Selecting the screen colours is just a matter of clicking on the 'Color' icon and following the instructions. You can choose from over 20 different preset schemes or design your own. The colours can be the standard range or you can select from a palette of several thousand.

Mouse operations
The mouse speed and its double click speed can be controlled from the mouse control box. Generally, once this is set you don't have to change it unless another user wants to use the system in a different way. If a different mouse is connected to the computer it may also need to be adjusted.

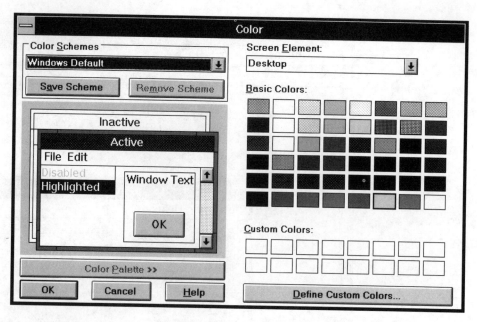

Figure 2.9 Selecting screen colours in Windows

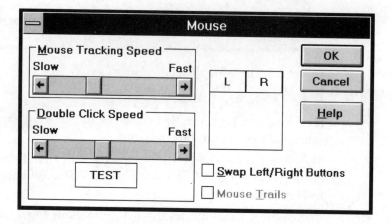

Figure 2.10 Mouse control dialog box

Desktop

The other main characteristics of the computer operation can be controlled from the Windows desktop control box. This box controls the screen background, the screen saver (a moving image which appears on screen after several minutes of inactivity to prevent the screen phosphor in the display being burned by a fixed picture), the cursor blink rate, etc. All of these functions are interesting to play with, although none of them directly affect the way in which the computer operates.

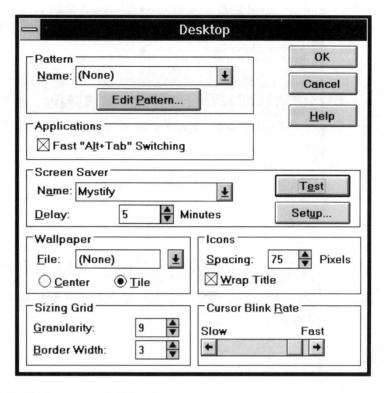

Figure 2.11 Desktop control dialog box

Connecting a printer

There are many different types of printer on the market and very few of them have exactly the same set of features or operate in the same way. It is therefore vital that each computer is set up correctly for the printer to which it is connected. There are some very different systems so that, for example, if the computer is set up for a laser printer and it is actually connected to a dot matrix printer, some very peculiar printing will result.

Printer drivers

Each computer includes a set of programs called 'printer drivers', either as part of the operating system or as part of an application package. These are special translation programs written for each of the printers that are likely to be used with the computer. They take the basic output from an application program like a word processor, and add all the correct control codes needed for a particular printer.

For example, the code to make letters appear bold on one printer may not be the same as those required on another. The printer driver for a dot matrix printer

```
┌─────────────────────────────────────────────────────────────┐
│ ▬                         Printers                            │
├─────────────────────────────────────────────────────────────┤
│ ┌─Default Printer──────────────────────────┐   ┌──────────┐  │
│ │ PostScript Printer on LPT1:               │   │  Close   │  │
│ └───────────────────────────────────────────┘   └──────────┘  │
│                                                                │
│ ┌─Installed Printers:───────────────────────┐   ┌──────────┐  │
│ │ Epson LQ-1000 on LPT1:                  ▲ │   │ Connect… │  │
│ │ HP DeskJet Printers on LPT1:              │   └──────────┘  │
│ │ PostScript Printer on LPT1:               │   ┌──────────┐  │
│ │                                           │   │  Setup…  │  │
│ │                                         ▼ │   └──────────┘  │
│ └───────────────────────────────────────────┘   ┌──────────┐  │
│                                                  │  Remove  │  │
│          ┌───────────────────────────┐          └──────────┘  │
│          │   Set As Default Printer  │          ┌──────────┐  │
│          └───────────────────────────┘          │  Add >>  │  │
│ ☒ Use Print Manager                              └──────────┘  │
│                                                  ┌──────────┐  │
│                                                  │   Help   │  │
│                                                  └──────────┘  │
└─────────────────────────────────────────────────────────────┘
```

```
┌─────────────────────────────────────────────────────────────┐
│ ▬                      Epson LQ-1000                          │
├─────────────────────────────────────────────────────────────┤
│ Resolution:   │ 120 x 180                           │ ▼ │   ┌────────┐ │
│ Paper Size:   │ Letter 8 ½ x 11 in                  │ ▼ │   │   OK   │ │
│ Paper Source: │ Lower Tray                          │ ▼ │   └────────┘ │
│                                                          ┌────────┐ │
│                                                          │ Cancel │ │
│ ┌─Orientation──────────────────────┐                    └────────┘ │
│ │        ⊙ Portrait                 │                   ┌─────────┐ │
│ │  A                                │                   │ Options…│ │
│ │        ○ Landscape                │                   └─────────┘ │
│ └───────────────────────────────────┘                             │
│                                                          ┌────────┐ │
│                                                          │ About… │ │
│ ┌─Cartridges (max: 1───────────────┐                    └────────┘ │
│ │ None                              │                   ┌────────┐ │
│ │ Courier                           │                   │  Help  │ │
│ │ Prestige                          │                   └────────┘ │
│ │ Script                            │                               │
│ │ OCR-B                             │                               │
│ └───────────────────────────────────┘                             │
└─────────────────────────────────────────────────────────────┘
```

```
┌─────────────────────────────────────────────────────────────┐
│ ▬                         Options                             │
├─────────────────────────────────────────────────────────────┤
│ ┌─Dithering──┐  ┌─Intensity Control──────┐   ┌────────┐      │
│ │ ○ None     │  │ Darker        Lighter  │   │   OK   │      │
│ │ ○ Coarse   │  │ ←│█████        │→      │   └────────┘      │
│ │ ○ Fine     │  │         Normal         │   ┌────────┐      │
│ │ ⊙ Line Art │  └────────────────────────┘   │ Cancel │      │
│ └────────────┘                                └────────┘      │
│                                               ┌────────┐      │
│                                               │ About… │      │
│                                               └────────┘      │
│                                               ┌────────┐      │
│                                               │  Help  │      │
│                                               └────────┘      │
│ Print Quality:  │ Letter Quality              │ ▼ │           │
└─────────────────────────────────────────────────────────────┘
```

Figure 2.12 Setting up a printer

will therefore add one set of control codes to the basic text, while the printer driver for a laser printer may add other codes.

Installing printer drivers

The correct printer driver *must* be installed as part of the operating system before any printing is attempted. Normally this would be done when the system is delivered, but it may also be done if a new printer has to be connected or an alternative printer is needed for a particular task.

The printer driver also needs to send its data to the correct port to which the printer is connected. This may be either a serial port, like COM1, COM2 or a parallel port such as LPT1 or LPT2. The ports can be set via the Control Panel but great care must be taken to get all of the settings right. Therefore you should not alter any of these settings unless you know exactly what you are doing. It is normally the job of a computer technician.

> Look back to Chapter 1 if you are not sure about the function of a port or the names which are used for them.

To install a printer you need a copy of the printer driver program. Some of these programs come with the operating system software, catering for most of the popular printers on the market. If an unusual printer has to be installed, the printer driver will probably be supplied by the printer manufacturer.

Figure 2.12 shows the three steps you have to go through to install a different printer. First, choose the printer in the top dialog box, then choose its basic set up with the 'setup' button and finally some of the more specialist options.

Once a printer has been installed, it can then be selected from any program by using the 'Print setup' option from the 'File' menu.

Progress check

Try some of the questions below before completing the rest of the chapter. You may need to try out some of the functions on your computer to check that they work correctly.

1. What is the name of the program that a DOS-based computer operates when it is first switched on? What is its function?

2. What happens if your computer is switched on with a floppy disk already in drive A:?

3. A friend has asked you to speed up the operation of the mouse on their computer. How would you do it?

4. What reasons are there for wanting a range of different screen colour schemes to be available?

5. What is the function of a 'printer driver'?

6. What printers can be operated from the computer you normally use? (N.B. In a computer using the MS-DOS operating system this may depend upon the applications programs.)

7. Try to find out what a 'PostScript' printer is and what type it is likely to be.

Keeping your work secure

It is important always to keep at least two copies of the files you have created on a computer, preferably in different places. This helps to prevent files being accidentally lost or deleted. Unfortunately, this lesson is usually learned when it is too late! Most people think it is impossible for coffee to be spilled onto their disk, or for the computer to display a message like 'Bad sector' or 'General error' when the vital page is about to be printed.

Most people learn the lesson the hard way, but eventually realise that keeping two copies of a file is a good idea. There are a number of ways in which this can be done, each of which requires only a small amount of extra time at the computer.

> **Remember:**
> Use the 'Copy' command or its equivalent to copy each file you have been working on before you leave the computer.

The simplest way to make an extra copy of a file is to copy it onto another disk with the 'Copy' command. If the computer only has one floppy disk drive, you may have to copy the file from the original disk onto the hard disk first before copying it onto another floppy disk. Copying can be done very easily with whatever operating system your computer uses. By developing the habit of copying all of your work onto a backup disk you will probably save yourself a good deal of frustration later.

Other security routines

The 'Copy' command is the one most frequently used to make an extra security copy of a file on disk. In addition, most software, particularly word processors, automatically makes its own backup copy of each file. These have the same file name, but have a .BAK extension. It is not a good idea to rely on this method however, since the backup may be the previous version of your file, and not exactly what you think it is.

For more extensive backups, MS-DOS has three other commands, 'Backup', 'Diskcopy' and 'Xcopy'. These will copy anything from a single file to a complete disk and all of its sub-directories. Their operation can be quite complicated, but is explained in detail if HELP is entered at the MS-DOS prompt followed by the command name. 'Diskcopy' will copy the whole disk irrespective of how many files are on it.

Whenever the 'Backup' command is used, the information stored on the backup disk has to be returned with the 'Restore' command before it can be used.

If you are using Windows, you can use the 'Copy' command to copy anything from one file to the complete contents of a hard disk. Highlight the files to be copied in the 'File Manager' window and hold down the Control key on the keyboard while selecting each one. Then drag the selection to the destination disk icon.

Removing unwanted files

No matter how big a computer disk is, it still seems to fill up very quickly. This may be because the software is creating automatic backup files, or simply because the files are much larger that you originally anticipated. This is especially likely to be the case if any graphics images have been created since they can easily occupy a few hundred thousand bytes of disk space.

Removing the unwanted files is another simple routine which many users either forget to do regularly, or do not know how to do. It is often forgotten until the disk gives an error message saying that it is full. This may mean that it is too late since some data could be lost.

In MS-DOS the 'Delete' or 'Erase' commands are the easiest way to clean up a disk. For example, to erase all of the .BAK backup files on disk A: type

```
C:>ERASE A:*.BAK or C:>DEL A:*.BAK
```

In Windows, open the 'File Manager' window and select the files to be removed by highlighting them. It may help to display only certain files by choosing them from the 'View' menu, 'By file type'. This will allow you to display only the selected files, such as the .BAK files. When the files have been selected, choose 'Delete' from the 'File' menu.

Passwords

Sometimes you need to keep the contents of a computer system secure from unauthorised access. Most computers contain a number of possible security systems which can keep data safe.

Some office computers have keys which can be removed to prevent casual users from tampering with the system. In addition some computers require a password to be entered before the keyboard can be used. This effectively stops anyone who does not know the password from looking at any files on the disk. Sensitive files can also be hidden so that they never appear in any directory listings.

In large organisations computers which may be connected to vast databases have elaborate security routines. All users need both a **user identity** and a **password**. If the wrong identity or the wrong password are entered the system can lock the user out. It does not usually indicate whether the identity or the password were wrong! This is particularly true when there is access via a network or the public telephone system. Even so, some people still regard computer 'hacking' as a game, and try to get through security systems, although this is now illegal. The consequences can be very serious, since convicted hackers have been sent to prison. Organisations whose systems have been 'hacked' may have to spend many thousands of pounds on checking their systems.

Running programs from the operating system

There are many types of file to be found on a computer disk but only a few of them are likely to be programs. In DOS-based computers these will have a file extension of .EXE, .COM or .BAT.

Running one of these programs is very easy with any of the operating systems.

In the MS-DOS system, it is usually best to change to the directory containing the program then just type its name, without its extension. For example, to run the application program called BASIC.COM, just type BASIC. It is also possible to start the same program without changing to the directory first by typing the full path name. If the program BASIC.COM is found in the LANGS subdirectory on drive C:, it can be run by typing **C:\LANGS\BASIC.**

In Windows, the programs are shown in the windows as icons so they can be run by double clicking on their icon with the mouse. These programs can also be started by clicking on their name in a list created by the 'File Manager' program, such as those shown in Figures 2.4 and 2.9. The icon of a program has a small bar over it, so they are easy to identify. Programs can also be started by clicking on a file name created with them. For example, clicking on the file name of a document will start up the word processor which created it.

Batch files

Batch files can be very useful in making the computer perform tasks automatically. One of them, the AUTOEXEC batch file, which controls the starting procedures, has already been considered. It is possible to make up your own batch files to speed up repeated operations and so improve efficiency. Use the MS-DOS 'Edit' program or the Windows 'Notepad' to write the batch file as a series of simple commands.

For example, the batch file shown below starts a program called 'banner' in the display subdirectory, which needs a mouse driver program to be loaded first. When the program finishes it returns to the root directory. The commands would be:

```
cd c:\dos
msmouse
cd c:\display
banner
cd\
```

Other batch files can be written to take care of many of the tasks needed to keep computer disks tidy, to do backup operations or to start many the programs on a typical hard disk. Some batch files can be used to make a very simple menu system.

What if things go wrong?

Sooner or later all computer users will experience some kind of fault with their system. It may be something simple – like not being able to read a disk file – or something more serious – like a complete system failure. In each case you will need to decide whether the fault is one that you can deal with yourself or whether you need assistance. There is a great temptation to switch off a computer if it does not behave properly but this is hardly ever necessary. It can seriously damage a computer if it is switched off and then back on again too quickly.

Before calling for help, check the most obvious things.

Check first that the commands you have entered are correct. Often when the computer does not perform exactly as expected, it is because it was given the wrong commands. There are many different sources of mistakes but by taking a few moments to try and work out why a computer is not behaving as expected you can save a lot of time waiting for help to arrive.
- Some formatting or typing problems in word processors can be reversed with the 'Undo' command from the Edit menu, if it is used straight away.
- Printers which give poor printouts may be using the wrong printer drivers or the margins may be set incorrectly. If they do not print at all they may be switched off or off-line.
- Files that cannot be found may have been saved in the wrong directories or onto the wrong disk.

If an error message like the one shown in Figure 2.13 appears, check that the right disk is in the drive first, then check that the file name was typed correctly.

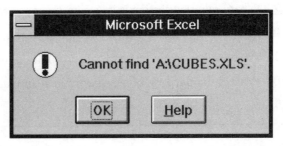

Figure 2.13 A typical error message box

Real faults

Sometimes real faults develop. Cables can become disconnected. The disk drive may not be able to read a disk or certain keys may not work correctly. There may be no response from the mouse or the printer may not do anything. When there are apparent faults like this, try the operation several times to check that it is a definite fault. Sometimes things seem to work the second time! If not, you may be able to find out whether the fault is with the computer hardware or with the program by trying another applications program if possible.

If you think that your computer has developed a fault, and you have checked the obvious things, leave it in its faulty state and ask for help. A technician or system supervisor is more likely to be able to diagnose the fault if it is still evident rather than having to recreate the same conditions again.

Rebooting – Control, Alt, Del

When software 'crashes', which it does quite often, it will probably not respond to normal keyboard or mouse commands. Pressing the keys usually simply makes the loudspeaker bleep. If this happens the best way to recover the situation is to press the Control, Alt and Del keys simultaneously. This restarts the system and is known as 'rebooting' it. It works in the same way as if the computer had been switched off. Sometimes the computer fails to respond to this, in which case, press the 'reset' button, located on the front of most machines.

Review questions

Try these questions if you are happy that you have understood most of the subjects covered in this chapter.

1. Setting the mouse speed may be quite difficult in a system which only uses MS-DOS. Why?

2. What are the basic rules for naming files in IBM-compatible computers?

3. What are the advantages of the Windows operating system compared with MS-DOS? How do these advantages improve the working conditions for users?

4. What is the difference between a serial port and a parallel port?

5. How could you make sure that a laser printer and a dot matrix printer would each print correctly when connected to the same computer and word processing software?

6. Why might you need to set up different directories on a floppy disk in the course of your studies?

7. What operating system is in use in the computer you normally work on?

8. How would you deal with a message on screen which said 'File not found'?

9. Why is it important to keep backup copies of files on a computer disk?

10. What is the purpose of a password in a computer system?

Exercises

Try the following exercises if you would like some practice at using the commands in your operating system. If you normally use Microsoft Windows, you can do all of the operations with the File Manager program. If possible also try the exercises with the MS-DOS commands. Click the MS-DOS prompt in the 'Main' window to start it.

You will need a floppy disk with about six files already on it, some with names beginning with letters A to K and others beginning L to Z. Your tutor may be able to supply one.

1. Using your floppy disk with a number of files already on it, make a sub-directory called ATOK, and another called LTOZ. Change to the LTOZ directory to make it active, and create another directory called COPIES.

2. With the disk created in Exercise 1, copy all of the files from the root directory into the ATOK directory. Now copy only the files beginning with the letters L to Z into the LTOZ directory.

3. Using the disk created in Exercise 2, delete all files which begin with the letters L to Z from the ATOK directory.

4. Using the disk as it is after Exercise 3, copy all of the files from the LTOZ directory into the COPIES directory. Now list each directory on screen and check their contents.

5. Write down the full path and file name for two of the files in the COPIES directory from the disk in Exercise 4.

6. Take a blank disk, preferably new, and format it using the 'Format' option on your computer. Give it a name, such as 'BACKUP' and put a suitable label on it.

7. Work out how to copy the files from another floppy disk onto the disk created in Exercise 6. This is very easy if your computer has two floppy disk drives, but you might need to copy them into a TEMP directory on the hard disk first. Make sure that any sub-directories on the original disk are accurately copied onto the backup disk.

8. Choose a disk with at least two unwanted files on it. Use the MS-DOS or a Windows command to delete them both from the floppy disk.

9. With Microsoft Windows, use the Control Panel to make the following changes to the system operation:

    (a) make the mouse speed as fast as possible

    (b) change the desktop wallpaper to a new pattern

    (c) change to a new Windows colour scheme chosen from one of the standards supplied.

10. While operating in Windows, press the Control, Alt and Del keys simultaneously, and follow the instructions on screen to restart the computer.

Assignment 1
Getting to know your computer

This assignment can be used to provide evidence for the following Performance Criteria:

Element 2.1   PC 4

Element 3.1   PC 4

Introduction

You have just started a new job and have been asked to use the computer which a previous employee has worked on for some time. It already has a number of programs installed but nobody seems to know exactly what they are.

The purpose of this assignment is to enable you to find out exactly what software is installed and what that software can do. Ideally, you will require access to the operating system commands, but you can omit Question 2 if your computer is connected to a network.

Your task

1. One way to find out what a computer will do is to check on the directory structure of the hard disk. Using the operating system installed on your computer use the appropriate commands to find out the complete directory tree. Draw a diagram of the directory tree or find out how to make the computer print one for you. With a networked computer, write down the basic menu structure instead.

2. Choose five directories on your disk and examine them in detail. List all of the file names they contain. The main programs in each of these directories will have file extension of .EXE or .COM. Indicate these files in your lists.

3. Briefly describe the function of each of the program files in the directories above. You may have to run them to find out what they do! Either type the file name at the prompt, or double click on their icon or file name in a Window. On a networked computer you can simply run the program from the menu.

4. If you have time, list the functions of the programs in the other directories on your hard disk so that you have a complete idea of the capabilities of your computer.

Complete a report on your findings, illustrated if possible by a computer printout of the files found and the tree structure of the directory.

Assignment 2 starts on the next page

Assignment 2
Computer programs which run automatically

This assignment can be used to provide evidence for the following Performance Criteria:

Element 2.4   PCs 1, 2, 3 and 4

Element 3.4   PCs 1, 2, 4 and 5

Introduction

There are many different ways in which a computer can be made to operate when it is first switched on. Each user is likely to prefer a different set of programs. However, many computer operators have no idea that they can make their computer behave in a way that suits them and so they simply leave them in the state in which they were first delivered or installed.

Your task

Your task is to conduct a simple survey of people who use computers as part of their job.

1. For each computer user (choose between five and ten people in different situations) find out what programs their computers run automatically when they are first switched on. Compile a table showing the make of computer, the operating system and the programs which run in order, until the point at which the system waits for a keyboard or mouse input.

2. Ask the users if they would prefer any different programs to start automatically, and note the results.

3. Ask the users if they know how to make their computer start any other programs automatically.

Write a short report as a result of your findings which will make recommendations about any training necessary to make the use of computers in the workplace more efficient. Include an explanation of why the computer is used to perform tasks for the users rather than other, manual, methods.

Assignment 3
Cleaning up a disk

This assignment can be used to provide evidence for the following Performance Criteria:

Element 2.4 PCs 2, 3 and 4

Element 3.4 PCs 2, 4 and 5

Introduction

Computers frequently run out of disk space. One solution to this problem is to periodically copy the files which are important onto a set of floppy disks, then erase the unwanted files from the hard disk. It is very important to obtain the permission of the computer owner before anything like this is attempted.

One way to try something similar is to clean up a set of floppy disks and make a backup of the important files onto another floppy disk. To undertake this assignment you will need at least two floppy disks with a number of files on them. If you have no files of your own yet, your tutor may be able to supply some.

Your task

1. Print a copy of the list of files on your disks and decide which of them are required and which are to be deleted. Erase any .BAK files and any others which you may not need. Make sure that *none* of the program files, .EXE, .COM or .BAT files are erased if there are any on the disks.

2. Use the 'Erase' command to remove as many of the unwanted files as you can using as few instructions as possible. This means that you should try to use the 'wild cards' * and ?

3. Now create a temporary directory called TEMP on the hard disk. Copy all of the files you wish to save from each floppy disk into it.

4. Check the contents of the TEMP directory very carefully to make sure that it contains all the files you need. Now delete all the files from the floppy disks. You may wish to reformat the disks, although this is not strictly necessary.

5. Copy all of the files from the TEMP directory back onto one of the floppy disks and label it as your working disk. Make sure it is dated.

6. Copy all of the files from the TEMP directory back to another of the floppy disks, and label this as your backup disk. Make sure it is dated so that you will be able to refer back to it later. Print a list of its contents.

7. Erase all of the files from the TEMP directory on the hard disk.

Produce a short report which lists the files before and after the disk clean-up on each disk. Give an indication of the time taken for the exercise and the amount of disk space now free for new files. Explain how the user's work is made much easier with a cleaned disk. Note any faults that occurred in the process.

Assignment 4
Setting up a new computer

This assignment can be used to provide evidence for the following
Performance Criteria:

Element 2.1   PCs 1, 2, 3 and 4

Element 2.2   PCs 1, 2, 4 and 5

Element 2.4   PCs 3, 4 and 5

Element 3.1   PCs 1, 2, 3, 4 and 5

Element 3.2   PCs 1, 2, 4, 5 and 7

Element 3.4   PCs 4, 5 and 6

Introduction

You are employed in the marketing department of a company whose manager
has decided that all new employees need access to a computer for word processing and for producing graphics. The computer and the software have
been ordered by the head office and have just arrived. Unfortunately there is
nobody available to set it up so you have been asked to have a go yourself.

The items below have been delivered:
- a computer with a copy of MS-DOS and Windows already installed on the
  hard disk
- an ink jet printer with a connecting lead
- a box with some word processing software in it
- a box with some graphics software in it
- a mouse
- a keyboard
- a computer screen.

Your task

Your task is to find out how to set up the computer, then to do it. Fortunately, the
installation of the software is just a matter of creating a suitable directory, then putting
the first disk in the drive and typing A:SETUP at the prompt. Alternatively you can type
this into the dialog box which appears when the Program Manager 'File, Run' command
is activated.

You will be required to produce a short report on how to set up such a computer for
the other new employees. The report will need to contain the following information.

1. How you decide where the cables from the power source, screen, keyboard,
   mouse and printer have to be connected.

2. How you create the required directories on the hard disk.

3. How you install the word processing program.

4. How you install the graphics program.

5. How you set up the new printer so that it will work with both application programs.

6. The contents of an AUTOEXEC.BAT file which will automatically start Windows when the computer is switched on.

Be sure to list in your report any problems you encountered, together with an explanation of how you overcame them.

CHAPTER 3

Introduction to word processing

Objectives

When you have finished this chapter you should be able to:
- Appreciate the basic functions of a word processor
- Understand how to enter text into a document using a typical word processor
- Understand simple terminology such as margins, blocks, justifications, word-wrap, tabulation, ruler etc.
- Use a word processor to enter text in a given format
- Understand how to use a range of printing effects such as italics, bold, underline and different fonts
- Understand how to number pages and date documents
- Understand how to achieve the required printed output from a word processor
- Include a picture in a document

This chapter covers the Performance Criteria and Range from all of the IT Core Skills Elements at levels 2 and 3 related to the preparation, processing and presentation of text, and the combination of information from different sources, with an evaluation of the techniques used.

Word processing in business

Almost every business now has at least one word processor. Word processors are used for all forms of written material that would have been produced on a typewriter only a few years ago. People like them because they allow anyone to produce good quality documents without needing to be an expert typist. Any mistakes can be easily corrected before the document is printed. A modern word processing program will check the spelling and the grammar to make sure that it is all correct and will even suggest alternatives in case of error. In addition, word processors can allow pictures, graphs and tables to be included in any documents very easily.

The most common uses for word processors in business are for:
Letters: Thousands of business letters are sent every day. They tend to follow a similar layout and other conventions about style and presentation.
Memos: Notes between staff inside companies are usually in the form of a memorandum or memo. These are less formal than letters but are intended to let people know what is going on.
Reports: Formal reports on aspects of business, research, proposals, enquiries, and many other subjects that demand a formal response.

Publicity material: Material for publication in the newspapers or as a brochure normally starts in the form of a word processed document.

Presentation material: Presentations to clients or customers about any aspect of a business are often made into slides or transparencies for display.

The many uses for word processors are limited only by the imagination of the user. Anything typed can usually be word processed.

Figure 3.1 shows some examples of documents created with the same word processor. One is a simple memo, the second is a business letter and the third is the header page for an overhead transparency used in a presentation. Note the totally different style used in each one.

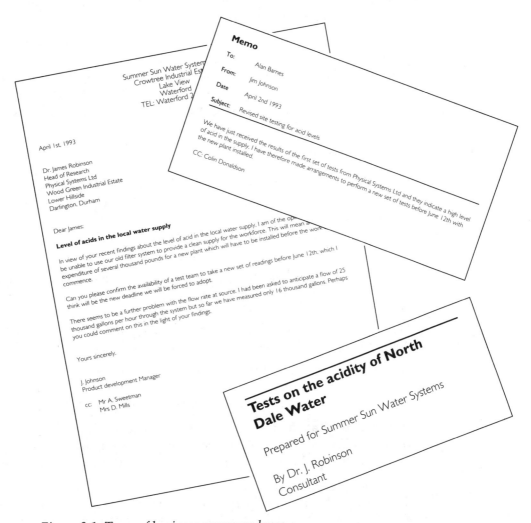

Figure 3.1 Types of business correspondence

Different word processors

Many different software manufacturers have designed their own word processing software. They have recognised that almost every computer will have a word processing package installed, so there is an enormous market for them. Each manufacturer then regularly updates their package to try to keep ahead of their competitors, so that the packages are becoming more and more sophisticated.

Some of the most well known titles include WordPerfect, Wordstar, Microsoft Word, and Ami-Pro. Popular integrated packages like Microsoft Works also include a powerful word processor.

The one you use will almost certainly have most of the features described later.

There are usually three versions of each word processor on the market, one for the MS-DOS operating system, one for Windows and one for the Macintosh. The version for MS-DOS is often more restricted than the other two and may not include all of the features mentioned in this chapter. The Windows version includes all of the features that make it very easy to transfer information between different programs. It is also likely to have many built in features of its own such as drawing, charts and table capabilities. The opening screens of some common word processors are shown in Figure 3.2

The quality of the output from any word processor depends mainly upon the printer that is used. A poor quality printer will always give poor results even with the best word processor on the market. For example, a dot matrix printer is unlikely to be able to produce photographic quality pictures, and an old daisy wheel printer is incapable of printing any graphics at all.

A window on a document

A computer screen is almost always too small to allow a complete page of text to be displayed at once, unless the print size is so small that it cannot be read. This means that the document has to be moved up and down, or from side to side on the screen so that it can all be seen. The process is known as 'scrolling', and is controlled with the 'direction' or 'cursor' keys on the keyboard.

Scrolling actually moves the cursor through the lines of the document so that the document appears to move up as the cursor moves down. In some word processors, this can also be achieved with the 'mouse'. Clicking the mouse pointer in a document moves the cursor to the point at which the cursor is pointing.

The cursor indicates the point in a document where the next character typed will appear. It is normally indicated with a flashing line, sometimes vertical, sometimes horizontal. This is sometimes called the 'insertion point'.

Text is entered at the insertion point or cursor position. Depending upon the word processor setting, new characters may either *overwrite* information already on screen, or may be *inserted* and push the old information out of the way.

Modern word processors allow more than one 'window' to be opened on the document and this allows parts of the computer screen to be used to display different sections of it at the same time. This is often a useful feature when blocks of text need to be moved or copied.

Word-wrap

The real advantage of the word processor is the speed with which text can be entered and corrected if necessary. Entering text is made easy because of a feature known as 'word-wrap'. This means that when a word is typed which is too long to fit onto a line, the word processor simply puts it on the next line automatically.

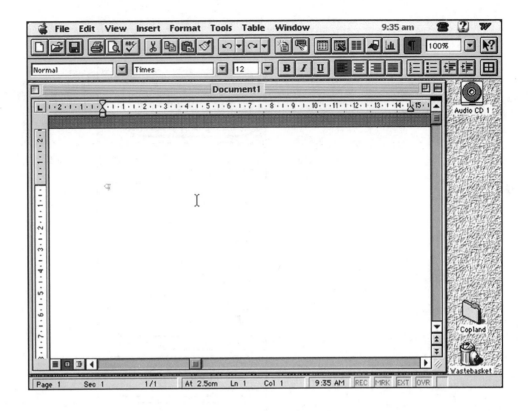

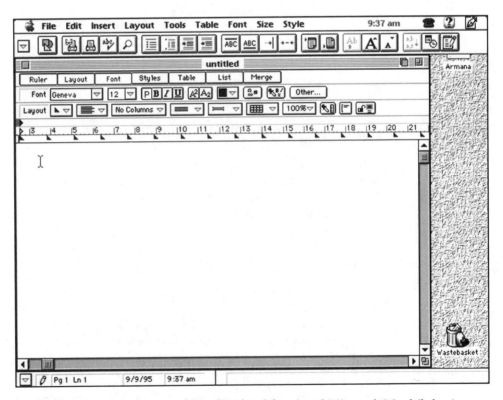

Figure 3.2 Opening screens of WordPerfect (above) and Microsoft Word (below).

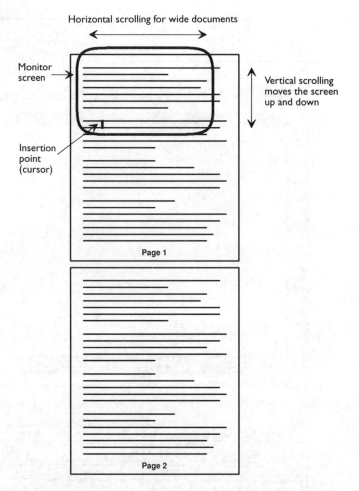

Figure 3.3 A window on a document

Justification

When the word processor decides to start a new line, it can also add extra spaces between words so that all the characters at both ends of the lines are aligned. This is known as 'justification'. Some people like it because it looks neat, but others find that the extra space between words makes the text more difficult to read.

Formatting

The process of setting out the text on a page to produce a neat layout is known as formatting the document. This may be necessary after corrections have been made or as a document is first being produced. Do not confuse formatting a document with formatting a disk – they are entirely different operations.

Formatting a document may include such things as:
- setting the line spacing
- changing the margins at the top, bottom and sides of the printed page
- using different type styles such as *italic*, **bold** or <u>underlined</u> text
- centring text on a page for headings or special emphasis
- creating columns of text or figures for tables or for a newspaper-like layout

- moving text between pages so that headings do not appear on the last line of a page
- adding page numbers, running headers or footers.

Some examples of formatting are shown in Figure 3.4.

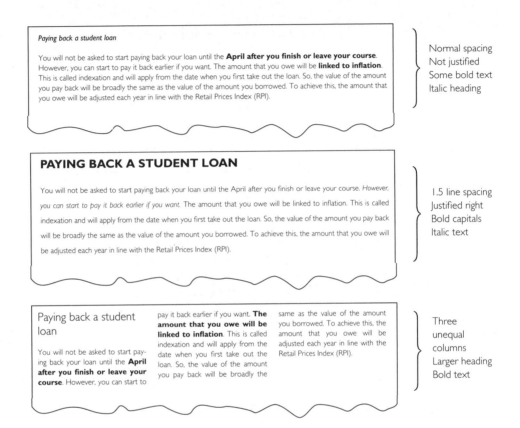

Figure 3.4 Examples of different text formatting

Entering and saving text

To make the most effective use of a word processor you will have to be able to type. Even if you can not type, you can produce high quality documents with a word processor – they just take a little longer!

It is well worth learning to type properly, using a typing tutor program if necessary. The time invested will be repaid many times over as you become able to complete documents much more quickly.

Entering text

The basic method of entering text is simply to type on the keyboard once the program has loaded. Word processors have a feature known as WYSIWYG, which stands for 'What You See Is What You Get'. It means that the text will be printed exactly as it appears on the screen. This unfortunately, is sometimes not quite true.

The keys to use when entering text are

Typewriter (alphanumeric) keys   enter text and numbers

Backspace key   erases the character to the left of the cursor

Delete key   erases the character at the cursor

Direction (arrow) keys   move the cursor around the text, but not beyond the last character

Return key   ends a paragraph

Shift key   prints a capital letter or special characters

If the word processor operates with a mouse, this can be used to position the cursor or insertion point anywhere in the document. It is generally much quicker than using the keyboard controls. Once the mouse has been positioned, click the mouse button to move the insertion point to the mouse position.

The best way to become familiar with the operation of the keyboard is to practice. Try to type some of your notes or an assignment. If you make a mistake, use the cursor keys or the mouse to go back to the error, then erase it with the backspace key.

Saving your work

When you type using a word processor, all of the information goes into the computer's memory – but this will be lost if the computer is switched off. The way to keep your work is to save it before leaving the word processor. Use the 'File save' or 'Save as' command from the pull-down menu or the menu bar and follow the instructions on screen. The document will have to be given a file name if it is to be stored on disk so that you can find it again later. Give it a file name that will help you to identify it. Generally the name is best linked with the title of the document in some way. Remember that the date and time of creation are automatically stored as well.

Check before printing

Reading text on a computer screen is quite a strange experience at first and it is not always easy to spot mistakes. Check the document carefully on screen before printing it. This will not only save time, because printing may take several minutes, but it will also help to reduce the amount of waste paper produced. It is a good idea to keep any original copies of material which is being typed just in case the printed document contains any errors that were not spotted on screen. Try to get everything right on the computer screen before you print the finished version.

Page layout

The documents produced by word processors generally end up on paper. This can have many different sizes and shapes, from small sticky labels to large sheets of computer listing paper.

Whatever the size of paper, your word processor will allow you to format the text so that it appears neatly in the right place. This is achieved by setting
- the page length   for whatever length paper is to be used
- the left and right margins   for the correct paper width
- the top and bottom margins   for headings and page numbers.

A typical page layout is shown in Figure 3.5.

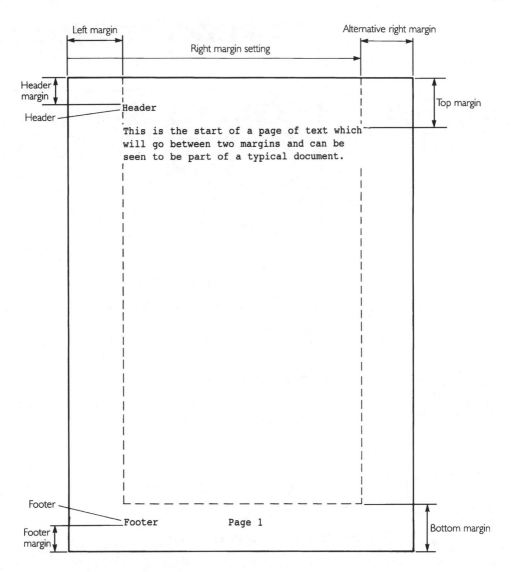

Figure 3.5 Typical page layout

A4 is the most common paper size and it can be used in either 'portrait' or 'landscape' positions. Portrait layout means that the long side of the paper is vertical. This is the most usual. Landscape layout means that the long side is horizontal.

Page length

The page length may be set with a command in the word processor package or it may be set as part of the printer set-up process. It must be set at precisely the same length as the paper being used in the printer or you will get very unpredictable results. This is because word processors decide how much text can fit each page and automatically start a new page when necessary. If the actual paper is a different size, the new page will start either too early or too late. Most word processors have a 'default' or standard value for page length built into the program which is set for A4-sized paper (295 × 210 mm). You should check the default page length, however, because some software defaults to US Letter size, which can cause problems if your printer is set up for A4. In a word processor, you will find the command in the 'Format' or 'Page Layout' menu.

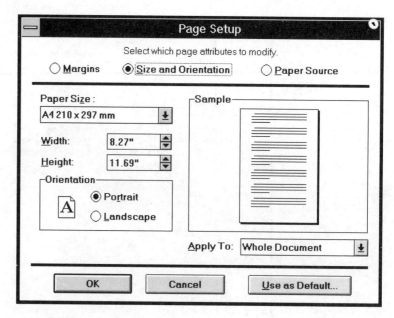

Figure 3.6 Setting the page length

Left and right margins

Margins have to be set so that the word processor knows how much text to fit onto each line. Printing which is too close to the edge of a page does not look very neat, so a margin of between 0.5" and 1" (1 and 2.5 cm) is normally left blank. The margins do not have to be the same width. For example, pages that will be bound into a book or folder frequently have wider margins on the binding side of the page. These commands are also part of the 'Page Layout' menu of most word processors.

Top and bottom margins

Top and bottom margins may not be obvious on the computer screen unless 'Page preview' is available. These margins are generally used for 'headers', which appear at the top of every page of a document, and for 'footers', which appear at the bottom of every page. Footers are often used to contain the page numbers.

Some printers are not capable of printing right to the top and bottom of each page and therefore they need a minimum value for the top and bottom margins which may be between 0.25" and 1" (0.6 and 2.5 cm). This is particularly true of dot matrix printers with single sheet feeders fitted. Laser printers can print to within about 0.2" (0.5 cm) of the edge of a sheet.

Page numbers

If page numbers are required in a document they normally have to be included as part of the header or the footer. They can usually be placed anywhere on the header or footer line. Numbering need not start at 1 each time, so separate documents can be combined to form a complete report. Most word processors allow numbering to be done in a variety of ways, such as 1,2,3 or i, ii, iii, Page 1. Look in the 'Insert' or 'Page layout' menu for the command.

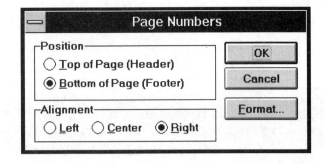

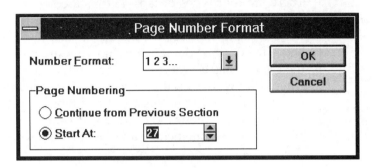

Figure 3.7 Page numbering options in Microsoft Word

Correct page numbering is very important in many types of document, including reports, assignments and essays. Unless there is a specific reason not to put page numbers on a document, it is better to include them so that information is easier to find if another person has to look at it.

Date stamping

Since all computers have a clock inside them, as long as it is correctly set many word processors can put the right date on any document it creates. This can save a secretary some time since the process can also be made automatic in some systems.

To add the date to a document, simply position the insertion point in the required place, find the command in the 'Edit' or 'Insert' menu and follow the instructions. You are likely to be offered a choice of date formats to suit all occasions and preferences.

Date stamping is a good habit to adopt as soon as you start to create word processed documents because it helps to keep track of when work was done. It can also help to locate the files by date if you forget to put their names on the documents.

The ruler

The ruler is an indicator at the top of a page on the word processor screen that helps to display the layout of the page being typed. Both the left and right-hand margins are marked in some way, for example with > and < signs or with square brackets [. . . . .]. The ruler is usually marked in inches or centimetres so that the position of the cursor can be seen at any time in relation to the page width.

The ruler can also be used to indicate the 'tabs' and 'indents'. Tabs can normally be inserted on the ruler by clicking the appropriate upward-facing arrow for the type of tab, in the ribbon, then clicking its required location on the ruler.

Tabs and work in columns

Tabulation marks (or 'tabs') are points along the line to which the cursor will jump when the tab key (⇄) is pressed. This feature allows tables or columns to be created easily because text or numbers on each line can be lined up vertically if they are aligned with a tab point. When most word processors start, the default tab settings are normally every 0.5" (1.25 cm), but these can be changed by resetting all or some of them. Using tabs is very important and will save you a lot of time when laying out documents that require information in columns.

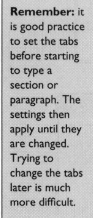

Remember: it is good practice to set the tabs before starting to type a section or paragraph. The settings then apply until they are changed. Trying to change the tabs later is much more difficult.

There are four types of tabs: left justified (normal), right justified, centred and decimal. Left justified tabs are used to align text so that the first letter of each word is kept in the same position on each line. Decimal tabs are used for numbers – the decimal point in a number is automatically aligned on each row. After the tab key has been pressed to move the cursor to a decimal tab, the numbers entered move left until a decimal point is entered, and then they continue to move right as normal. Right justified tabs align the right hand letters of words with the tab position, and centred tabs centre each word on the tab position. Not all word processors include all types of tab.

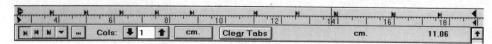

Figure 3.8 The ruler and tabs in Ami-Pro

Indentation (indents)

Indents increase the left margin for a paragraph or section. By setting an indent the text will still have its left edge aligned, but the extra left margin will move it further to the right. Indenting is used particularly for sub-sections of documents or where special emphasis is needed, because it can make sections stand out.

An example of the use of an indent is shown in Figure 3.9. Each of the paragraphs is indented by 1" (2.5 cm), so that they appear to be aligned with the text in the columns above them.

Progress check

Answer the following questions about word processors. Try to relate them to the work that you are doing at the moment so that you can best see how to apply the features of your word processor.

1. Page layout is very important. What features of your word processor would you need to use to ensure that the pages of your reports are properly laid out?

2. What types of tab are available on the word processor you use?

3. What is the meaning of the following terms?
   (a) word-wrap
   (b) right justification
   (c) font
   (d) scrolling

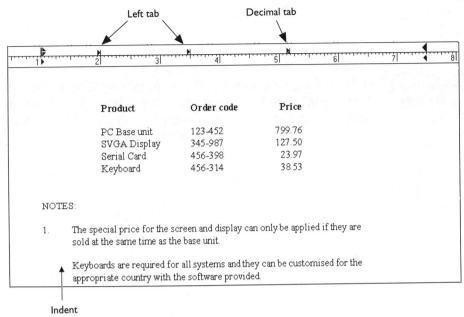

Figure 3.9 *Examples of tabs and indents*

4. You need to create a set of paragraphs which are indented by 1″ (2.5 cm) from the left hand edge of the paper. How would you do this on your word processor?

5. Is it possible to start the page numbering of your document at number 12 with your word processor? If so, find out how to insert the page numbers at the top of each page starting at 12. When might this be necessary?

6. When would you need to set the left and right margins of a page to different values? Give two examples.

7. How does your word processor display the edges of a page on the ruler? Find out how to set the page width to 14″.

8. How would you add the date at the bottom of a page with the word processor you normally use?

Printing effects add impact

The first impression given by a page of text is decided mainly by its layout. However, important text can be made to stand out with printing effects such as centring, underlining, bold, italics and changes in the size or type of lettering (fonts). Some word processors have a much wider range of facilities than others, such as double underlines and bullet points. Not all printers can print all of the effects that the word processor includes.

Centring

Centred text is used for many headings and can be a way of giving a professional-looking appearance to things like menus, business cards or name badges.

Note: With a Windows-based word processor, all of these effects can be achieved by highlighting the text, then clicking the appropriate icon at the top of the screen. They will also have menu entries.

Remember that centring of any text takes place between the margins that have been set for the line. It can also be affected by pictures or other objects on a page of text.

Underlining

Underlining also adds emphasis to important words or paragraphs in a document. For example, an underlined heading is quite common in a business letter, although many typists now prefer to make headings bold instead. In printed material such as books, underlining is very rarely used.

Figure 3.10 Examples of centred text

Bold text

Creating bold characters is probably the most effective way of making some words stand out from the rest. Bold words are frequently used for headings or titles in books and reports.

Italics

Italics are sloping versions of the normal characters and are also used in circumstances that require a different emphasis to be attached to the letters. For example, a computer manual may use A:>**cd** *directory* to mean that the bold characters **cd** have to be typed as written, but the italic characters, *directory*, should be replaced with your own directory name.

Subscript and superscript

Subscript and superscript letters are positioned slightly lower and slightly higher than the normal text, respectively. These features are common in maths, science and engineering where formulae have to be typed. Some systems also make the relevant letters slightly smaller than the normal text.

For example:
$$x^2 - 7x + 12 = 0$$
$$R_1 + R_2 + R_3 = 1800$$

Fonts

'Font' refers to the shape of the letters that appear on a page. Many different kinds of letters have been designed, some of which go back to the very early days of printing and some of which are very modern. A few examples are shown in Figure 3.11.

Avalon

Brochure

Courier

Frankenstein

Kids

Modern

Paradise

Roman

Surreal

Switzerland

Times New Roman

USA Black

Figure 3.11 Some of the different fonts available in word processors

Not all printers and word processors are capable of reproducing all fonts, but a reasonable selection is generally available. By including one or two fonts in a document the overall impression created can be improved, but it is a mistake to include a large number of fonts. This simply makes the document look untidy. A better impression will be created by employing the same font throughout a document, simply changing its size to add emphasis to headings, titles or other parts that need to be highlighted.

The size of the letters is normally given as a 'point size'. A 'point' in printing terms is about $\frac{1}{72}''$ (0.35 cm) and point sizes of 10, 18 and 24 are simply multiples of this. Normal type is generally between 8 and 12 point.

Unfortunately, not all word processors display on screen the range of fonts that is available on the printer. This means that the text that appears on screen might not be what is finally printed – you have to believe that the font will be different when printed or check with the 'Page preview' mode of the word processor if that is available. Most Windows-based word processors give a good on-screen impression of what will actually be printed.

Many of the features of a word processor can best be illustrated with a specific example. One of the normal methods of applying for a job is to send prospective employers a CV (curriculum vitae) and a covering letter.

Worked example

CV and covering letter

INTRODUCTION
You wish to apply for a job with a local company. No vacancies have been advertised but you intend to make a general initial enquiry. The normal way would be to write a letter explaining that you are looking for employment and enclosing your CV to tell the employer what you have done and what you are capable of doing. Both the letter and CV are to be typed on a word processor and printed. Their address is Brown and Baker Ltd, Twin Hills Industrial Estate, LEEDS, L5 3JJ.

PROBLEM
1. Your task is to produce both a CV and a covering letter on a word processor. Two documents are required and so it makes sense to use two different files, one for the letter and one for the CV. This will allow you to update your CV as you gain experience and also allow you to modify the letter easily for different potential employers. It is likely that you will have to apply for more than one job.

   Even though different files are used, the styles should be similar and the same type of printer should be used for them. The best size for both is probably standard A4 paper.

2. The covering letter should be in the format of a standard business letter. It can be on plain paper, with 1″ (2.5 cm) margins, no page number, with a centred and underlined heading. It must be short and to the point.

3. The CV should be a one or two page document summarising your personal details, skills and experience to date. Its layout and style should be consistent with the covering letter: on A4 paper, using 1″ (2.5 cm) margins, no page numbers, centred titles, indented paragraphs and tabulated data.

SOLUTION
Typical examples are shown in Figures 3.12 and 3.13, although the order and presentation of each section may be adjusted according to individual requirements.

15 Green Lane
Walkhampton
Leeds
LI7 3QY

The Personnel Manager
Brown and Baker Ltd.
Twin Hills Industrial Estate,
LEEDS
L5 3JJ

12th June 1994

Dear Sir

Vacancies for Full Time Staff

I have noticed in the local paper recently that your company has been successful in obtaining a major export contract with a Dutch company. If this extra work will enable you to take on extra staff, I would be very grateful for the opportunity of an interview.

You will see from my CV enclosed that I have recently completed a General National Vocational Qualification in Manufacturing at Level 3 and I am sure that my training could be of value to you in your production department.

I look forward to hearing from you in due course.

Your faithfully

JOHN SMITH

ENC

*Figure 3.12
Sample
covering letter*

| EXPERIENCE: | When I was in my final year at school I decided that I wanted to find a career linked to technology because I so much enjoyed my technology project. My work as a part-time salesman in an electrical wholesalers has given me a good idea of different types of electrical equipment and small hand tools. I often had to test appliances and rectify simple faults, under supervision. |

My GNVQ study in Manufacturing has given me an insight into the maufacturing process which I find very interesting. It has given me experience of team work and project management. My training included the basic use of hand tools and a milling machine as well as some electronic circuit construction.

I have achieved my Duke of Edinburgh's Silver Award, which included courses on First Aid and fire fighting.

INTERESTS: Computers, music, walking and football.

REFEREES:
Mr A. Johnston
Technology Department
Lakeside College of Further Education
Still Lane
LEEDS

Mr M. Swan
B. Slade Ltd
6 Grant Close
Blackwell
LEEDS

CURRICULUM VITAE

JOHN ROBERT SMITH

SUMMARY: **A keen and enthusiastic young man with some experience of work and a special interest in manufacturing processes. He has an Advanced GNVQ qualification in Manufacturing which provided training in teamwork and in producing work to meet deadlines.**

ADDRESS: 15, GREEN LANE, WALKHAMPTON, LEEDS, YORKSHIRE

TELEPHONE: (01132) 391120

DATE OF BIRTH: 12th March 1976

NATIONALITY: BRITISH   STATUS: SINGLE

EDUCATION: LAKESIDE COLLEGE OF FURTHER EDUCATION
September 1992   June 1994
HOLLAND ROAD COMMUNITY COLLEGE, LEEDS
September 1987   July 1992

QUALIFICATIONS:
GCSE English Language	Grade C	1992
GCSE English Literature	Grade D	1992
GCSE French	Grade E	1992
GCSE Mathematics	Grade C	1992
GCSE Geography	Grade E	1992
GCSE Science	Grade B	1992
GCSE Technology	Grade A	1992
Advanced GNVQ Manufacturing		1994

EMPLOYMENT:
September '92   January '94   B. Slade (Electrical Wholesales) Ltd
Part-time salesman

July '92   August '92   Trust House Forte
Temporary kitchen porter

October '90   January '92   Marks and Spencer PLC
Part-time warehouse assistant 1 day/week

*Figure 3.13
Sample
curriculum
vitae*

71

Progress check

Answer the questions below before proceeding with the rest of the chapter to check that you have understood the basic features of the word processor you use.

1. How many different ways are there of emphasising text with your word processor? Produce a list of them.

2. What features of a word processor are likely to make the production of typed documents a much more efficient operation?

3. What is the maximum point size which your word processor can produce?

4. When would you need to use a subscript in a document or letter? What command is required for your word processor?

5. What features of a word processor would have been used to produce the CV in the previous worked example?

If you would like some practice at a practical exercise in word processing, try some of those at the end of this chapter now, or have a go at Assignment 1 on producing your own CV.

Document styles and templates

The features of a document, such as the page layout, the margins, the orientation, the font and font sizes, and the typing effects all combine to give it a certain style. Some word processors can store these features as a 'template,' which can be used many times to produce similar work.

Some word processors refer to templates as 'Style sheets'. Check the 'File', 'New' menu to find them.

For example, if a company always wants the same style of business letter, a particular template can be created for it. Every time a typist produces a letter, he or she does not need to remember which font has to be chosen because it has all been stored and will be selected automatically. The template provides the basic settings for the main features of the document – this saves a lot of time whenever new work is created. The use of document templates can help to improve office efficiency.

It is also possible to give individual paragraphs a certain style. These may include the font and size of the text, the indentation or centring, any bullets used, etc. Paragraph styles allow headings to be styled (large, bold or centred) all with one command. This is another way in which word processor features can help to improve efficiency.

Examples of templates

When you start a new document look for the different templates that may be available – they are not available on all word processors. If various templates are available on the word processor you use, try to use them to save time when creating different documents. For example, if you need to produce a business letter, there may be several templates already available. This can also apply to Fax sheets and layouts for overhead transparencies.

Some examples are shown in Figure 3.14

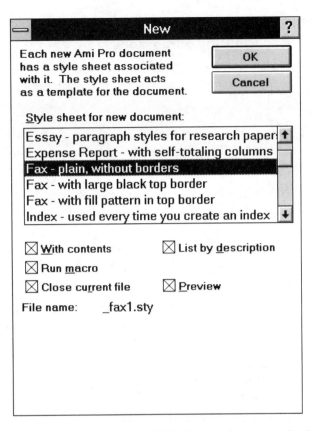

Figure 3.14 Different style sheets are available for new documents in Ami-Pro

Speeding up the operation

One of the advantages of using a word processor compared with a typewriter is that changes to the text can be made very quickly and easily. These changes include moving, copying, deleting or modifying both single words and whole sections of text. They also allow other documents to be inserted or created while the word processor is operating.

The commands are normally found in the 'Edit' menu, and may be called 'Cut', 'Copy' and 'Paste'. The method is basically the same for all the commands:
• mark or highlight the text to be used
• carry out the operation.

Moving text

Moving text from one place to another within a document is one of the most useful functions of a word processor. If the order of words or paragraphs has to be changed, the 'Move' command prevents whole sections of the document from having to be retyped.

In Windows-based word processors moving text can be a two-step operation. First the section is 'cut' from its original position, then it is 'pasted' into its new location. There is a short-cut, however, because highlighted text can usually be 'dragged' to its new location with the mouse.

Worked example ——

Reorganising paragraphs

The author of a report on influenza has decided that it would be better if the second paragraph came first and the last paragraph came second. How would you do it?

```
Facts About Flu

Flu viruses are easy to catch. They are far tinier than
bacteria and linger on surfaces touched by infected people or
in the air for hours after the sufferer has coughed.

The more you know about flu, the better you can protect your-
self. Influenza is not bacterial, but viral, so antibiotics
have no effect.

Once the virus enters the throat or nose it burrows inside a
cell. There, it tricks the cells reproductive mechanism to
make millions of copies of itself.

The first signs of cold and flu are similar. If it is flu
however, you will soon feel other symptoms such as fever,
fatigue, aches and pains.
```

SOLUTION

This change can easily be accomplished with the 'Move' or 'Cut' and 'Paste' commands, as follows:

1. Highlight the second paragraph

2. Choose the move or the cut and paste commands to move it to the beginning – the space left is automatically filled by the word processor

3. Highlight the last paragraph

4. Move it into the space after the first paragraph.

The same operation could be carried out in other ways.

——

Copying text

Text can be copied by highlighting it, moving the cursor or insertion point to the destination, then using the 'Copy' command. With Windows-based word processors, the text may be 'dragged' to the new location while the Control key is held down. This exercise can be repeated many times over to create multiple copies if necessary.

For example, you may want to create a small invitation that occupies only about half a page of typing. By copying the text, it would be possible to print two invitations on a page and save a lot of paper.

Deleting text

The backspace or delete key can be used to delete small blocks of the text. For longer sections, the 'Delete' command is better.

The section to be deleted is simply highlighted in the same way as for the 'Move' or 'Copy' command, and is then deleted using either the menu option or the delete key.

Some word processors have an 'Undo' feature , which allows the procedure to be reversed in case the wrong section has been deleted, but it is always better to double check the operation before pressing the keys in the first place. Even with an 'Undo' feature, some blocks of text may be too large to be restored if they have been deleted by mistake. In cases of serious errors, the only solution is to abandon the document and revert to the previous version saved on disk.

Saving blocks of text on disk

Sometimes sections of text (standard paragraphs or headers for memos or press releases, etc.) need to be saved on disk as separate files. The basic operation is to mark the block and then execute the required command. The word processor will ask for the text to be given a new filename before it is stored on disk.

In Windows-based word processors such as Microsoft Word and Ami-Pro, the 'Copy 'command places the text on the 'Clipboard', from where it can be inserted into another document and saved as required. This is also the basic method of transferring sections of text between documents.

Inserting text

Inserting other documents from disk into a file is a useful feature of a word processor, since it allows common information to be typed once and included many times. The operation is simply a matter of placing the cursor where the text is required and then issuing the command to retrieve the information from the disk.

For example, headers for reports, memos and press releases, etc. can be stored as paragraphs on disk. Legal documents are often based on standard paragraphs, and by keeping each of these on disk slightly different versions of contracts can be drawn up with minimal re-typing.

Find and replace

Find and replace facilities allow words or phrases to be changed throughout a document without the need for the writer to search painstakingly for each occurrence. In long documents visual searching for text is very difficult, so it makes sense to allow the computer to do the hard work. Trying to find every time 'which' occurred in report and changing it to 'that' would take a long time.

Different systems provide slightly different facilities for the search and replace function. Follow the screen instructions carefully or you may find a lot of words have been changed by mistake – and it can all happen very quickly!

The computer needs to be given a word or phrase – this is known as the 'search string' – which it will then attempt to match with each group of letters in the document. Capital letters can be ignored or not, according to the options selected. An exact match may also be chosen so that words within other words may also be ignored. For example, if it is necessary to replace the word 'gold' with the word 'silver' it would probably not be wise to alter the word 'golden' even though it contains the word 'gold'.

Moving quickly around a document

If you want to go to a particular word in a document, the 'Find' facility of most word processors allows you to find it very quickly. If you enter the word to be

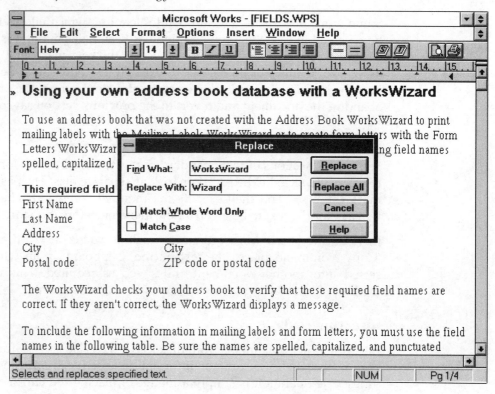

Figure 3.15 Using the 'Find and replace' function in Microsoft Works

found, the word processor can quickly move you to the page on which it appears and save the time it would have taken to search through manually. Be careful to enter the word *exactly* as required however, or the system may find many other occurrences.

If you know that you want to go straight to a particular page, use the 'Goto' command. This is often located in the same menu as the 'Find' command and allows you to move through a document quickly. Enter the page number required and the software will put it on screen almost immediately.

Your word processor may also allow you to store 'bookmarks'. These are named points in a document. Once set, they can be found very quickly with the 'Goto' command.

Progress check

These questions are on the subjects just covered in this chapter. Try to answer them by thinking about the word processor you normally use.

1. How can you include a complete document as part of another one with your word processor?

2. What is meant by the 'style' of a paragraph?

3. Give three examples of the type of document which may be created by a company in a particular style.

4. What special things need to be taken into consideration when producing an overhead transparency for a presentation?

5. How would you copy a paragraph from one document to another with your word processor?

6. Why do you need to be careful when using a 'find and replace' facility in a word processor?

7. What is a 'search string'?

8. What facilities does your word processor provide to allow you to move to a particular place in a document quickly?

Including graphics with text

Until recently it was not very easy to include pictures in word processed text because the MS-DOS based software was not designed to allow it. The only way it could be done was to transfer both the text and the pictures to a desktop publishing (DTP) package such as Aldus PageMaker or Corel Ventura Publisher.

Desktop publishing

DTP packages can produce exceptional results for many types of high quality publications. They bring the basic capabilities of many commercial publishing organisations into the offices of other companies. Because of their complexity they also require trained operators to achieve the best results – in the hands of novices the results can be quite poor! With a good deal of practice however, publicity material, handouts, invitations, posters, news sheets and many other forms of literature can be produced to a high standard, both cheaply and easily. More advanced DTP packages can be used for newspapers and books, which are rarely produced by 'traditional' methods any longer.

Graphics built into word processors

Fortunately, simple DTP has now been incorporated into the latest generation of word processors. It is now possible to include pictures, charts and diagrams in documents very easily.

Windows-based word processors normally have a built-in drawing facility, which is very good for most of the simple drawings and diagrams needed in documents. The precise features of each system depend upon the particular word processor, but they can all carry out the basic tasks of drawing lines, boxes, circles, arrows, etc. and then filling them with colour or patterns. Text can also be added to illustrate the drawings.

If a drawing is required as part of the text, just click on the 'Drawing' icon and a drawing frame will appear on the screen. Use the grid feature if you want all of the lines to join precisely. Finish the diagram, and when you leave the drawing mode, the image will appear on the page of your document. If you need to make changes, simply click on the drawing and make the alterations as required. A typical example is shown in Figure 3.16

Charts in documents

Some word processors also provide built-in charting facilities that may save you the trouble of using a spreadsheet for some simple charts. The 'Chart' icon can be used to open up the chart drawing facility with a simple spreadsheet to enter the data. Naturally this is not as comprehensive as a full spreadsheet, but for

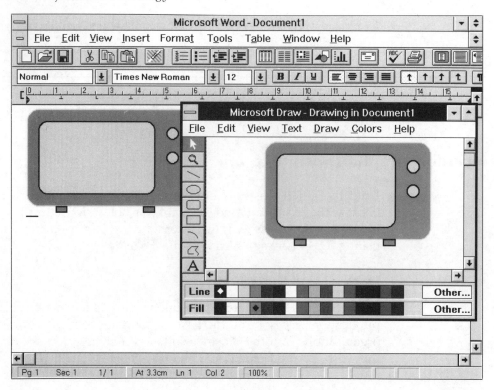

Figure 3.16 Drawing facilities in a word processor – Microsoft Draw inside Microsoft Word

simple charts it can be much quicker. If the data that forms part of a document is changed, it is possible to make sure that the chart also changes automatically.

Pictures from other sources

There are many other possible sources of pictures, but they all need to be in the form of a picture file before they can be included in a document. Here are a few:
- Charts from spreadsheet packages or special charting software like Corel Chart.
- Drawings from CAD packages like AutoCad.
- Pictures from 'paint' packages such as Windows Paint and Corel Draw.
- Photographs from images captured with a document scanner and suitable software.
- Video pictures – stills of video displays captured off-air or from video cameras and tape with suitable software.

As long as the picture information is stored in a file format that the word processor can read, the picture can be included, positioned and often modified before finally being printed. With modern colour printers, even coloured pictures can be put into documents and printed with very high quality.

Adding pictures to a document is reasonably straightforward as long as a few simple rules are followed. Pictures in documents are like pictures on a wall – they are usually best in a frame. The basic process is as follows.

1. Create a frame of the size and in the position required.

2. Import the picture into the frame.

Frames

Frames are like sub-documents within the main document and can often cause what appears to be confusing behaviour of the text. They can be arranged so that

- text on the page flows all around them
- text on the page does not flow around them but stays behind them (and is then only visible if the frame is transparent)
- text does not appear at the side of them.

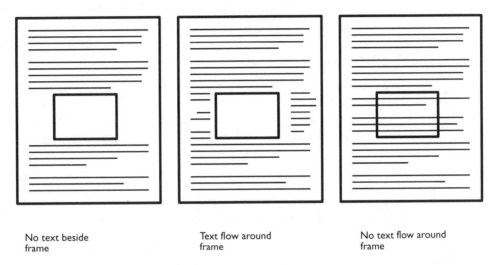

No text beside frame

Text flow around frame

No text flow around frame

Figure 3.17 Text flow and frames

Frame outlines can also be changed to achieve a variety of effects. Pictures could be shown with a thick or thin line around them for emphasis or a 'shadow' behind them to make them appear to stand out from the page. Some examples are shown in Figure 3.18.

Figure 3.18 Frame types with various shadows

The important thing to remember is that, for best results, pictures and drawings need frames, and when they are placed in a document it is like pasting them onto the page that contains the text.

When moving a frame or changing its size remember that alterations will change the position of the text already on the page. Sometimes this is desirable, such as when a picture must cross the columns in a newspaper style layout. At other times it can be a nuisance if text that is already exactly right is displaced.

If the size of a picture has to be changed, the usual method is to click on the picture or frame, then drag the corner 'handles' with the mouse until the right size is achieved. Exact sizes may also be set from the menu. A picture can often be cropped by holding down the shift key while moving the 'handles'.

Mixed text and graphics

Figure 3.19 shows how a number of different types of graphics can be included in a document to make it more interesting. The first paragraph is standard text. Below it, two frames have been created to hold the picture on the left and the 'Facts and Figures' on the right.

NEW YORK

As a tourist destination, New York has a lot to offer. The view from the top of the Empire State Building or any of the other monsters is a breathtaking spectacle which is unsurpassed by any other city. For those who adore grandure New York is a monument to man's skill with steel, concrete and glass.

Facts and Figures:
Largest city in the USA, industrial port and commercial centre.
Population: about 8 million
Skyscrapers include:
World Trade Centre: 412 metres
Empire State 381 metres

Established 1631 by Dutch and named New Amsterdam. Captured by English in 1664 and renamed New York.

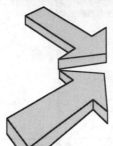

HOW to get there .....

Figure 3.19 Text and graphics combined in a document

The photograph was imported as a .PCX file from a graphics package and was automatically scaled to fit in the frame that had been drawn. The text frame is a standard feature of the word processor but a background shade has been added for emphasis.

Below the photograph, part of a piece of line art has been included. The original contained four arrows, so the picture had to be cropped to show only two. Positioning the text next to it in exactly the right place required a frame of its own.

Review questions

The following questions are intended to check your understanding of the main topics covered in this chapter. If you can, try to think about the way in which you need to apply word processing techniques to the work you are doing in your course.

1. In the business you are learning about, what are the main uses of word processing? Do all of the employees have to operate a word processor at some time in their work?

2. How can business efficiency be improved with a word processor? Are there any ways in which you think a word processor can reduce efficiency?

3. If you are applying for a job, what are the advantages of using a word processor to write your CV? Why do you think some companies ask for hand-written letters of application?

4. Why is it important to have the right type of printer with a word processor?

5. What is the function of a frame in a word processed document? How can they be used to improve the layout of a page?

6. How would you include page numbers in the bottom right-hand corner of your documents with the word processor you normally use?

7. What factors must you take into consideration if you want to include pictures or other graphics in a document?

8. How would you move quickly to page 9 in a 13-page document with your normal word processor?

Exercises

The following exercises are intended to provide a short introduction to the set of techniques that you will need to be able to use in general word processing. They will serve only as a starting point since most techniques have to be practised with a wide range of documents.

1. Create a new document with the page length and width set to the standard A4 values of 8.27" × 11.69" (21 cm × 29.6 cm). These may be the default settings for your word processor, but check them anyway.

   Set the top margin to 1.5" (3.81 cm)

   Set the left and right margins to 1.2" (3.05 cm)

   Now type the following paragraphs, or some text of your own which is of similar length.

   Moods, say the experts, are emotions that have become fixed, so they influence your outlook for hours, days, or

```
weeks. Fine, if the mood is pleasant, but a problem if
you are sad, angry or anxious. However, scientists have
discovered several new approaches to release you from an
unwanted mood.

Exercise is one way of altering a mood. The key is aero-
bic exercise such as swimming, running, cycling, and
similar activities which boost the heart rate.

Colour can also have a powerful influence. To diffuse
irritability and anger, stay away from red. To help
depression, avoid dark colours. Go for warm, bright
active colours.

Music can help. Experts have found that by first matching
the type of music to your current mood, you can gradually
change your mood by changing the type of music you are
listening to.
```

Save the results with a file name of your choice and then print a hard copy.

2. Using the document from Exercise 1, change the left margin to 3.5" (8.89 cm) and print the document again.

3. Using the document created in Exercise 2, add the following title, centred and bold.

```
Beating a bad mood
```

Below the title, but above the main text, add the following sub-heading, in bold and left justified.

```
Lift your spirits with these techniques
```

View a 'Print preview' of the page on your computer screen to check that it will look correct before printing it.

4. Set up a new document in landscape format, using A4 paper and a 1" (2.54 cm) margin all round. Set up tabs at the following distances from the left margin – 0.5", 5.0", 7.0", 8.0" (1.27 cm, 12.70 cm, 17.78 cm, 20.32 cm).

Using tabs between the columns for the title, author, publisher and ISBN number, enter the following list:

```
All quiet on the Western front  Erich Remarque  Random
House  0-224-04220-3
Noble House  James Clavell  Coronet Books  0-340-26877-8
Kane and Abel  Jeffrey Archer  Coronet Books
0-340-25733-4
Murder on the Orient Express  Agatha Christie  Fontana
0-00-617006-4
Into the Blue  Robert Goddard  Corgi Books
0-552-13561-5
Paddy Clarke  Ha Ha Ha  Roddy Doyle  Minerva
0-7493-9735-7
```

Make sure that the tabs set for each line are continued onto the next by pressing the return key after the final entry on each line.

5. Below the table created in Exercise 4, add the following paragraph. It should be indented by 0.5" to line up with the left edge of the text in the columns above it.

This selection of books represents only a small selection of the range from our new catalogue. They represent exceptional value at up to 25% discount on their original published price. By choosing more than five books from our enormous range, valued customers also qualify for our special free gift – an invaluable magnifier for checking the small print.

6. Using the document created in exercise 5, add a bold title of your choice above the table, then make the '25% discount' in the paragraph below the table italic text.

   Now increase the size of the font for the whole paragraph to 18 point, and the size of the title to 24 point.

7. If your word processor has the facility to use templates or style sheets, create the following overhead transparency, or something similar of your choice.

   The advantages of travelling by train are:
   • More relaxing than travelling by car
   • People can walk about
   • 99% are on time
   • Refreshments are available
   • Toilet facilities

   If your word processor does not have a suitable template, create your own. Use large bold text, wide margins to ensure it fits the projector, bullet points and a small reference number in the corner.

8. On the transparency created in Exercise 7, change the order of the bullet points. Use the cut and paste or block move features to place them in the following order:

   • Refreshments are available
   • More relaxing than travelling by car
   • Toilet facilities
   • People can walk about
   • 99% are on time

9. Look, either in the 'File' menu or the 'Insert' menu of your word processor, for any pictures which may be available with your system. If you can find any, create a frame in a new A4 document and choose a picture to put in it. The size of the image can be adjusted to be a square, about half the width of the sheet, and placed in the top left corner.

   Now create another frame to the right of the frame with the picture in it. Put lines round the frame, and inside it write a five line description of the picture you have chosen and the reason for choosing it.

Assignment 1 starts on the next page

Assignment 1
Producing your own CV

This assignment can be used to provide evidence for the following Performance Criteria:

Element 2.1 PCs 1 to 4

Element 2.2 PCs 1, 2, 4, 5 and 6

Element 2.3 PCs 1, 2, 3 and 5

Element 2.4 PC 3

Element 3.1 PCs 1 to 4

Element 3.2 PCs 1, 2, 4, 5 and 6

Element 3.3 PCs 1, 2, 3, 4 and 6

Element 3.4 PC 4

Introduction

Your 'ideal' job has just been advertised in the local paper. The hours would suit you well and the pay seems to be very good. You decide that you must get it.

Your task

Write a letter of application, saying how much you would like the job and enclose a copy of your CV. Make sure that you emphasise all of your good points that would help you to be successful in your application. Prepare a hand-written copy first then type it once you are happy with the results.

1. Use A4 paper with 1″ (2.5 cm) margins, no page numbers and whatever other typing effects you think will give a good impression.

2. Before and after any major changes in the CV, save disk copies of your work.

3. Format your CV in two different ways using different effects, then choose the most appropriate one to give the impression you wish to create. Print two copies.

In a short report list the word processing effects that you have used in the CV. For example, has it included bold text, italics? Annotate the second copy of the CV to show how you input the information to make it easy to edit – for example, where you used tabs, indents, word-wrap and returns.

Assignment 2
Producing a transparency for a presentation

This assignment can be used to provide evidence for the following Performance Criteria:

Element 2.1	PCs 1 to 4
Element 2.2	PCs 1, 2, 4 and 5
Element 2.3	PCs 1 to 5
Element 2.4	PC 3
Element 3.1	PCs 1 to 5
Element 3.2	PCs 1, 2, 4, 5 and 7
Element 3.3	PCs 1 to 6
Element 3.4	PC 4

Introduction

Use of overhead transparencies is one of the most effective ways of presenting information to an audience. They must be made with reasonably large characters, and only a few main points can be put onto each one. The best quality is obtained from a laser printer. If a colour printer is available, some very impressive results can be achieved by using coloured text to create maximum impact.

Your task

Choose a topic from your course on which you have to present some information either as part of a group or individually. Follow the steps below.

1. Decide the main headings for the transparencies. Take care not to try and include too much information on each one.

2. Check your word processor and find out if it has a template for transparencies. If it does, use it to create each one as required. If not, create your own style sheet for them. It will be most effective if it has large text, possibly using bullet points under a main heading. You may like to number the transparencies in small characters in one corner so that they can be sorted out if they get mixed up. Include some colour if you can. Save the template file.

3. Print each transparency on plain paper first. The size of overhead projectors is not the same as A4 paper, so you may need to adjust the margins to make sure everything fits correctly.

4. Check the type of transparencies that are needed for the printer you have. Laser printers and ink jet printers use different types, which cannot be interchanged. Print each one by loading the transparency into the printer according to its instructions. Check the quality of each one as it is produced.

5. Use the transparencies as part of your presentation.

Assignment 3
Including text and graphics in a document

This assignment can be used to provide evidence for the following Performance Criteria:

Element 2.1	PCs 1 to 4
Element 2.2	PCs 1, 2, 4 and 5
Element 2.3	PCs 1 to 5
Element 2.4	PC 3
Element 3.1	PCs 1 to 5
Element 3.2	PCs 1, 2, 4, 5 and 7
Element 3.3	PCs 1 to 6
Element 3.4	PC 4

Introduction

You have decided that the covers of all of your future assignments need to be more impressive, so you will create them on the computer. They will all be very similar, with a large border round the page and then some centred text with the title about half way down. At the bottom you want to include a personal logo beside your name to give a special impact. This can be included in a frame and will be a piece of graphics, either a photograph or line art from any sources that are available.

Your task

This assignment involves the design and production of a suitable front page for your future assignments. It requires the use of your basic word processing skills and the use of both text and graphics on the same page.

1. Design a basic assignment front sheet by sketching it on a sheet of paper first. If you cannot find any suitable pictures yet just draw an empty box where the logo will go.

2. Open a new document in your word processor and create a frame large enough to cover the whole page. This can be used for the border. Choose a suitable line style so that it stands out. Keep away from the edge of the paper for the best results. Save the basic template file for use later.

3. Add the text for the assignment title inside the frame. This will be changed every time a new assignment front page is needed.

4. Create another frame to hold the graphic logo in the bottom left corner of the page. Make it as large as you like.

5. Choose a suitable logo from the images you have available. If you can find nothing that you think is suitable, you will have to design one using a graphics package or the word processor facilities. Load the image into the document when it is ready.

6. Add your name and a space for the date on the page together with any other information you may need. It may be best to include all of this information in frames so that it can be moved around the page as required.

7. Save the file with a new filename as it is being created. If changes are made, save them with a version number in the file name so that you can tell which is the most recent. Back up your finished work.

Keep all your source information in your portfolio together with the text and graphics before and after they have been combined. Create at least two assignment front sheets using the same template. Indicate on one of them the word processing features you have used – frames, large font sizes, etc.

CHAPTER 4

Advanced word processing

Objectives

When you have finished this chapter you should be able to:
- Use column format in a document to create simple tables
- Understand how to include data from a spreadsheet in a document
- Appreciate the best type of printer to use for different documents
- Use a word processor to complete pre-printed forms
- Use a word processor to create a document outline
- Understand how to combine text from different sources to create multi-chapter documents
- Understand how to create form documents for mail-merge purposes
- Combine the output from a database into a word processed document
- Compile an index automatically
- Solve simple problems with word processed documents.

This chapter covers the Performance Criteria and Range from all of the IT Core Skills Elements at levels 2 and 3 related to the preparation, processing and presentation of text, and the combination of information from different sources, with an evaluation of the techniques used and an introduction to automated operations.

Advanced word processing facilities

The combination of a word processor and the right type of printer can produce virtually any document required in normal business and domestic life. Modern word processors can now give good results in operations where they were traditionally poor, such as in the creation of text with high quality graphics or in multi-coloured documentation. Tables of many types can now be added to text and both pictures and charts can be included with ease.

Only by thoroughly learning all the features of a word processor can you use its power to the full. Many people can use only a fraction of the capabilities of even the most mediocre software. The more advanced the facilities, the more likely they are to be neglected unless the proper training is undertaken.

Text in columns

Many kinds of document look best with their text in a number of columns. For example, publicity material is often printed on a landscape A4 sheet, arranged so that it can be folded into three. Newspaper style formats are often used by people who produce information bulletins for staff or students as well as in many of the most popular magazines.

Reading narrow columns can be very easy, and the density of the page can often be broken up with pictures crossing a number of columns or by including wide, bold headlines.

Other types of text often produced in columns includes sets of figures or tables of numerical data. Sometimes it is vital that all of the columns line up properly or the figures could be meaningless.

Multi-column text

Most Windows-based word processors can create documents that have up to eight columns and some are capable of creating up to 100. The format can be applied to a whole document, a section or just a paragraph. Use multi-column text if you are creating a document that needs to have special impact or which needs to include a lot of information in a small space. It is often possible to reduce the font size to squeeze more in.

> **Take care:** What you see on screen may not be what you get on paper! This can depend upon the view chosen for the screen display. The lines between columns may not appear on the screen either. Some word processors only allow the whole document to be given a multi-column format and sections with other formats have to be included in a frame.

One way to improve the presentation of your proposal is to separate the explanation from its justification. Itemise what is in the proposal first, then explain or justify its contents. Do not mix the two together otherwise the explanation can sound just like an apology.

Single-column format

One way to improve the presentation of your proposal is to separate the explanation from its justification. Itemise what is in the proposal first, | then explain or justify its contents. Do not mix the two together otherwise the explanation can sound just like an apology.

Two-column format: narrow gutter, line between columns

One way to improve the presentation of your proposal is to separate the explanation from its | justification. Itemise what is in the proposal first, then explain or justify its contents. Do not mix | the two together otherwise the explanation can sound just like an apology.

Triple-column format: wide gutter, no lines between columns

Figure 4.1 Examples of multi-column text formats

The space between columns in a document is known as the 'gutter' and it can normally be set to different widths for different purposes. In addition, lines can be drawn between the columns if necessary.

Older types of word processor operating under MS-DOS do not all have facilities for multi-column text work. This means that if a multi-column format is needed, the only solution might be to produce each part separately then stick them together on a single sheet. However, all word processors can handle multiple columns of figures – they are actually formed simply by using the tabs correctly.

Figures in columns

Tables of figures are needed in many documents. Financial statements, orders, invoices, lists of materials, forms, etc. all contain figures in columns.

They can easily be created by carefully setting out the tabs on the 'ruler' on the word processor page. This topic was introduced in Chapter 3. Figures need to line up with those above them in a column, so right-justified or decimal tabs have to be used. Use decimal tabs only if all of the numbers contain decimal points. Some examples are shown in Figure 4.2.

Secondhand cameras - Price guide

MAKE	Excellent	Good	Fair	Part Exchange
Current Compacts				
Canon AS6 - outfit	95	83	73	53
Fuji DL - 250	80	70	62	45
Fuji DL - 400	120	104	92	67
Konica MR 640	120	100	88	64
Leica M4P/50mm f2	1050	910	804	593
Minolta AF-DL	80	70	67	45
Minox 35GT	116	101	90	65
Nikon AD3	95	83	73	53
Olympus AF1	95	83	73	53
Pentax Zoom 70 - S	140	121	107	79

Right-justified tabs

Figure 4.2 Columns of numbers created using tabs

It is vital to set the tabs before creating the table. Trying to change the settings after the numbers have been entered can cause terrible problems.

Table creation

One of the most useful features of Windows-based word processors is the ability to create tables automatically. One click on the 'Table' icon allows tables of almost any shape and size to be created. Lines can be added around each entry if required so that they are easy to read, or the lines can be omitted for a less formal presentation. All the hard work is done for you. There are no tabs to set and no column widths to work out, just specify the number of rows and columns required, and the sizes are worked out by the word processor. Column widths can be changed by dragging with the mouse.

Simple formulae can sometimes be added to the tables to make them operate like a basic spreadsheet. This means that they can be made to calculate totals in columns of figures or multiply others together, etc. In the table shown in Figure 4.3, for example, the total number of points for each team has been calculated by inserting a formula in the table, just as you would do in a spreadsheet. Although the table shown has a border showing the row and column identification, this would not normally be printed. The borders show on screen only if the right option is selected to assist in formula entry.

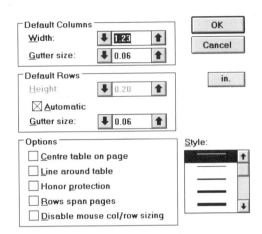

TOP FIVE POSITIONS AT THE END OF LAST SEASON

	A	B	C	D	E	F
1	NAME	P	W	D	L	POINTS
2	WEST PARK UNITED	20	16	2	2	50
3	BRIMLINGTON RANGERS	20	12	5	3	41
4	POST OFFICE MESSENGERS	20	12	3	5	39
5	LEAF LANE WANDERERS	20	9	4	7	31
6	OLD CENTRALIANS	20	8	6	6	30

Figure 4.3 Creating a table inside a word processor

Importing data from spreadsheets

If the word processor you use does not have a table facility, or if it does not allow formulae to be included, you may need to import numerical data from a spreadsheet. With complex spreadsheets this is often the only way to include the data in a complete report. You may be able to print from the spreadsheet directly, but if a lot of extra text is needed, importing it into a word processor is the only option. This also allows the charts produced by the spreadsheet to be included with the text to improve the clarity of the data. Before importing information from a spreadsheet, you need to be reasonably familiar with spreadsheet concepts.

Whether importing numerical data or charts, there are a number of pitfalls for the unwary. Probably the simplest systems that allow spreadsheet data to be imported into word processors are integrated packages such as Microsoft

Works. These include a complete spreadsheet, database and word processor, and have all the necessary facilities built in to exchange data. However, the procedure is not so simple with information from Lotus 1-2-3 or Microsoft Excel.

With older word processors, which were not really designed to import data from other sources, the process is possible but is rather more cumbersome.

Spreadsheet size

The size of the spreadsheet data to be transferred is the first thing to think about. Many spreadsheets are made up of large number of rows and columns. When this information is transferred to a word processed document, normally only a selected range is copied. The maximum size that can be accommodated depends upon the format of the document, its page orientation and the font size being used. If the selected data is too large to fit the space allowed, some rather unpredictable formatting problems will result.

The length of the data may also be important. If it stretches over more than one page, it may have to be modified so that a second set of column headings is inserted at the top of the columns on the second page.

Table format

Behind the numbers on a spreadsheet there is other hidden information, such as the formulae used to obtain the results and formatting commands to show how the numbers and text are displayed. When data is transferred to a document usually only the *values* are moved. The formatting of cells and their layout on the spreadsheet will therefore not always be the same as that in the document. In particular, bold or italic letters, currency signs and formats and cell borders may not appear exactly as they should. Perhaps more importantly, the alignment of columns may depend more upon the tabs set in the word processor than in the columns set in the spreadsheet.

In addition, although the data in the cells of most spreadsheets can spill over into adjacent empty cells, this may not be the case if the cell contents are transferred to cells in a word processor table. They may be limited to one cell, which means that the text will probably wrap round and form more than one line, which may not be the desired result.

An example of this is shown in Figure 4.4.

Importing data into a table

This method only applies to word processors with a 'Table' facility. It is achieved by creating a table with the required number of rows and columns on the page in the right position. The file containing the spreadsheet information is then opened and either the entire spreadsheet or a selected range of cells is imported. Data fills the cells in the table corresponding to the cells of the spreadsheet from which they came. By selecting different ranges of a spreadsheet it is possible to combine different parts of it in a single report if necessary.

Importing cell data as text

If a formal table is not required, it is still possible to import the spreadsheet data. The text and values of the spreadsheet are transferred to the word processor, with the contents of each cell separated by a tab. The tabs then align the data

(a)

Site	Operating Exp	GL #	Q1	Q2	Q3	Q4	Year
Blackpool			£85,525	£90,125	£95,600	£98,325	£369,575
	Salaries	1-1002	£30,000	£33,000	£36,000	£36,000	£135,000
	Supplies	1-2310	£8,500	£8,000	£9,400	£8,900	£34,800
	Equipment	1-2543	£13,725	£13,725	£13,725	£13,725	£54,900
	Lease Pmts	1-7862	£28,800	£28,800	£28,800	£28,800	£115,200
	Advertising	1-8752	£4,500	£6,600	£7,675	£10,900	£29,675

(b)

Site Operating Exp	GL #	Q1	Q2	Q3	Q4	Year
Blackpool		£85,525	£90,125	£95,600	£98,325	£369,575
Salaries	1-1002	£30,000	£33,000	£36,000	£36,000	£135,000
Supplies	1-2310	£8,500	£8,000	£9,400	£8,900	£34,800
Equipment	1-2543	£13,725	£13,725	£13,725	£13,725	£54,900
Lease Pmts	1-7862	£28,800	£28,800	£28,800	£28,800	£115,200
Advertising	1-8752	£4,500	£6,600	£7,675	£10,900	£29,675

Figure 4.4 (a) Data in a spreadsheet table. (b) The same data presented in a table created inside a word processor

with the current tab settings in the document. If these are wrongly set the results may be unpredictable. However, by carefully selecting the correct number of cells for the number of tabs set, then the results should be as expected.

Worked example

Types of light bulb

Consider the following questions, which may be part of an assignment that requires both a table and a chart to be included in a document.

Light bulbs are available in two forms, conventional and low energy types. The conventional bulbs cost 50p, last 1000 hours and cost 0.85p an hour to run. Low energy bulbs cost £9.00, last 8000 hours and cost 0.2p an hour to run.

1. Construct a simple spreadsheet showing the cost of running each of the bulbs over a period of 8000 hours. Include both the purchase cost of the bulbs and the running costs in the calculations.

Time	0	1000	2000	3000	4000	5000	6000	7000	8000
Conventional									
Purchase	0.5	0.5	0.5	0.5	0.5	0.5	0.5	0.5	0
Running	0	8.5	17	25.5	34	42.5	51	59.5	68
Total	0.5	9.5	18.5	27.5	36.5	45.5	54.5	63.5	72
Low energy									
Purchase	9	0	0	0	0	0	0	0	0
Running	0	2	4	6	8	10	12	14	16
Total	9	11	13	15	17	19	21	23	25

2. Use the data to create a line graph showing the total cost of using each bulb.

3. Write a short report in a new document explaining the differences between the two bulbs. Include in the document the table of spreadsheet information and the graph which illustrates the costs. Conclude the report with the results of your findings on which bulb is the cheapest to use.

SOLUTION

A part of the solution to the assignment is shown in Figure 4.5

Table showing the relative cost of using Conventional and Low Energy light bulbs.

It is assumed that the conventional bulbs cost 50 pence, last 1000 hours and cost 0.85 pence per hour to run (100 watts). The low energy bulbs cost £9.00 to buy, last 8000 hours and cost 0.2 pence per hour to run (25 watts)

The rows show the cost of purchase, runnung and the accumulated total per 1000 hours of use.

	0	1,000	2,000	3,000	4,000	5,000	6,000	7,000	8,000
Con Purchase	0.5	0.5	0.5	0.5	0.5	0.5	0.5	0.5	0
Con Running	0	8.5	17	25.5	34	42.5	51	59.5	68
Con Total	0.5	9.5	18.5	27.5	36.5	45.5	54.5	63.5	72
LE Purchase	9	0	0	0	0	0	0	0	0
LE Running	0	2	4	6	8	10	12	14	16
LE Total	9	11	13	15	17	19	21	23	25

It can be clearly seen from the table that the cost of running the low energy bulb, although initially higher for the first 1000 hours, eventually works out to be £47.00 cheaper over the 8000 hours.

The results are shown graphically below

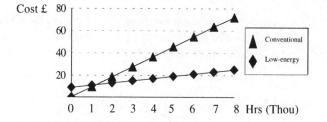

Graph of the cost of running conventional and Low Energy light bulbs

---

Figure 4.5 Presentation of text and graphics in the Light Bulb Assignment

Creating drawings in documents

Most Windows-based word processors allow drawings created with special drawing packages, such as Paintbrush, to be put into documents. The drawings can be placed anywhere on a page or in a frame that can be moved or adjusted in size. This allows the size of drawings to be changed to suit the rest of the page layout. Pictures and photographs can be added in the same way if there is some way of converting them to the required disk format first. For example, photographs can be converted to computer images with a desktop scanner or a special digital camera. Their size can be changed and they can be cropped if they contain unwanted parts.

Another convenient way to create simple drawings to insert into documents is to use the built-in drawing facilities of the word processor. These are really designed for basic drawings, but they can be very useful because they are part of the word processing software. One of the best drawing facilities comes in the Ami-Pro word processor.

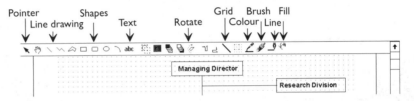

Figure 4.6 Drawing within Ami-Pro

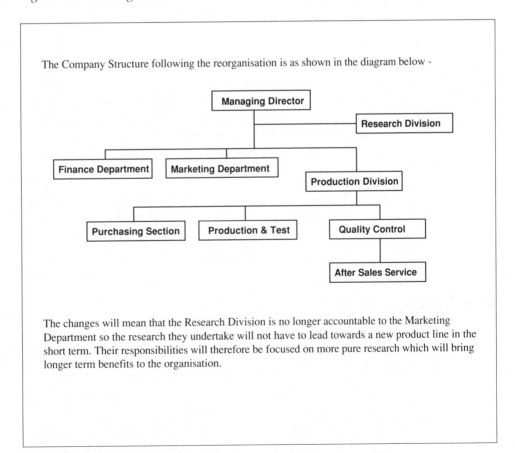

Figure 4.7 The finished result

Drawing features

When the 'Drawing' icon is clicked, another set of icons appears along the top of the screen that control the main drawing operations. They provide line and shape drawing, including rectangles and circles, and move, copy and rotate facilities.

One of the most useful features is the ability to superimpose a fine grid on the screen and to make all of the lines snap to one of the grid points. This means that all of the lines and boxes can be made to align automatically, which gives a much more professional look. Naturally, the grid of dots will not appear on the printed version.

A special feature of the Ami-Pro drawing editor is that it can be made to place its drawing anywhere in the main document. This is because the drawing is actually in a frame which can be put anywhere, and which can be transparent so that the text underneath it shows through. So, if you want to include a picture on a page, but need to draw some arrows to point to the important features of it, Ami-Pro allows you to do it.

Progress check

Now that you have covered some of the more advanced features of word processors, try to answer the following questions by relating them to the work you are doing on your course.

1. If a spreadsheet can be used to create tables of figures and perform calculations, why are tables needed in word processors?

2. Think of at least two examples of documents you have to create that may require a table.

3. Does the word processor you normally use have a 'Table' facility? If so, find out how it works by creating a simple document with a four-column, eight-row table in it. Fill the columns and rows of the table with information on the price of goods similar to that shown in Figure 4.2.

4. How would you create a simple table in a word processor without a 'Table' facility? Assume that the table has to contain text in some columns and numbers in others.

5. Find out if your usual word processor has any built-in drawing facilities. If it has, use them to produce a simple block diagram of your choice as part of a report. If there are no facilities built in, use a drawing package to create the illustration, then transfer it into the report instead.

Printing documents

Good presentation takes very little longer to achieve than poor presentation. Most of the hard work can be done by the computer – as long as the right commands are entered. The page layout, page numbering, spelling and even the grammar can be checked by the computer. This means that there is very little excuse for mistakes and poor quality.

The quality of the final printed documents may depend more upon the printer than on the software itself. If an old printer with limited capability is all that is available the printed output will probably be poor, but with some of the latest laser printers, the same software may be capable of producing professional quality results. Details of the main types of printer available were given in Chapter 1.

Choosing a printer

Most computers have only one printer attached to them so the question of choosing a printer does not arise. In an office, or sometimes when a network is being used, there may be several printers to choose from.

Always choose a printer which best suits your needs. If you need to print on sticky labels for a mail shot then it is best to choose a dot matrix printer with a tractor feed mechanism or a laser printer. If glossy paper is needed to give a very professional looking finish to a presentation or to print the front cover of a report, then choose an ink jet printer, preferably in colour, because a laser printer may smudge.

When good quality printing is needed, for example for publicity material or anything which will be copied a number of times, choose a laser printer. Lasers are also the best type of printer to use for transparencies – as long as the right kind of film is used.

Choosing the right printer not only saves time but also prevents wasting paper.

Printer drivers

Not all printers work with all software because they need special programs, called 'printer drivers', to run them.

Remember: Always be sure that the choices you make when answering on-screen questions actually correspond with the equipment you are using.

If your word processing or database software does not happen to have the right printer driver for the printer you wish to use, it might not work correctly. The most common problem arises when a laser printer is being used because there are two common types: 'PostScript' and 'non-PostScript'. The people responsible for setting up your computer system should be able to tell you which type you have and be able to make sure that all of your software works with the printer.

In the same way, it is no good choosing a laser printer from the list given by the software if only a dot matrix printer is attached to the computer. Unpredictable results will occur!

A summary of the types of printing which each type of printer can do is shown in Figure 4.8.

Printer type	Fan-fold paper	A4 paper	NCR paper	Sticky labels	Envelopes	Transparencies
Dot matrix	Yes	Yes	Yes	Yes	Some	No
Colour dot matrix	Yes	Yes	Yes	Yes	Some	No
Ink jet	No	Yes	No	Yes	Yes	Yes
Colour ink jet	No	Yes	No	Yes	Yes	Yes
Laser	No	Yes	No	Yes	Yes	Yes

Figure 4.8 Summary of printer capabilities

Which way round?

Most software can print on paper in either 'portrait' or 'landscape' mode. *Portrait* means that the paper has its short side at the top and *landscape* means that its short side is at the side. This is called its **orientation**. Choosing which is the right way round depends upon what has to be printed. Normal pages are in the portrait mode. If you would have to turn the paper round to get everything on one sheet, such as when you have to print a wide spreadsheet table, it is better to choose the landscape mode.

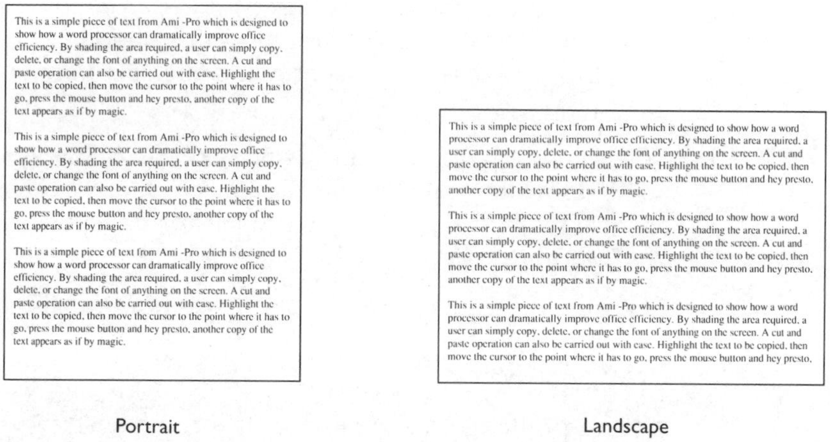

This is a simple piece of text from Ami -Pro which is designed to show how a word processor can dramatically improve office efficiency. By shading the area required, a user can simply copy, delete, or change the font of anything on the screen. A cut and paste operation can also be carried out with ease. Highlight the text to be copied, then move the cursor to the point where it has to go, press the mouse button and hey presto, another copy of the text appears as if by magic.

This is a simple piece of text from Ami -Pro which is designed to show how a word processor can dramatically improve office efficiency. By shading the area required, a user can simply copy, delete, or change the font of anything on the screen. A cut and paste operation can also be carried out with ease. Highlight the text to be copied, then move the cursor to the point where it has to go, press the mouse button and hey presto, another copy of the text appears as if by magic.

This is a simple piece of text from Ami -Pro which is designed to show how a word processor can dramatically improve office efficiency. By shading the area required, a user can simply copy, delete, or change the font of anything on the screen. A cut and paste operation can also be carried out with ease. Highlight the text to be copied, then move the cursor to the point where it has to go, press the mouse button and hey presto, another copy of the text appears as if by magic.

Portrait

This is a simple piece of text from Ami -Pro which is designed to show how a word processor can dramatically improve office efficiency. By shading the area required, a user can simply copy, delete, or change the font of anything on the screen. A cut and paste operation can also be carried out with ease. Highlight the text to be copied, then move the cursor to the point where it has to go, press the mouse button and hey presto, another copy of the text appears as if by magic.

This is a simple piece of text from Ami -Pro which is designed to show how a word processor can dramatically improve office efficiency. By shading the area required, a user can simply copy, delete, or change the font of anything on the screen. A cut and paste operation can also be carried out with ease. Highlight the text to be copied, then move the cursor to the point where it has to go, press the mouse button and hey presto, another copy of the text appears as if by magic.

This is a simple piece of text from Ami -Pro which is designed to show how a word processor can dramatically improve office efficiency. By shading the area required, a user can simply copy, delete, or change the font of anything on the screen. A cut and paste operation can also be carried out with ease. Highlight the text to be copied, then move the cursor to the point where it has to go, press the mouse button and hey presto,

Landscape

Figure 4.9 Page orientation

Headers and footers

If you have to produce a multi-page document such as a report, one of the easiest ways to give it a professional appearance is to include headers or footers on each page. **Headers** are the lines of text which appear along the top of each page of a document generally containing the title of the document or the current chapter title. A header may also include the page number. In books, a common style for headers is to include the book title on the even-numbered pages and the chapter title on the odd-numbered pages.

Footers can be used for the same purpose but are placed at the bottom of each page. They tend to be more common in publications which are not professionally printed. It is unusual to include both headers and footers on the same page unless the footer contains only the page number. Footers are often made a slightly smaller size than the rest of the text.

Page numbers are generally part of either the header or footer. For example, if the chapter title appears in the top left-hand corner of a page, the page number may appear at the top right. Figure 4.10 shows how headers and footers can be selected in Microsoft Word.

Note: Some word processors do not display the header or footer on the screen unless you are in 'Page preview' mode. You will only see them on the printed copy.

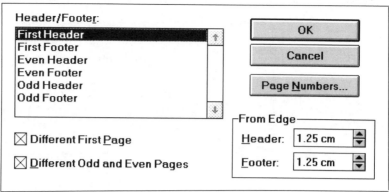

Figure 4.10 Choosing a header or footer in Microsoft Word

Preparing to print – page preview

You should only print a document when you have made sure that everything will turn out exactly as you expect. It is easy to waste pages and pages of paper by printing documents which have not been properly checked on screen. This also wastes a lot of valuable time since every page will take time to print and check.

The best way to make sure that the printed page will be correct is to make use of the 'Page preview' (or 'Print preview') feature of most software packages. This gives you the opportunity to see what the printed page will look like before it is printed. It may not be possible to read every word on a page preview, but it *is* possible to get a good idea of the layout. You can check for obvious mistakes such as a heading on the last line of a page, or a bad piece of formatting. Sometimes by adjusting the margins or the page length settings it is possible to correct these mistakes before printing.

Occasionally it is necessary to print a document to check it properly. For example, if information has to be checked between different pages, it is easier to print them and place them side by side on a desk than to constantly switch between them on a computer screen or even between windows on the screen. In cases like this it is often possible to do a quick print by using the 'draft' printing quality of the printer, which usually prints about twice as fast as the 'letter' quality.

Pre-printed forms

One of the most difficult problems for a word processor user is to make the printing line up exactly with a pre-printed form. Sometimes the problem is so complex that it is better to align each part of the text on a typewriter. However, simple alignment problems can be undertaken on a word processor with a suitable printer.

For example, consider the problem of providing a small certificate for about 25 people who took part in a series of fund-raising events for local charities. To make the certificates attractive they have been specially printed, but they need to be overprinted with the name of each participant. The printing is to be in a special 'script' typeface, so it would not look very good if a typewriter were used. The solution is to use a word processor and a suitable font to overprint a blank certificate.

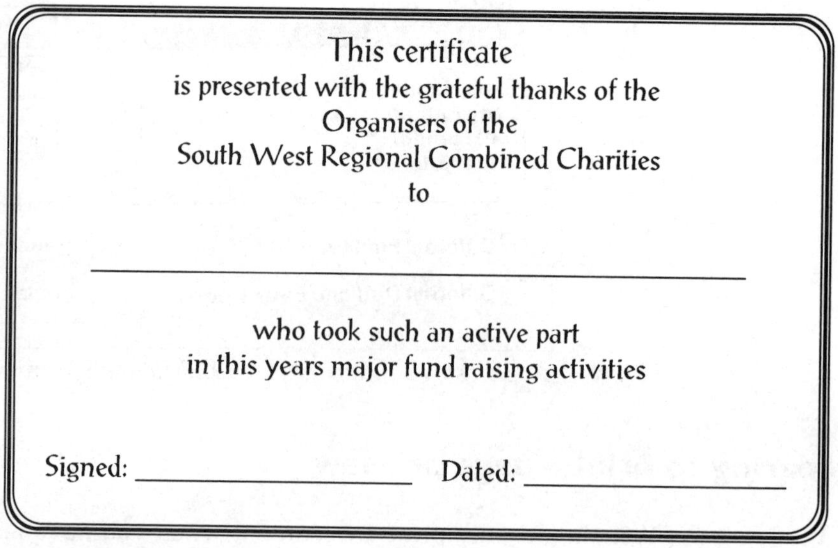

> **This certificate**
> is presented with the grateful thanks of the
> Organisers of the
> South West Regional Combined Charities
> to
>
> _____
>
> who took such an active part
> in this years major fund raising activities
>
>
> Signed: _____   Dated: _____

Figure 4.11 A blank certificate ready for personalising

Alignment

Aligning the name and the date depend upon making the word processor print on the right line and start at the right place along the line. One way to find out which line to print on is to print a test page in the same font, with a complete line of numbers on each line. This is a good method of calculating which line number has to be used and the character position where the text has to start. Once these have been calculated, the page can be set up using tabs to align the text positions along each line. It is very important that this is done, since names will cause alignment problems because of their different lengths. Use the minimum number of tabs possible by removing unwanted tabs from each line.

Centred tabs are best for the name on a certificate, whereas left-justified tabs can be used for all other text.

If vertical alignment is a problem, one trick is to use subscript or superscript letters, which move the text up or down by half a line. Alternatively, with some word processors, the text could be included in a frame, which can be adjusted in position very precisely. Remove any pre-set frame margins, however, if this technique is to be successful.

> **Hint:** Some laser printers have problems printing on very glossy paper such as certificates, since the letters smudge. Use an ink jet printer instead.

Large documents

Writing a large document such as a multi-chapter report can be quite difficult, particularly when deciding what to include and what to leave out. One way to solve the problem is to write an outline of the document first. This initially contains only the main headings and none of the detail.

The headings are arranged in order of importance so that the main chapter or section headings are decided first, then the subheadings and then any further subdivisions. Finally, the detail is added to complete the whole project.

Working out the outline first helps to keep the main points in order so that it becomes clear what detail has to be added later. It also means that if you decide to alter the layout by moving sections from one chapter to another, you can do it at the design stage rather than at the final writing stage.

Outlining tools

Most modern word processors include some special tools which allow documents to be developed from a basic outline. For example, both Microsoft Word and Lotus Ami-Pro include an 'Outline' view of the text.

To develop an outline using either of these word processors, switch to the 'Outline' view instead of the 'Normal' view. Then type the main headings of your text. These may be chapter headings or the main section headings. As each one is entered it is given a 'Heading 1' style. This means that it is the highest level, or the most important type of heading.

Next, under each one, insert the sub-headings. After the first sub-heading is entered, click on the right arrow in the 'ribbon' just above the text area to move the subheading to the right. It automatically becomes a 'Heading 2' style. This process can then be repeated for all of the headings and sub-headings until the outline of the document is completed. Each lower level of subheading is given a slightly different style to distinguish it from the others. Whole sections can be moved or changed in importance simply by dragging them around with the mouse or by using the icons provided. Parts of the document can be 'collapsed' to show only particular levels of heading and hide the detail.

When the outline is finished, 'body text' can then be added to complete the report.

Figure 4.12 shows an example of some of the headings of a report done with an outliner. Each level of heading can be clearly seen.

<u>Chapter 1</u>
    The basic premise is expounded
        The theory explained
            <u>The arguments for and against</u>
            <u>The evidence</u>
    Comparison with the old theory
        Fitting the facts
            <u>Changing viewpoints</u>
        The weight of testimony
            <u>Letters and research from around the world</u>
<u>Chapter 2</u>
    First principles of the new theory
        Correcting the basis of old thinking
            <u>Extending to the ultimate conclusions</u>
            <u>Errors and miscalculations</u>
    Fighting to preserve the status quo
            <u>Long established beliefs</u>
            <u>The reluctance to change</u>
    Explanation of deviations from the expected
<u>Chapter 3</u>
    How the modern system cannot allow the changes necessary

Figure 4.12 An outliner in operation

Joining files to make large documents

It is sometimes very convenient to create all of the parts of a large document in different files. For example, if a number of people are working on a project at the same time or if information has to be drawn from different sources, it is best to keep the files separate. The only problem arises when all of the files have to be combined to form the final report. This will need to be properly numbered for pages and sections, have a complete contents list and have a proper index.

It may not be necessary to combine all the files that make up a complete document into one file, but if it is, wait until each part has been checked thoroughly. Working on large files can be a very slow operation. Choose a suitable file, either the first chapter or a new file altogether, then gradually insert the other files at the end of it until they are combined. This can then be numbered and finally checked before printing.

A little thought before starting such report can save a lot of time later. For example, make sure that if different people type different sections, they all use the same font size, the same types of heading and the same margins.

This is where an outliner comes in handy. If the basic page layout of each section is the same, then the complete document will at least *look* as if it belongs together.

Section numbering in large documents

It is usual to number the sections of a large document to make it easier for the reader to refer to specific parts. The main sections can be numbered according to the chapter number 1, 2, 3, etc. Subsections are normally given a second decimal number 1.1, 1.2, 1.3, etc. Further subdivisions can be created with a third series of numbers – 1.1.1, 1.1.2 – but this can create a very complex numbering system and should be used with care.

Some large publications, such as government documents, number all of the paragraphs. This makes it simple to refer to specific points if changes are required or comments need to be made.

Page numbering large documents

The page numbering facilities of all word processors allow the numbers to start at any value. This means that each chapter can be numbered consecutively. The manual method of doing this is probably easiest for a small number of chapters or sections. Print the first section, note the number of the last page, and change the first number of the next section accordingly before it is printed.

The automatic method depends upon the capabilities of the word processor. Some require a master document to be set up, which includes a list of all the chapter or section files that make up the whole work. If the first page is numbered, when the master document is printed it consecutively numbers each of the files included in the list. Figure 4.13 shows a typical master document which has only a title page. If the page numbers are set to 1 for the first page of chapter 1, all the following chapters will be correctly numbered. Furthermore, if there are index references or headings for contents lists in any of the files listed, they will also have the correct page numbers attached to them.

The special fields, shown in curly brackets ({ }) are called 'Field codes' and have to be inserted from the 'Insert' menu in Microsoft Word.

THE COMPLETE REPORT

ON GLOBAL WARMING

```
{include CHAP1}
{include CHAP2}
{include CHAP3}
{include CHAP4}
{include CHAP5}
{include CHAP6}
{include CHAP7}
{include BIBLIOG}
```

Figure 4.13 Master document, including a number of chapters

Index and table of contents entries

A 'Table of contents' at the beginning and an 'Index' at the end of a document are very important if it contains more than one chapter. They help readers to make sense of the layout and can save a lot of time looking for particular parts of it later.

Both 'Table of contents' entries and 'Index' entries can be made by placing special field codes near the text they refer to on a page. These references have to be specially inserted as the text is being written, but the page number on which they occur is automatically calculated by the word processor when the document is printed. This means that if changes are made to the text, the page references are also recalculated.

If large documents with a number of sections or chapters are produced in the way described above, their complete contents list and index can be created in much the same way. Each word processor has a slightly different method of doing this, so it is worth taking a little time to find out exactly how to do it before starting on a large project.

Care with large documents

Dealing with large documents is one of the more difficult operations with a word processor, and it is easy to get into a mess. Always take the sensible precaution of working with a copy of the files and not the only masters. Keep a set of backup files in a safe place before starting major operations.

If possible, avoid having to create one large file from several smaller files. This can save time because the word processor can deal with smaller files much faster than large ones. Several files created by different people are the most awkward to combine because they are likely to be in slightly different styles. For example, some people may have indented the paragraphs, some may not and different fonts and type sizes may have been used. These types of problem are best avoided by agreeing on a complete style before typing, or by agreeing that no formatting will be used at all. The document can then be formatted at the final stage so that all the formatting is the same.

Save your work very regularly, or arrange the word processor to do it automatically so that, if things go wrong, only a small amount of work will have to be redone.

Mail-merge for customised documents

A few years ago it was considered to be very clever marketing for a document to include the recipient's name and address and perhaps other details in the text. The whole document looked as though it had been personally written and was therefore worthy of special attention. Unfortunately, nothing could have been further from the truth since most of the original 'personalised' documents were the products of massive mail-shots from large companies who could invest thousands of pounds on marketing. Most word processors can achieve the personalised effect by merging a form letter or template containing blank 'slots' with a data file which includes the information to be added. This process is called 'mail-merging'. The result is a copy of the letter or document customised for each entry in the data file.

Customising documents can be very useful if similar information is required by a large number of people, each of whom has a slight variation from the others. Examples are the names and addresses of students on college reports, with the names of the various subjects studied; the names, addresses and appointment dates and times at a dentist's practice; 'thank you' letters for donations to a charity; acknowledgements for conference bookings.

When large numbers of customised documents are required, it is generally a good idea to use a database to store all of the information to be added to the template.

Built-in databases

If only a few documents are needed, then the data can be stored in a special file created by the word processor. For example, in Microsoft Works the integrated database would normally be used to store the variable data, and the word processor would create the document file. Most modern word processors have a built-in database facility especially for mail-merging operations

Sticky labels

Mailing labels are created from a special type of template document and printed on a different type of paper. The format of the label can be created in almost the same way as any other customised document. However, special formatting commands are needed to ensure that the labels are created in the right places on each page. Some may have only one across the width of a page, others two, and some have three.

Normally, the word processor system will ask you to choose whether you want to create a letter or a set of labels during the mail-merging process.

Worked example

Customised letters

As part of a month of work experience in the Careers Office, you have been given the task of writing to about 50 people to set up an interview with their careers counsellor, at fixed times over a period of a few weeks. The task would take too long if each letter were typed individually and it would also lead to a lot of potential errors, so the best solution is to set up a database of appointments, then extract the information to put into each letter.

SOLUTION

THE DATA FILE

The data file contains all the information required for each letter, but it may also contain extra information which is needed for other purposes.

In this case it requires:

> title, first name, surname, address (may be several lines), postcode, appointment date, appointment time, counsellor's name.

The file may also contain information such as date of birth and telephone number, although these are not required for the letter. The database is created in the manner described in Chapter 5, with field names appropriate to the contents. In this case the database fields may be:

> Title, FName, Surname, Add1, Add2, Add3, PCode, DoB, Tel, Appdate, Apptime, CName.

Each field must be long enough to hold the longest entry required for any data. When typed, each field is separated by a comma, a style known as a 'comma delimited' file. The database would be typically like that shown in Figure 4.14.

Title	Fname	Surname	Add1	Add2	Pcode	DoB	AppDate	AppTime	CName
Mr	James	Newton	12 Sandringham Court	Monwearmouth	S12 8JK	14/3/79	21/10/95	10.00	J. Hoult
Mr	Henry	Wilson	3 Archer Court	Whitburn	S33 1MK	3/4/79	12/10/95	2.15	K. Hanson
Miss	Linda	Bridges	77 Abingdon St	Barnes	S6 7RG	1/10/78	21/10/95	10.30	J Hoult
Miss	Jenny	Clark	15 Gower Rd	Pennywell	S21 3TD	18/2/79	12/10/95	3.00	K. Hanson

Figure 4.14 The database file

THE TEMPLATE

The template is the letter which will be sent to each person on the database, but in the place of specific names, addresses etc. the template contains special entries known as 'place holders' or 'data fields'. In the final version of each letter these are replaced by real data from the database.

A suitable form letter or template is shown in Figure 4.15.

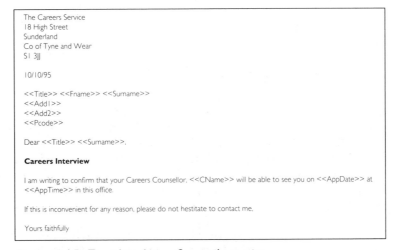

Figure 4.15 Template letter for mail-merging

THE CUSTOMISED LETTERS

The output from the merging process is illustrated in Figure 4.16. Each letter has been customised with the name and address of the recipient as well as the time and date of their appointment. Most systems will print one letter for each database entry, so it is important to ensure that the database is correct and complete before printing. It is sometimes difficult to go back to the database and reprint only one or two letters if mistakes have occurred.

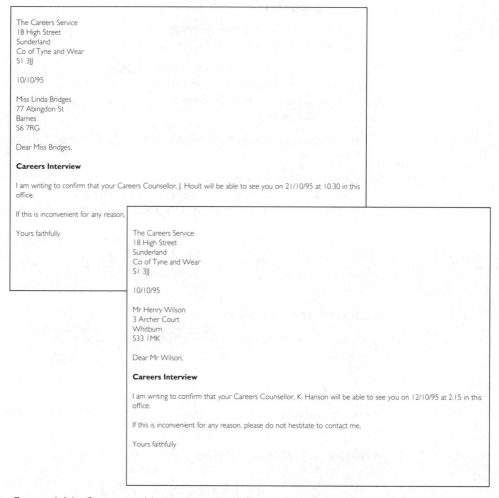

The Careers Service
18 High Street
Sunderland
Co of Tyne and Wear
S1 3JJ

10/10/95

Miss Linda Bridges
77 Abingdon St
Barnes
S6 7RG

Dear Miss Bridges,

Careers Interview

I am writing to confirm that your Careers Counsellor, J. Hoult will be able to see you on 21/10/95 at 10.30 in this office.

If this is inconvenient for any reason,

Yours faithfully

The Careers Service
18 High Street
Sunderland
Co of Tyne and Wear
S1 3JJ

10/10/95

Mr Henry Wilson
3 Archer Court
Whitburn
S33 1MK

Dear Mr Wilson,

Careers Interview

I am writing to confirm that your Careers Counsellor, K. Hanson will be able to see you on 12/10/95 at 2.15 in this office.

If this is inconvenient for any reason, please do not hestitate to contact me.

Yours faithfully

Figure 4.16 Customised letters prepared from a template using mail-merging

Precautions using mail-merge

Take special care, because word processors will automatically reformat each paragraph in which the variable data occurs so that it appears to have been typed individually. This means that the text looks good, but can lead to unexpected results if a long data entry creates an extra line in the text, or a short entry creates one line less. Try to use tabs to keep certain parts of the text at fixed points if necessary and make sure that the page is terminated by a fixed 'page break' instruction.

If the data file is created by a database program which is not connected to the word processor in any way, you may need to indicate to the word processor the name of the file and the field names that need to be read into the template. This is sometimes called the **data header**.

The format of the data file may be important. Although most word processors can now read files directly from databases, they may need a special format such as a 'comma delimited file', in which variables are surrounded by quotation marks " and separated by commas – "Mr", "James", "Smith", etc.

Progress check

The following questions are designed to check your knowledge of the topics covered since the last set of questions. Write down your answers if you can without referring back to the text just to see how much you have remembered. If you are really stuck, look at the previous pages rather than the answers for some help.

1. List some of the ways in which a word processor can help with the presentation of an important assignment.

2. How does the type of printer used for a document affect the quality of the finished result?

3. What type of printer would be able to produce
   (a) an overhead transparency
   (b) a printout on 14" wide paper
   (c) a sheet with high quality text and a colour photograph on the same page
   (d) the high quality master for a publicity handout
   (e) a bill on NCR paper
   (f) a set of mailing addresses on sticky labels?

4. What is the typical resolution of a laser printer in dots per inch?

5. Which of the statements below are true?
   (a) A PostScript laser printer will produce high quality printing from any computer program.
   (b) Printer drivers are software programs which control the printer connected to a computer.
   (c) Dot matrix and laser printers require different printer drivers.

6. Give one purpose of a 'footer' on a printed page.

7. How could you find out whether or not your printer was able to print a document exactly as you planned it?

8. What problems are you likely to come across if you are asked to print the details on several lines of a pre-printed form, and how would you overcome them?

9. What is the purpose of an 'outline' facility in a word processor?

10. How would you create an index entry for a document with the word processor you normally use?

11. What problems are you likely to encounter in page numbering a document which contains several chapters in separate files?

12. What are the two files needed before a letter can be customised for a large number of different people?

Improving the content

One of the best features of a word processor is that it can help to improve the content of what is written as well as displaying it in an attractive layout. Some word processors include spelling checkers which look up every word in an electronic dictionary, a thesaurus which provides synonyms for most words if required, and grammar checkers which highlight text which does not obey grammatical rules.

Spelling

Spelling checkers have only been introduced as standard features of word processors in the last few years. The word processing software is supplied with a complete dictionary of words which are correctly spelled, although some may only have American spellings. Typically 20,000–30,000 words are included, but most have the facility to add extra words into a 'personal dictionary'. Technical terms, names of friends, businesses, addresses and many other words not normally found in a dictionary but frequently typed would be added to the personal dictionary over a period of time.

Whenever the word processor is asked to check the spellings in a document, it looks up every word in the dictionary. If the word is found, the next word is checked, but if no matching word is found, the spelling checker stops and offers alternatives which are guesses at what the word may be. These suggestions are not only based on similarly spelled words, but also on similar sounding words.

If any of the suggestions is the word which was intended, then a simple replacement can take place. However, if none of the suggestions are correct, the word can be ignored, added to the personal dictionary or re-typed from the keyboard.

Always make use of a spelling checker if your word processor has one. A misspelled document reflects badly upon its author.

Checking every word in a document may seem like a long job even for a computer, but with the speed of modern machines, a page of A4 text can be checked in less than one second if there are no mistakes. However, even if all the words in a document have been spelled correctly, the results may not be perfect. For example, if the wrong word is used in a sentence, such as 'their' instead of 'there', but it is spelled correctly, no error will be reported. Only a grammar checker will detect these types of error.

Alternative words

A thesaurus is included in some word processors to help find words of similar meaning (synonyms). When writing it is often necessary to vary the words used to provide added interest for the reader. Frequently, the first word which springs to mind does not have the exact meaning that you wish to convey. In these cases, a thesaurus provides the means of finding an alternative.

The word to be checked is normally highlighted in the text and the thesaurus is then selected. It provides a list of words with similar meanings and allows the writer to select one to replace the word in the document. In addition, for each of the alternatives it provides more words which have similar or related meanings so that it is possible to generate many alternatives to any word in the original document.

For example, if the word 'selected' has to be replaced with an alternative, the thesaurus will provide a number of possible alternatives – picked, chosen, elected, named, preferred. Not all of them fit every sentence, so the most appropriate alternative has to be chosen.

Grammar checkers

Grammar checkers are available on only a few word processors, but are likely to become popular as a way of ensuring that all text appears to be well written. Grammar checkers look at the sentence structure in a document and apply a series of grammatical rules according to the type of writing which the document contains.

For example, different sets of rules are applied for business writing, legal writing, technical writing, fiction writing, academic, formal or casual writing. Over twenty different rules of grammar and the same number of style rules may be applied to a sentence, together with other rules regarding word order.

By selecting which rules to apply, according to the type of document, the word processor can quickly highlight any possible errors and make suggestions about how they can be corrected.

Grammar rules check each sentence so that they would suggest that, for example:
- 'we has not time to go', should be changed to 'we have not time to go'
- 'partners explains themselves' should be changed to 'partners explain themselves'
- 'the box which I bought' should be changed to 'the box that I bought'

Style rules check for:
- Wordy expressions – for example it may suggest that 'which could be supposed, in the first instance to be the answer' is replaced by ' which could be the first answer'
- Redundant expressions – suggesting that 'it is, in fact not true' is replaced by 'it is not true', for example.

Even though they break some grammatical rules , some writers prefer to leave their text as it is to achieve a special effect or to emphasise a writing style.

Grammar checkers are also capable of calculating 'readability statistics'. These allow writers to discover how easy it will be for the intended reader to understand what is written.

The effect of word processors on work

The development of the word processor has changed the way in which offices work. In the past, typing was a very specialist skill which could be done only after a fairly long training. Typing a lot of information still requires a fast typist, but with a word processor anyone can produce a document that looks good if they have enough time to spend at it. The word processor can work out all of the margins, correct the mistakes and the spellings and so make the job of typing much easier for everyone. Because of this, many more people in an office do their own typing if they have a computer available. Even some top managers like to be able to make their own corrections to text which other people may have typed.

Publicity and calculations

However, the word processor can do very much more than this. It can add to the facilities available in an office because it can be used to produce masters for publicity information (including pictures), which would previously have been produced at a printers. Some systems also provide basic mathematical capability so that tables can be created and calculations performed automatically. This helps to reduce the mistakes which can creep in when using a calculator.

Mailshots

Mailing several people with the same or similar information is another job at which the word processor excels. The rapid and easy production of personalised letters is a great advantage only brought about with computer power.

Drawings

Including drawings in text has always been a problem. With a good word processor the ability to add drawings to a document at any point means that technical reports, organisation charts, line diagrams, etc. can all be done within the word processing package. The need for manual drawings which have to be stuck in place is now largely a thing of the past.

Review questions

Now that you have completed the work on word processing, take some time to reflect on how some of the things learned apply to the work you are doing.

1. From your experience, apart from the difficulty in learning to type, think of a number of disadvantages of a word processor and things it can not do.

2. What are the limitations of the word processor and printer combination you normally use?

3. How would you include a picture in a report for one of your assignments? Give a brief explanation of the steps involved and the details of the packages you would use.

4. Briefly describe the process of creating entries for an index for one of your documents. How is the process of compiling the index carried out with your usual word processor?

5. What changes have to be made to the indexing process if more than one file is involved?

6. What would you do if your word processor spelling checker kept stopping on a lot of technical terms in a report which you knew were spelled correctly?

7. List the precautions required before starting a multi-chapter document to ensure that the minimum of re-formatting will be needed when the complete document is compiled?

8. How does a word processor improve the efficiency of an office?

Exercises

If you need to practice some of the techniques introduced in this chapter, these exercises may prove useful.

1. Create the following table to go in a document using the table facility of your word processor if it has one. It should be placed in the centre of an A4 page, just after the introductory paragraph.

   The following data has been extracted from the published university information but can only be used as a guide

Name of university or college	Total number of undergraduates	Percentage of mature students	Male to female ratio	Percentage of first years in managed accommodation
Aberdeen	7324	26	53/47	100
Aberystwyth	5230	17	50/50	100
Birmingham	10873	11	53/47	95
Bournemouth	5600	28	54/46	8
Bradford	5529	18	59/41	100
Brighton	7063	35	50/50	50

2. Using the table created in Exercise 1, add an extra five rows and add the following information in the appropriate columns

Bristol	8463	13	53/47	97
Central Lancashire	7453	48	50/50	75
Dartington College	405	41	40/60	90
Essex	3756	34	55/45	100

Ensure that a line is drawn round each cell in the table. Make the titles a slightly larger font size than the rest, and use italic print.

3. Find a league table for any sport in a newspaper, and enter the top part of it into a simple spreadsheet. Begin a newspaper-style article using your word processor, with the following text:

```
At the end of last week's fixtures, the top of the table
looks like this:
```

Now import the table you have created from the spreadsheet. If you are not using a Windows-based spreadsheet, you may need to set up the tabs very carefully first. With a Windows-based system, the word processor will probably create a table for you automatically.

If the import does not work correctly, try to analyse what went wrong and try again.

4. Find one of the documents you have already created on disk, which is more than one page long and which has fairly basic presentation. Make a copy of it and give it another file name.

Open the file and add both a header and a footer to each page. The header should be on the left for even-numbered pages and on the right for odd-numbered pages. It should contain the document name in 8 point, italic text. The footer should contain the page number as 'Page . . . ' in the centre of each page.

5. Use the 'Outline' view, if your word processor has one, to create the headings for a report as follows:

Introduction
Chapter 1
    The human being
        Dimensions
        Origins
        Longevity
        Reproductivity
Chapter 2
    The living world
        Mammals
        Birds
        Reptiles
        Fishes

Chapter 3
   The natural world
         Natural phenomena
         Weather
         Structure and dimensions

After you have created the outline, enter one further subheading for each section. Then add a sentence or two as the body text for the report itself.

6. Type the names and addresses of five of your friends into a simple database. You may be able to use the facilities built into your word processing package or any other database package.

Now lay out the following invitation with your word processor. Centre the text within a frame with rounded corners and draw a line round it.

```
To . . . . . . . ..(name) of . . . . . . . . . . . . (town)

I have great pleasure in asking you to accompany me to
Paris for the weekend to celebrate my . . . . ..th (choose
a number) birthday. I will be able to pick you up at . .
. . . . . . . . . . . . . . .(address) at 0830 on Saturday
morning which will give us plenty time to be able to
catch the Eurostar at 10.30.

RSVP
```

In the gaps, use the 'mail-merge' feature of your word processor to automatically enter the names and addresses of the people on your database.

Assignment 1
Designing a questionnaire

This assignment can be used to provide evidence for the following Performance Criteria:

Element 2.1	PCs 1 to 4
Element 2.2	PCs 1, 2, 4 and 5
Element 2.3	PCs 1 to 5
Element 2.4	PCs 1 to 4
Element 3.1	PCs 1 to 5
Element 3.2	PCs 1,2 , 4, 5 and 7
Element 3.3	PCs 1 to 6
Element 3.4	PCs 1 to 5

Introduction

You are part of a team which has been asked to do a survey to attempt to collect opinions from members of the public on the construction of a new superstore. The task of designing the questionnaire has been given to you, so you decide to try your new skills with the word processor. There will be about 12 questions that can all be contained on one side of an A4 sheet of paper. Each question will need three tick boxes beside it for the responses 'Yes', 'No', and 'Don't know'.

Your task

1. Design the layout of the questionnaire using one of the methods described below.

    -   Use of tabs to create the table and use square brackets [ ] for the tick boxes.

    -   Use the word processor 'Table' facility to create a table with boxes at the end of each line for the responses.

    -   Use the built-in drawing facility to draw the response boxes at the end of each line of text, but don't enter any text yet.

    A typical question should look like the illustration below

Yes	No	Don't know

    1. Do you agree with the proposed location of the new superstore?

2. Lay out the rest of the response boxes in the same way, then save your work as a style sheet or template for later use.

3. Write the questions in each of the boxes.

4. Save the document about half way through, and then again at the end. Use a different file name from the style sheet created in Step 2.

5. Print the completed questionnaire, preferably after you have had a 'Print preview'.

Write a paragraph to add to your questionnaire describing how you would have undertaken the same task without a word processor. Comment on the alternative ways of creating the same questionnaire, and, if possible, give examples of two methods in use.

Assignment 2 starts on the next page

Assignment 2
Printing your National Record of Achievement

This assignment can be used to provide evidence for the following Performance Criteria:

Element 2.1	PCs 1 to 4
Element 2.2	PCs 1, 2, 4 and 5
Element 2.3	PCs 1 to 5
Element 2.4	PCs 1 and 2
Element 3.1	PCs 1 to 5
Element 3.2	PCs 1, 2, 4, 5 and 7
Element 3.3	PCs 1 to 6
Element 3.4	PCs 1 and 2

Personal Details

National
Record of
Achievement

Name:

Date of birth

Address

Post Code

List of Secondary Schools, Colleges, Higher Education Institutions attended

Accreditation or validation, where applicable

Signature   Position   Date

Figure 4.17 The National Record of Achievement form

Introduction

You have been asked to complete the 'Personal Details' page of your National Record of Achievement so that it can be included in your file as soon as possible. The document itself is pre-printed with spaces for your name, date of birth, address and postcode, then it has a large space for the list of educational establishments you have attended. It will only be possible to print it once, so it must be exactly right.

Your task

Your task is to work out how to align the text on a blank A4 page so that if it were printed on the Record of Achievement it would all line up exactly with the spaces provided. Always test the results on normal paper, then hold the printout up to the light with the actual document behind it to check the alignment.

1. First, work out which line number is required for your personal details. Do this by printing a test page with the line number as the first text on each line.

2. Either measure the distance from the left edge of the paper or calculate the correct character position needed for the text on each line by printing a test page. Then set a tab to the correct value in each case. These may be different for each line. Make sure you make allowance for the left margin setting.

3. Enter your text and check that each entry is on the correct line. Use the tab key to align the start of each line with the tab stops set.

4. Print a copy of the text on a sheet of normal A4 paper. Hold it up to the light in front of the Record of Achievement to check its alignment. The top left-hand corners of each sheet need to be held exactly together. Alternatively, you could print on a photocopy of the actual record, but in this case make sure the copy is exactly the same size as the original.

5. If everything is correctly aligned, put the Record of Achievement sheet into the printer, making sure it is the right way round, then print it.

How does the result you have produced compare with any alternative ways of doing it? Make some brief notes on how easy or otherwise the process was. Comment on any problems you encountered and describe how you overcame them. Print a spare copy of your Record of Achievement details onto plain paper and annotate it with the word processing features you have used.

Assignment 3 starts on the next page

Assignment 3
Checking a document

This assignment can be used to provide evidence for the following Performance Criteria:

Element 2.1   PCs 1 to 4

Element 2.2   PCs 1, 2, 4 and 5

Element 2.3   PCs 1 to 5

Element 2.4   PCs 1 to 4

Element 3.1   PCs 1 to 5

Element 3.2   PCs 1, 2, 4, 5 and 7

Element 3.3   PCs 1 to 6

Element 3.4   PCs 1 to 5

Introduction

This assignment is based upon some work which you have already done, preferably when you did your first assignment on a word processor. You will need a disk file of a report or something similar. The word processor you use will need to include a spelling checker, a thesaurus and, if possible, a grammar checker. The assignment will show you how to improve the quality of your work for future assignments, as long as it was not perfect in the first place.

Your task

The task involves the use of some of the more advanced word processor facilities.

1. First make a copy of the file you intend to work on so that you can see the corrections which have been made later. Work on the copy, not the original.

2. Check the spelling in the file by running the spelling checker of the word processor. Take care with the corrections if it finds any – not all of them might be mistakes.

3. Find a few words which could be improved. Perhaps the same word has been repeated a number of times or an alternative expression could be employed. Start the thesaurus by highlighting a word then clicking the icon or selecting it from the menu. Pick one of the alternative words and put in into the file. Try the same thing several times.

4. Now, if possible, check the grammar in the file. Select the style for 'business use'. Take each suggestion carefully and see if there are any corrections to be made. It may surprise you.

5. Print a copy of the file after the corrections have been completed as well as a copy of the original. Highlight the changes on the revised version.

Write a brief report on the process you have gone through, including comments on the use of IT to perform the tasks compared with manual methods, the efficiency of the operation and the effects on the work of IT users who have access to similar facilities.

CHAPTER 5

Introduction to databases

Objectives

When you have finished this chapter you should be able to:
- Understand the functions of databases and why they are important
- Recognise the terms field, record, index
- Create a database with a given structure
- Devise a database structure for an application
- Select items from a database that fulfil search criteria
- Delete records from a database
- Understand the value of some of the large sources of data.

This chapter covers the Performance Criteria and Range from all of the IT Core Skills Elements at levels 2 and 3 related to the preparation, processing and presentation of text and numbers in databases, the reorganisation of data and an evaluation of the types of software used.

Why are databases important?

Try to work out how many people have your name and address and any other personal details – think about your school, college, library, doctor, dentist, bank, employer, Department of Social Security, etc.

The more you think about it, the longer the list becomes. Many of the people and organisations that keep personal information about you will have it on a paper-based system of cards. This forms a simple database, but is rather inefficient by modern standards. Others will keep information about you on a computer.

The information in a computerised database can be retrieved much more rapidly than that in a paper system, so it is much more efficient. Its most important advantage, however, is that the information it contains can be analysed.

A commercial example

The sales department of a large company keeps a database on the company's computer that stores the name, address, telephone number, post code, date of each order, value of each order, a discount level and credit rating of all of its customers. In addition, each customer is given a unique customer reference number. There are over 12,000 altogether.

Why does the company use an electronic database?

REF	NAME	TOWN	DISCOUNT LEVEL (%)	CREDIT LIMIT (£)	LAST ORDER (£)	DATE OF ORDER
952133D	Mr J. Stephens	Reading	10.0	250		
931288M	Mrs L. Briers	Sunderland	10.0	250	122.00	23/04/94
942255G	Miss G. Shaw	Whitby	5.0	200	25.87	1/04/94
893577S	Mr G.Willis	Hartlepool	15.0	2000	1255.80	27/05/94
931109E	Mr D.Small	Lowestoft	0.0	0	85.99	20/01/93
931110C	Mrs K. Grearson	Hull	0.0	0	5.85	13/3/93
903188P	Mrs W Knowles	Grimsby	15.0	2000	1509.00	24/2/94
914421D	Mrs S. King	Sandwell	10.0	1000	863.25	12/4/94
952557M	Miss J. Jones	Leicester	0.0	0		
926194A	Ms A. Wales	Swansea	10.0	250	66.44	3/05/94
914472K	Dr. Q. Frank	Kingston	15.0	2000	1322.99	3/05/94
932790H	Mr T. Harris	Grimsby	5.0	200	100.75	13/3/94
931969G	Mrs Y. Cowell	Hastings	10.0	1000	23.33	20/01/93

Figure 5.1 Part of a company database

Storage capacity

The size of the database is the first reason. If each customer had an entry on a card index system, the 12,000 cards would probably fill several filing cabinets. On a computer, if each customer's information requires up to 500 characters, the whole database needs only 6 MByte. It could be stored on five floppy disks or a fraction of a hard disk.

A 320 MByte hard disk could store the same information on 640,000 customers.

Rapid retrieval

If the sales staff need the name and address of a customer, it can be found in seconds. The computer can search the entire database and compare each name with the one required until a match is found. The system has an electronic index, and the name is looked up first in the index, so the full record can be found more quickly.

Looking up the same information in a manual system is likely to take several minutes at best, as long as all the names are kept in strict alphabetical order. If not, it could take hours.

Selection of particular information

The company launch a new product, and wish to obtain feedback from recent customers in a small area. They want the sales department to select recent customers from one of three towns. For each one they need a printed label with the name and address.

With a computer database this is no problem. By entering 'search criteria' including the date of last order and town, the computer can print the names and addresses of all those who match the requirements. The longest job is printing the labels.

With a manual filing system, the task could take weeks. Every card would have to be checked then the name and address of those selected would have to be typed on an envelope.

Analysing the data

The managing director wants to find out how much the average daily order is, to calculate the projected income. Asking the computer database to add all of the order values for one day and to calculate the average takes only a few minutes. Doing the same task manually would take days of work and would be subject to many possible errors. The computer calculation will probably be correct if all the input information is accurate.

Increased efficiency

In each of the situations above, the computer can perform the task much more quickly than doing it any other way. This considerably improves the efficiency of organisations for whom extra time means more money. The computer also makes it possible to do things that would otherwise be almost impossible.

For example, selecting particular information is very difficult in a manual system. Suppose the company need to find all the customers who have ever placed orders over £1000, or all of those who have not placed an order in the last six months. The computer can work it all out in a few seconds but to do the same thing by hand may take weeks!

Potential problems

However, the database output is only as good as the information that is put in. A mailing list in which half the addresses are wrong is hardly worth having. Therefore time and effort must be spent on keeping any database up to date whether it is electronic or paper based. In some organisations database management is a full-time job for many people.

Data Protection Act

It is very easy for the information held on an electronic database to be inaccurate or out of date if the system is not properly maintained. Sometimes this can have disastrous consequences.

One man was arrested on two separate occasions for crimes he had not committed. He discovered that the Police National Computer had confused him with a known criminal of the same name. Unknowingly, he had been given a police record. Another person was refused credit when she went to buy a new television. The shop manager claimed that she was a bad debtor because she had a County Court judgment against her. It turned out that the credit reference agency used to check her credit rating had confused her with someone else who had previously lived at the same address.

To protect individuals against this type of error, the Data Protection Act gives us all important rights. If you think the data held on a computer system about you is incorrect, you can request a copy of the record. It may cost up to £10 to obtain it, but you have the right to have it corrected or erased if it is wrong. If the company refuses, you can complain to the Data Protection Registrar.

All electronic databases holding personal information must be registered, and the owners must provide basic security for the data. Users need to have secure access with passwords which they change regularly, and they must always switch terminals off when not in use.

Key ideas

The most common way to think of a database is to imagine that it is like a card index system. Some computer databases, such as Windows Cardfile, actually use graphics which makes entries look like index cards. The important terms are illustrated in Figure 5.2.

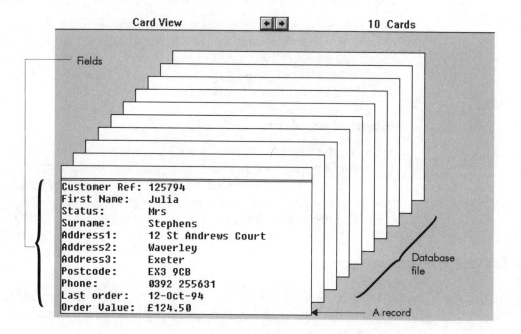

Figure 5.2 Database presented as a card index system

Database file

The whole group of electronic cards makes up the database file. In a simple system all of the information is kept in one database file. More complex databases can get information from several files.

Records

Each database entry is known as a record. It is the electronic equivalent of a single record card. Electronic databases can contain millions of records, limited only by the size of the computer disks that store them.

Fields

Each record can have many fields. These are like the spaces on a pre-printed record card which are waiting to have the data entered into them. In an electronic system, the computer creates the equivalent of a blank record card with all of the fields empty whenever new information is to be added.

Data

The information to be stored in the database is put into the empty fields of a record card. It is important that the same type of information is put into corresponding fields on each card. For example, if a person's name is put in the field for an address the whole system will be confused.

Figure 5.3 shows a simple database that could be part of a library system. It has fields for name, address, membership number, number of books on loan, book titles and return dates, etc.

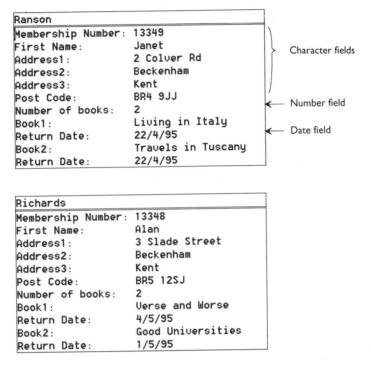

Figure 5.3 *A simple library database system*

Types of data

By examining the library data, you can see that it is necessary to be able to enter different types of information into the various fields. Some fields need letters and other characters, some need numbers and others need dates. The most usual types of information to be stored are as follows.

Characters

The most common database information is simple text or characters, such as the names of people, towns and cities. Text can include both letters and numbers. If numbers are entered as characters they can not be used in any calculations. House numbers, reference numbers and telephone numbers are the numbers most commonly entered.

Numbers

Numbers entered can be used as part of a calculation if necessary. For example, quantities may be included in a stock control database, prices may be included as part of an order processing database. Numbers can be simple data entries or they could be part of a calculation for the value of an order or the number of items left in a store.

Most systems allow numbers to be used with or without decimal places.

Dates

In systems like the basic library database shown in Figure 5.3, dates are very important. Often they are needed for dates of birth or the dates of transactions. Dates are stored in such a way that they can be used as part of calculations. For example, it is possible to calculate someone's age from their date of birth.

Other types of field

Some database systems allow other types of entry in the system, such as:

Logical values	True or False, Yes or No
Memos	longer sections of text about an entry
Pictures	for systems which need visual identification on screen
Video	for advanced information systems
Sound	either speech or music may be used

Creating a database

Creating a good database needs careful planning. It is important to anticipate the probable future requirements so that any expansion later is not limited by the initial design. You have to know what you want to store, the reason for storing it and the format it needs to be in.

Worked example

Simple database for computer software

PROBLEM

Your IT Department has mislaid the list of the software it has purchased over the last three years and has asked you to help recreate one from the old orders. You have been asked to create a database to hold the information so that it can be easily updated in future.

The basic information to be held includes:
- Software title
- Supplier name
- Order number
- Quantity purchased
- Date of purchase

SOLUTION

1. First you need to decide the fields required to hold the information and their sizes. They may be either character fields, numeric or date fields in this case.

   The size of each field depends upon the maximum entry that it is likely to contain. Generally this is only a problem with character fields because numbers and dates are much more predictable. Estimate the longest title or supplier name you think you will have to enter.

2. Choose a name for each field which is different from all the rest but which is easily distinguished. You may need to be able to remember what the field contains many months later. The names are normally restricted to ten characters and may not contain any spaces. Often an 'underscore' character is used instead.

   The chosen fields with their sizes and types for the IT database are

Field Name	Type	Size	Decimals
TITLE	Character	30	
SUPPLIER	Character	30	
ORDER_NO	Character	10	
QUANTITY	Numeric	3	0
DATE	Date	8	

Note that although the ORDER_NO field will contain a number of digits, it has been set up as a character field because it may also contain letters. In addition, it will not be part of any calculations.

The DATE field is automatically set to eight places so that dates can include separators, such as 20/10/94.

3. The third step is to use the 'Database create' command or its equivalent in your system to set up the new database to the specification you have worked out.

   Different software will do this in different ways so it is best to refer to a manual or ask you lecturer how to do it. This is sometimes called creating the database 'Structure'. It will involve typing in the field names, their types and sizes in a format similar to that shown above.

4. When the structure has been entered and saved on disk, the data can then be entered. Most systems provide what looks like a blank card containing the names of the fields and an empty box of the maximum size next to it. The data can simply be typed in to the correct spaces. If you make a mistake, use the backspace or delete keys to correct it.

   Figure 5.4 shows the data entry screen for the IT database with one of the entries complete.

Figure 5.4 Data entry screen for the IT database, showing one completed entry

Keeping the information accurate

As soon as a database has been set up, it needs to be properly maintained or it will quickly become out of date. This may be nothing more complicated that correcting a few errors, or changing an address every so often. However, with a large database, particularly one based on personal information, the task may be a full-time job.

All database software contains a number of tools that help users to keep the information accurate. These include editing existing data, adding or appending more data and deleting information no longer needed.

Editing data

The usual method of correcting mistakes and making small changes is to edit the existing data. All of the corrections are made to the data while it is stored in the computer memory, and are then stored back on the disk when the database is next saved.

Each database system has its own way of editing so you will need to check the manual to see exactly how it can be done. If the software is Windows based there will probably be an 'Edit' item on the menu bar, so this is the most likely place to start. Some systems allow almost anything displayed on the screen to be edited by over-typing, which makes the task quite easy. Figure 5.5 shows one of the ways of editing the data using Microsoft Access.

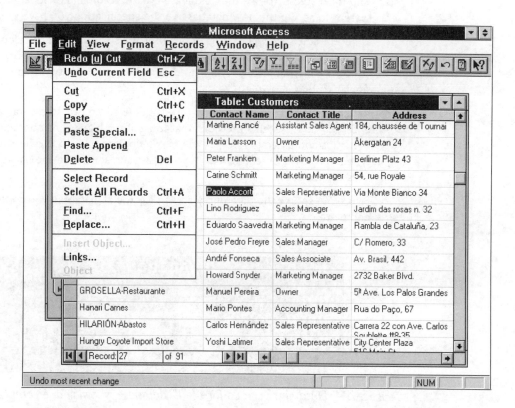

Figure 5.5 Editing using Microsoft Access

Adding more data

New records can be added to the existing database in the same way as the original entries were made. The computer software presents you with a data entry screen to be filled in with the new entries. When the new records appear on the screen they may appear to be mixed up with the original entries since the computer may display all of its data in alphabetical or numerical order.

If a new field is needed in an existing database, the whole structure of the database has to be changed. The computer creates a new database and adds all of the original entries to it before deleting the old one.

Deleting data

Old records can usually be removed with the 'Delete record' command. In some databases this immediately removes the record, but in others a second command may be needed to 'Pack' the database before those entries marked for deletion are actually removed. This is an added security measure to prevent accidental removal of vital information.

Browse facility

Checking a lot of database records for errors can be a very difficult task. Most software gives the users the ability to browse through the data on screen in a way that is easy to read. This makes the task of checking very much easier.

Backing up the data

You may not find a 'Backup' command on your database software menu, but backing up is a vital part of maintaining the database. Backing up the data simply means taking an extra copy, either on a floppy disk or on a tape. Before you leave a database system, make sure that you have two copies of the data. It is very difficult to check the accuracy of the data later because much of the information is unconnected to anything else in the system. Use the 'File copy' or the 'Save as' command to create an extra copy if there is no 'Backup' command available.

Data validation

Trying to make sure that only the correct information is entered is known as **data validation**. It is very important to enter the correct information the first time because every subsequent change takes time and the incorrect information may be used before it can be corrected.

When a database is set up, each field can contain only one type of information – characters, numbers, dates, etc. The system normally prevents a user from putting a character into a numeric field, so avoiding a mistake.

Some sophisticated systems may check the values entered in numeric or date fields to see that they are in the right range. For example, dates of birth can be checked to see that they are within the age range expected. A common mistake is to enter today's date on a form instead of a date of birth. If incorrect dates are entered, a database warning indicates that a manual check should be made.

Some errors, however, cannot be prevented. There is little to stop a wrong postcode being entered in an address or someone's surname being misspelled, other than careful typing. It is a good idea to keep the original copies of the paper records until they have been checked against the information entered into the computer.

In professionally managed databases, errors may be prevented by having critical data entered by two people. It is highly unlikely that they will both make the same mistake, so only the data which is the same will be entered into the system without further checking.

Viewing the data

Selecting information from the database to display on screen or to print is a vital part of database operation. It is very unusual to be able to display the whole database at once, so some form of selection must be undertaken.

Selecting fields for the screen

A computer screen can normally display only about 80 characters on each line. This means that if the size of the database field is larger than this only parts of the data will be visible on screen at once. When selecting data to view, choose only the most important fields. For example, if addresses are important choose only the city rather than the full address or choose a surname rather than a person's full name, etc.

Figure 5.6 shows part of the database created for the Worked example on page 132. Only a few fields have been selected so that each record can be displayed on each line of the screen. Other fields can be selected depending upon the user's requirements. For example, if it is necessary to view all of the barcodes, they can be added to the display instead of one of the other entries.

TITLE	TYPE	STOCK	ON_ORDER	DELIV_DATE	RET_PR
The Premiere Collection Encore	CD	5	6	21/09/95	12.99
Sgt. Pepper's Lonely Hearts Club Band	CD	1	3	24/09/95	10.99
The Premiere Collection	Tape	3	4	26/09/95	10.99
Carreras Domingo Pavarotti in Concert	CD	10	0	/ /	14.99
Canto Gregoriano	Tape	1	0	/ /	5.99
Glen Miller – The Legend	CD	2	5	02/11/95	8.45
Great Blues Guitarists String Dazzlers	Tape	0	4	26/09/95	5.99
The Singer and the Song	CD 2	6	0	/ /	15.99
Miss Saigon	CD 2	2	0	/ /	14.49

Figure 5.6 Fields selected from a larger database

A selection showing only part of a database is sometimes called a 'View'.

Printing the data

Printing information from the database carries the same problems as those that apply to the screen display. Unless very small fonts are used, or the paper is in landscape mode, the width of an A4 sheet of paper allows only about 80 characters per line. When the margins are taken into consideration, this may be reduced to only 66 characters. Longer lines will appear to be wrapped round on each other and will probably not be easy to read.

The solution is, again, to select only the information that is absolutely necessary to be printed. There are only a few occasions when it is essential to print out all of the main information held electronically.

Databases generally print the information in columns, with the field name as the column heading. Each column is as wide as the maximum width set up in the database. It may be possible to select a different column width, but this depends upon the software used.

Reports

Much more sophisticated ways of printing database information allow the data to be laid out in any way required on a page. These are known as 'Reports', and are dealt with in more detail later in the book. Reports allow data to be selected and grouped in different ways, columns to be totalled and other calculations done on the numerical entries.

Reports are the usual way of extracting particular information. It is normal to set up a series of standard reports then choose the one that will provide the required data when it is needed.

Progress check

Try to answer the following questions and do some of the exercises before continuing. They will check your understanding of the topics covered so far. If you have access to some database software, use Exercises 1 to 5 at the end of the chapter to make sure that you understand how its basic functions work.

1. What are the main advantages of an electronic database system over a card index system? Does the card index have any advantages over the electronic system?

2. Without looking back at the text, write down the meaning of the following terms:
   (a) Record
   (b) View
   (c) Field
   (d) Data types.

3. What protection does the Data Protection Act give to individuals?

4. What are the three steps that you would need to go through to create a simple database?

5. What would normally restrict the amount of data that could be stored in a computer database?

6. What is meant by 'data validation' and how could it be achieved in a large database?

7. What is the name of the command that is needed in the database system you normally use to do the following tasks?
   (a) Add extra records to an existing database
   (b) Remove records from an existing database
   (c) Correct errors in a data entry.

8. What must be taken into account before trying to display data records on a computer screen?

9. Why is a 'report' from a database likely to be more useful than a simple printout?

Selecting specific information from a database

The most useful feature of a database is that it allows the data to be analysed to provide valuable information from a simple set of data entries.

For example, consider the database held by a bank on all of its customers. It will hold all the usual personal facts for each account holder, such as their name and address. In addition, the account details for all of the customers will be stored. Some of the other kinds of information which may be obtained include
- the number of customers who are overdrawn
- the total amount deposited in a day
- the average balance of all its personal customers
- the number of business customers who use the bank.

Using this type of information the bank can begin to make policy decisions and predictions, such as the trigger point for bank charges and the probable receipts following a change in interest rate. It can begin to compare its performance with other banks and make special offers to attract more customers.

Analysis of any database has to be undertaken very carefully to ensure that the right questions are being asked. In general, all analyses start by selecting records from the complete database which meet certain 'search criteria'. The process is sometimes known as 'querying' the database.

Search criteria

Searching the database for all the entries that meet certain **conditions** or **criteria** is the first step towards obtaining useful information. Great care must be taken in setting up the conditions, or the information obtained may not be exactly what was anticipated.

Single conditions

The most basic search lists all records that have a certain value in one of the fields. For example, this may be 'All the people who have a postcode containing PL2', or 'All the entries that are over 1000'.

When a simple search condition like this is entered, the database lists each entry that meets the conditions and omits all of the others. If the database is very large it may not be necessary to list all the entries – it may be enough to just *count* the number of entries that meet the conditions. Figure 5.7 shows a listing of the members of a leisure centre who play in the Squash league. At the same time it may be necessary to limit the number of fields printed so that the information fits onto the screen or paper.

Each database has a slightly different way of entering the search conditions so you will need to check with your lecturer or the software manual for the exact procedure. In some cases you may be able to enter the conditions by selecting directly from a menu. Other systems require you to enter the conditions in the form of a request, such as

```
LIST FIELDS MEMNUMBER, SURNAME, TITLE, FOR LEAGUE =
'SQUASH'
```

Complex conditions

For more complex searches a number of conditions can be applied at the same time. This begins to show the power of the computer database over the manual system since the analysis can be very rapid.

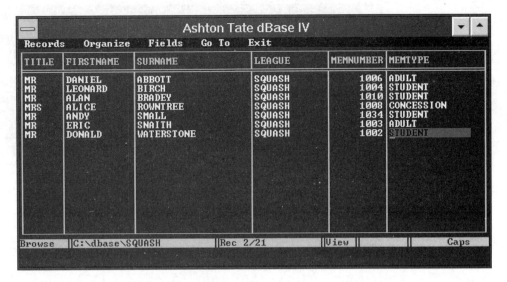

Figure 5.7 Listing the members of a leisure centre who are in the squash league by selecting the required field

For example, some typical search conditions on a database may be

```
All records with Credit_limit greater than £2000 AND
Last_order before 1/1/94
All records with Surname beginning with B AND Town
equal to Worthing OR Brighton
All those with Title equal to Miss OR Title equal to
Mrs
```

The records can normally be made 'Equal to', 'Greater than', 'Less than', or 'Not equal to' the desired condition. Conditions are combined with AND or OR. These are known as the **logical operators**. In some systems, they have to be written as .AND. and .OR. to distinguish them from normal data or field names.

You must take great care when combining conditions since there is a great difference between 'All those with cars OR bicycles' and 'All those with cars AND bicycles'. If the wrong condition is entered, the wrong information will be produced. Queries on large databases with hundreds of fields have to be handled by professional programmers. They write the query, then thoroughly test it to see that it gives the right results before any of the information it produces is used.

Figure 5.8 shows how two search criteria have been used in a leisure centre database. The printout has been produced for all the members with INTEREST1 OR INTERST2 EQUAL TO FITNESS.

Improved efficiency with an index

When entries are made to a database over a period of time they are usually put in in a random order. It would be normal in a manual paper-based system to store the cards in alphabetical or numerical order so that they can be found easily when necessary. Records in a computer database can be sorted alphabetically or numerically with a 'Sort' command, but this is not usually the best way to

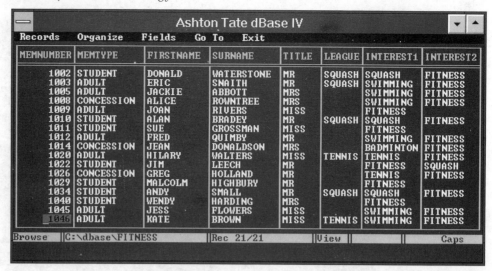

Figure 5.8 Records selected for INTEREST1 .OR. INTEREST2 = 'FITNESS'

keep the data in order. Instead, an **index** is created which can achieve the same thing much more effectively.

Each record in the computer database has a record number that may or may not be visible. If an index of surnames is created in alphabetical order, for example, the computer creates a special index file containing the record numbers in the order that is the same as the surnames in alphabetical order. A simple example is shown below.

Record number	Surname	First name
1	James	Bob
2	Abbott	Andrew
3	Bell	Colin
4	Robertson	Julia
5	May	Caroline

If an index were created for the surnames in alphabetical order it would contain record numbers 2, 3, 1, 5, 4. This order would then be used to display the records on screen or in a printed list, like this:

2	Abbott
3	Bell
1	James
5	May
4	Robertson

If a search for a particular name is required, the computer would not need to search through every record to find the right one. Instead, it would look up the name in the index file, starting with the first letter, then the second, in the same way that you would use the index of a book. When it finds a match it could go directly to the correct record in the database.

Two indexes

If two entries are identical they will appear in the order in which they were entered unless **primary** and **secondary indexes** are used. The primary index is used first, and if there are two identical records the secondary index is then used to decide their order.

For example, if a database contains the names James Clarke, Fred Brown, Albert Clarke and John Brown, a primary index could be used for the surnames and a secondary index for the first names. This would give an index order of Fred Brown, John Brown, Albert Clarke, James Clarke. The two Browns come first, but Fred comes before John. The two Clarkes come next, but Albert comes before James.

Always try to select at least one field of your database as the index field so that the records appear in the most convenient order. If your database software does not provide an index facility, use the sort command instead to put the records into a convenient order.

Database design

The structure of a database must be carefully considered before it is created. It depends not only upon the data that has to be stored, but also upon the type of output required. Sometimes it is necessary to anticipate the sort of questions that may need to be answered and to design the database accordingly.

How many fields?

Consider a simple example of a database that stores names and addresses. How many fields are required for a name?

One field could store the whole name   `NAME: Mr John Smith`

Two fields could be used   `TITLE: Mr; NAME: John Smith`

Three fields could be used   `TITLE: Mr; FIRSTNAME: John; SURNAME: Smith`

Four fields could be used   `TITLE: Mr; INITIAL: J; FIRSTNAME: John; SURNAME: Smith.`

Each method has its advantages and disadvantages. The first method (using one field) means less storage is required but, without special programming, every occurrence would have to be the whole field. Letters would begin 'Dear Mr John Smith'. The label on the envelope would be 'Mr John Smith'.

The last method is the most flexible but requires most storage. Letters can begin 'Dear John', while the address label can say 'Mr J. Smith'.

The last two methods would also allow any analysis to show very easily how many people on the database had a surname of Smith.

The methods of using only two or three fields are possible solutions that may be adequate for some tasks but they also have some limitations.

Database fields and their structure

Choose field names that are long enough to be understandable, but short enough to minimise the amount of typing required.

When the number of fields has been chosen, the content of each one has to be decided. First select the type of data – characters, numbers, dates, etc. – then the size. The size of each field has to be sufficient to allow the largest expected entry to be contained. It is pointless having fields that are very wide, but very frustrating if they are too small. As a rule, in a typical database 'Surname' and 'Address' fields could each be up to 32 characters.

Some databases allow indexes to be created at the same time as the database and it may be necessary to decide which fields are to be used for an index. If one main field is chosen, such as 'Surname', the entries will be displayed in alphabetical order however they are entered.

Data content and format

What is actually entered into each field is also important if the job of searching for information is to be made easier. The importance of consistency cannot be over-emphasised. This means sticking to certain allowed entries in fields that will be used in the selection criteria.

For example, consider a database that shows whether an address is in England, Scotland, Wales or Northern Ireland. The address entries have been restricted to a single character – E, S, W or N. This allows the user to search the database for all of the addresses in Scotland by typing a condition like ADDRESS = 'S'. If the field contains all sorts of variations such as Eng, E/Land, Scot, NI, Northern I, Wa, N-I, Wales or S/land, the job of finding all the addresses in Scotland would be very difficult indeed.

The same principle applies to all databases where selections have to be made. You will need to keep a record of the allowable entries in each of the database fields.

Worked example

Simple database for a music shop

PROBLEM
The database for a music shop was originally held on a card index system but it is proving too slow for the number of customers. It also needs to be linked to the barcode system to make stock control and reordering easier. Although you only do part time work at the shop, you have been asked for your advice on the new system. It has to use the existing database software to save money.

SOLUTION
To create the new database you have to ask yourself several questions.

1. First, decide what information needs to be kept.

   The basic data on each article includes:

Stock number	in some cases this could be the same as a barcode number
Description	the title of the music
Artist	the name of the artist or band
Reference number	the publisher's reference number
Publisher	the publishing company name
Type	whether it is a tape, CD, video, etc.
Supplier details	the name and address of the supplier
Number in stock	current stock level
Number on order	numbers expected

Delivery date	when stock on order is expected
Barcode number	if different from the stock number
Price	retail price
Wholesale price	price from the supplier

2. Next, decide the format of each data field. It is best to plan the structure on paper before trying to enter it into a computer to save time on correcting mistakes.

   Each field has to have a different name which may be restricted to ten characters and must not contain any spaces (use the 'underscore' character instead). The maximum size of each character field has to be chosen at this stage. In some systems it can be changed later, but it is better to choose about the right size from the start. If the longest title for a CD, for example, is likely to be 45 characters, then make the 'Description' field 45 characters long. Remember that the larger the number of characters the more storage space will be needed on the computer disk.

   Choose whether each entry has to be a number, with or without decimal places, a set of characters, a date, or something else. For the music shop, the following database structure could be used.

Field name	Type	Width	Decimals
STOCK_NUMB	Numeric	5	0
TITLE	Character	45	
ARTIST	Character	45	
PUB_REF_NO	Character	8	
PUBLISHER	Character	30	
TYPE	Character	6	
SUPP_NAME	Character	30	
SUPP_ADD1	Character	30	
SUPP_ADD2	Character	30	
SUPP_ADD3	Character	30	
STOCK	Numeric	30	
ON_ORDER	Numeric	3	0
DELIV_DATE	Date	8	
BAR_CODE	Character	12	
RET_PRICE	Numeric	5	2
WHO_PRICE	Numeric	5	2

3. Now the database has to be set up on the computer by using the 'Create new database' facility. The precise method of doing this will depend upon the database software available, but the result will be the same in each case. The structure of the fields will be set up and the system will then be ready for data to be entered.

4. The last step is to enter the data. Often this will be the most time consuming and boring part of the operation. However, it is the most vital part since without the data the database cannot function.

   Most databases have a special data entry screen. They present a set of fields that have spaces next to them to indicate the maximum size of the entry that is expected. Some error checking is also done. The system will probably bleep if too much data is entered, and it will generally not let you put letters into numeric fields.

   Figure 5.9 shows the data entry screen for Dbase 4, with the music shop data being entered.

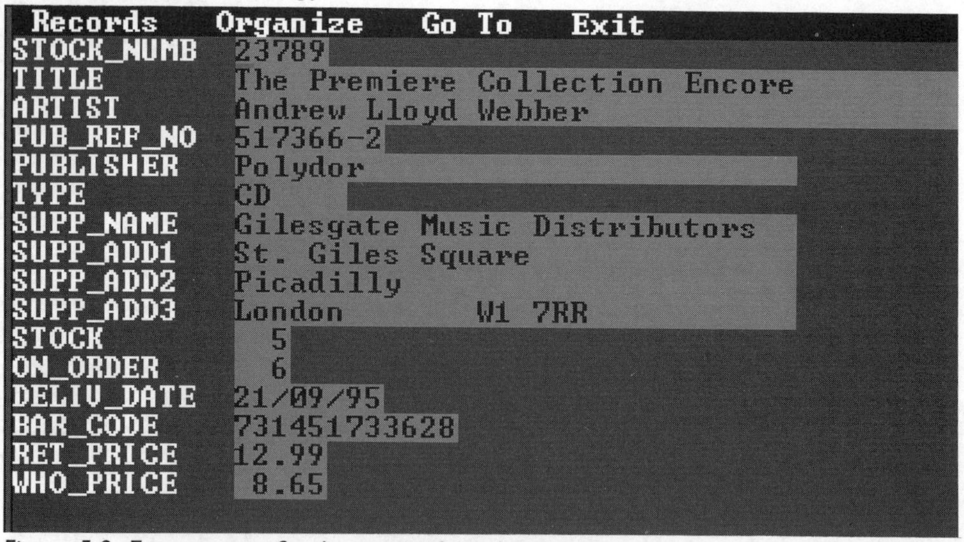

```
 Records    Organize    Go To    Exit
STOCK_NUMB  23789
TITLE       The Premiere Collection Encore
ARTIST      Andrew Lloyd Webber
PUB_REF_NO  517366-2
PUBLISHER   Polydor
TYPE        CD
SUPP_NAME   Gilesgate Music Distributors
SUPP_ADD1   St. Giles Square
SUPP_ADD2   Picadilly
SUPP_ADD3   London          W1 7RR
STOCK        5
ON_ORDER     6
DELIV_DATE  21/09/95
BAR_CODE    731451733628
RET_PRICE   12.99
WHO_PRICE    8.65
```

Figure 5.9 Entry screen for the music shop database

Databases in action

If you have ever received 'junk mail' then you must be on someone's mailing list. Hundreds of companies throughout the world maintain databases of customers and regularly send out all sorts of advertising material. There is quite a trade in mailing lists, which can be bought and sold for large sums of money. Lists of lists can be bought which provide information on the types of mailing list available and there are many specialist lists of doctors, dentists, schools, colleges, people in different social groups, special interest groups, Lords, MPs, football managers, etc.

All of these lists are held on databases, which may be run on a large mainframe computer in a big company, or on a desktop PC. The value of the database is not the data itself because this is normally available free in reference books. Its value lies in the use to which the data may be put once it is on a computer. In the hands of a book club, the data may be used to sell books to certain sections of the population. A political party may use its database to take samples of opinions on particular issues. A television channel may use it to work out audience ratings.

DVLC Vehicle Database

One of the most well known databases is held in the Driver and Vehicle Licensing Centre (DVLC) in Swansea. This enormous database holds the records for all the cars, lorries and motor bikes in the country, together with information on their owners and drivers. With so many vehicles being bought and sold every day, the task of keeping it up to date requires an army of staff. Security is also an enormous problem. The records have to be kept safe to prevent fraud, so access has to be strictly controlled. However, information must also be readily available for those people who are authorised to access it, such as the police. Such people may be given limited authority to access the data so that they can perform functions that read the data, but cannot change it by writing new information. This is called **read-only access**.

CD-ROMs

Some large databases are now available on a CD that can be inserted into the CD-ROM drive of a personal computer. For example, instead of sending out a massive paper catalogue every three months, some suppliers of electronic parts are now sending a CD. This contains more information than can be supplied on paper, and is considerably cheaper to produce in large numbers. Postage is a fraction of the price.

Databases available on CD include lists of books in print, postcodes for the whole country, software catalogues, and many others. CDs are likely to become one of the most widely used sources of large volumes of information available to anyone with a personal computer.

Remote information

All over the world, large databases store useful information. Research establishments, universities, companies and many individuals use a large computer network that permits users to search for specialist information on each other's computers. This is known as the 'Internet'.

Security of information on such a system is only maintained by several levels of passwords that must be typed correctly before the system allows access. Naturally these passwords must be changed regularly by all users so that the level of security is maintained. Databases of this type can be entered via a telephone connection to the public data networks using a modem. A modem is a device that converts the computer data into a format suitable for transmission down a telephone line. Unfortunately the cost of such connections can be quite high. Not only are users charged per minute for access to the information or to perform database searches, they are also charged for the telephone line and the time used by the connection. Some information can be very expensive to access.

Personnel records

All firms are required to keep records on the people who work for them. Such records are used to ensure that all the employees are paid at the right time, and to inform the Inland Revenue of the amount of tax deducted from each person. The records must always be accurate and up to date so that when a new appointment is made or when an employee leaves the new information is rapidly entered into the system.

With personnel records, the historical data is also very important, so records usually go back many years. These can be required when calculating pensions, sickness benefits and other matters related to conditions of employment. Because personnel records and payroll information are confidential they must be kept very securely with limited access to those people who work on them. This data is also subject to the rules in the Data Protection Act – that the database owner must register the database and allow people access to their own data.

Although the basic information is held in a database, the computer software that is used to manipulate it may not be a commercial database package. Often, software has been specially written to deal with this type of information only. However, modern commercial databases can be 'programmed' to make specific applications like this semi-automatic. This aspect of their operation will be covered in the next chapter.

Review questions

Try these questions when you have completed the chapter. They are mainly based on the work in the second half of the chapter, but you need to apply the ideas to the work you are studying throughout your course. If you have access to some database software, attempt the exercises and the assignments that follow.

1. If a database field has to contain a number, what other information must be entered to completely define the field, before data can be entered?

2. Why is it useful to be able to select specific information which meets certain conditions, from a database?

3. A database has been designed to hold the answers to questions about political parties which members of the public have been asked in the street. The answers were anonymous. How could such a database be used?

4. What is a 'logical operator' and when would it be used?

5. Explain the difference between sorting a database and creating an index.

6. If a number of records in a database have the same data in the field used for the index, what determines the order in which they appear on screen?

7. Give the advantages and disadvantages of including the postcode in the last line of an address rather than giving it a separate field in the database.

8. Why is it important to restrict the data entries that can be put in certain fields of a database?

9. What equipment would you need to be able to access information from a remote database?

Exercises

These exercises have been designed to cover the basic skills you need to have to use a database system. They can be completed as you work through the chapter or left until you have completed it. The later exercises require greater understanding and skill than the earlier ones. In all cases these exercises need to be supplemented by those which naturally form part of the GNVQ being studied. These may be stand-alone exercises or part of larger assignments.

1. Use your normal software to set up a simple database for a piano tuning business. The field descriptions are given below, but you will need to choose a suitable name, size and data type for each one. The reason for using a database is to provide a simple way of finding out when each customer needs to be sent a reminder letter for the next appointment.
Customer name
Customer address (three fields)
Make of piano
Value of piano
Date of next visit
Last price charged

2. Set up the database you have designed for the previous question and enter about 12 customers. The makes and values of the pianos are not important as long as some data is entered. If you cannot think of any names of piano manufacturers, use Steinway, Bluthner, Welmar, Young Chang, Evestaff, Zimmermann, and Bremar. Values start at about £2000.

When the database is set up, find out how to display only a few of the fields on the screen.
(a) Display the customer name and the make of piano
(b) Display the customer name, and the date of the next visit.

3. Two of the customers on your database have moved and their new addresses have to be entered.

   Use the editing facilities of your database software to change each of the addresses.

   List the customer names and their addresses on screen to check that the changes are correct.

4. The piano tuner finds that the database is very useful in making sure that each customer receives a regular reminder about the next tuning date. If the business expands so that three people are employed for both tuning and repairs, how could the database be expanded to provide more information?

5. Think of at least two applications of a database in your main subject area. They may be related to an assignment you have to do or simply something you have studied already.
   (a) For one of the applications, decide what type of data will need to be kept on the database. Write this down in the form of field descriptions, as in Question 1, then translate them into precise database fields.
   (b) Calculate the maximum number of characters each record will occupy by adding together all of the sizes for the fields.
   (c) Calculate roughly how many records could be stored on a floppy disk with 1 MByte of free space, assuming it can all be used for the database records.

6. Look at Figure 5.1 and set up a simple database using suitable field names instead of the column headings in the figure.

   When the database has been set up with the seven fields shown, enter the data from the figure and add some extra records of your own. You will need between 12 and 20 records with the same data in some of them.
   (a) Enter the commands necessary to display on screen only those records which have a credit limit of £2000
   (b) Change the commands to display those who have a credit limit of £1000 or more.
   (c) Enter the search criteria to display those customers who have a discount level of 10% *and* whose last order was over £50.
   (d) Enter the search criteria to select those customers who live in either Grimsby *or* Whitby.

7. Use the database set up for Question 6. With your database software set up an index on the TOWN field so that the records appear in alphabetical order according to the town in which the customer lives.

8. Using the database as it is after Question 7 arrange the records in the order of the highest to the lowest order value.

9. With the database as it is after Question 8, delete from the database all of those customers who have a zero credit limit.

10. Use your computer system to make a backup copy of the database file you have after Question 9. Make sure that the file is on a different disk to that on which the original database was created. This is a security copy that can be stored in a safe place in case the first is damaged in any way.

Assignment 1
Planning a new database

This assignment can be used to provide evidence for the following Performance Criteria:

Element 2.1	PCs 1 to 4
Element 2.2	PCs 1, 2, 4, 5
Element 2.3	PCs 1, 2, 3, 5
Element 2.4	PCs 1 to 4
Element 3.1	PCs 1 to 5
Element 3.2	PCs 1, 2, 4, 5, 7
Element 3.3	PCs 1, 2, 3, 4, 6
Element 3.4	PCs 1 to 5

Introduction

You have been asked to help with the design of a database for a small company that is having trouble with its suppliers. They buy about 1000 different products from about 100 suppliers and a simple database is required to keep all of the information up to date. In addition, by placing the information on a computer they hope to allow several buyers access to the same data.

Your task

1. Your task is to design the structure for the database that will meet the needs of the company. It can be fairly simple to start with, but needs to include the following fields as a minimum.
   Product reference number
   Product description
   Supplier reference number
   Supplier name
   Supplier address
   Minimum order quantity
   Delivery time
   Payment terms (days credit)
   Discount (if any)

2. Add some other fields if you think that they will be useful and help to identify the best supplier for each product.

3. When you have designed the database on paper, try to enter it into your computer with some suitable database software. Save it with a suitable file name in case of accidents. Keep a backup copy.

4. Enter about ten or 20 products with their supplier's information to see if there are any problems with your design. Correct any errors you notice on input as you go along.

5. Browse through your database information to check that it has all been entered correctly.

6. Print out four or five selected fields from the database to provide a list of the records entered. Make sure that the chosen field widths can be fitted onto the sheet of paper used in the printer.

Write a brief report to explain why the electronic database may be an improvement over a manual system. What effects could the new database have on the people employed by the company? Comment on both the benefits and the drawbacks for both individuals and the whole company.

Assignment 2
Conducting a survey on a sensitive issue

This assignment can be used to provide evidence for the following Performance Criteria:

Element 2.1 PCs I to 4

Element 2.2 PCs I, 2, 4, 5

Element 2.3 PCs I, 2, 3, 5

Element 2.4 PCs I to 4

Element 3.1 PCs I to 5

Element 3.2 PCs I, 2, 4, 5, 7

Element 3.3 PCs I, 2, 3, 4, 6

Element 3.4 PCs I to 5

Introduction

Shops in the city centre seem to be losing a lot of trade because of the construction of a number of superstores on the edge of town. A proposal for another store is now being considered by the planners and you have a feeling that this could make matters worse. Since your opinion would carry more weight if it was backed up by others, you decide to carry out a survey of local people to find out what they really think.

The survey form carries the following questions:
1. Do you live within the city boundary?   Yes/No
2. Are you a car owner?   Yes/No
3. Are you a regular user of the bus service?   Yes/No
4. How often do you visit the city centre?   Daily/Weekly/Rarely
5. Do you buy most of your food within the city centre   Yes/No
6. Do you shop in 'out of town' superstores?   Always/Sometimes/Never
7. Would you be happy to see more city centre shops close?   Yes/No
8. Do you think more 'out of town' superstores are required?   Yes/No
9. What is your age group?   Under 20/20–40/41–60/over 60

Some of your friends design the questionnaire and conduct the survey for you, then hand you 200 forms to analyse. Since you have just studied databases, you decide to design one to help you.

Your task

1. The first task is to set up a database that will allow the survey forms data to be entered. It will need one field for each of the questions. Choose field names which are appropriate. Note that it may not be very wise to use Q1, Q2, Q3, etc. because you will have to refer to the questionnaire every time you need to know what a question was. Use names like 'City', 'Car', 'Bus', etc. Save the empty database structure with a suitable file name and print a copy.

2. Decide the possible responses to be entered for each question. Some will be a simple Y or N, whereas others may have several answers.

3. Enter the data from about 20 fictitious questionnaires and save the results.

4. Write down at least five of the questions that you think the database will help you to answer. For example, you may ask 'How many of the people who are over 60 visit the city centre weekly?' This means those who answer 'Weekly' to question 4 *and* 'over 60' to question 9.

5. If you can do it, try to enter some of the questions you described in Question 4 as queries on your database. Rather than display or list all of the records which meet the criteria, you could count them instead.

Think about the process you have just undertaken, and answer the following questions:
(a) Could you have found out the same information by looking through the questionnaires and selecting responses manually? If so, how long would it have taken to answer the same questions?
(b) Could the database be structured any better to make the analysis any easier?
(c) How has an IT system made it easier for people involved in market research to derive useful information?
(d) What other applications might there be for such a powerful analysis tool in the area of work you are studying?

CHAPTER 6

Advanced databases

Objectives

When you have finished this chapter you should be able to:
- Produce a report from a database
- Create mailing labels using a database
- Transfer data to a word processor
- Understand the advantages of relational databases
- Understand how database operation can be automated with a 'macro'
- Understand how to use data from a remote database
- Access a CD-ROM database

This chapter covers the Performance Criteria and Range from all of the IT Core Skills Elements at levels 2 and 3 related to the preparation, processing and presentation of text and numbers in databases, the reorganisation of data, the use of automated routines and access to remote data sources.

Reporting on database contents

The most usual way of extracting information from a database is to ask it to print a **report**. The report selects some of the records or fields from the whole database and prints them in a convenient format. Someone has to have designed the layout of the report and, in large commercial databases, some reports may be included as part of the system. Other reports can be designed by users to their own requirements.

Once a report has been designed, it can be used many times with different data selected from the database. Each report is simply the template into which the information is placed.

Reports in business

A company keeps all of its customer, supplier and sales staff information on a database. This includes all the orders and invoices, who made the sale, delivery dates. Such a large amount of information is actually held in a number of different 'tables' within the database. The types of report that they are able to produce include:
- an alphabetical list of products
- a product catalogue
- customer mailing labels
- sales invoices
- products on order
- sales by date

- sales by salesperson
- a summary of sales by month, quarter or year
- employee sales by country.

Each report is stored with the database and can be printed as many times as required, each time using the latest information.

A typical report from a food wholesaler's database is shown in Figure 6.1. Here the database of products has been grouped into different categories, such as beverages, condiments. These have then been listed with their products, product ID, quantity per unit, and units in stock. These are not the only fields held on the database for each product, but they are the only ones selected for this

Product Name:	Product ID:	Category Name:	Units In Stock:
A			
Aniseed Syrup	3	Condiments	13
B			
Boston Crab Meat	40	Seafood	123
C			
Camembert Pierrot	60	Dairy Product	19
Carnarvon Tigers	18	Seafood	42
Chai	1	Beverages	39
Chang	2	Beverages	17
Chartreuse verte	39	Beverages	69
Chef Anton's Cajun Seasoning	4	Condiments	53
Chocolade	48	Confections	15
Côte de Blaye	38	Beverages	17
E			
Escargots de Bourgogne	58	Seafood	62
F			
Filo Mix	52	Grains/Cereal	38
Fløtemysost	71	Dairy Product	26
G			
Geitost	33	Dairy Product	112
Genen Shouyu	15	Condiments	38
Gnocchi di nonna Alice	56	Grains/Cereal	21
Gorgonzola Telino	31	Dairy Product	0
Grandma's Boysenberry Spread	6	Condiments	120
Gravad lax	37	Seafood	11
Gudbrandsdalsost	69	Dairy Product	26
Gula Malacca	44	Condiments	27
Gumbär Gummibärchen	26	Confections	15
Gustaf's Käckebröd	22	Grains/Cereal	104
I			
Ikura	10	Seafood	31
Inlagd Sill	36	Seafood	112
Ipoh Coffee	43	Beverages	17
J			
Jack's New England Clam Chow	41	Seafood	85
K			
Konbu	13	Seafood	24

Alphabetical List of Products
11-May-95

Page 1 of 3

Figure 6.1 A database report for a food supplier

report. Each category has been counted to give a total for the number of products in each one. Headings have been added to each column to give the finished report a neat layout.

Creating a report

Different database programs have different facilities for creating reports, so you will need to consult your supervisor for the exact commands you need. However, most of the basic features are common to each package.

Linking a database

Before planning the layout of the report, it is necessary to link the report to a database. This allows the fields from the database to be selected for the report – opening the database or the table containing the data is usually all that is needed. The fields selected from the database can then be easily placed in the report at the most convenient location.

In large databases, it is often possible to link a report to a selection from the database known as a 'Query'. The query pre-selects part of the data to make the task of producing the report much easier. For example, if a report is required on the products of a company, it is easier to select the fields only from those that deal with the products rather than others that may relate to customers, orders, invoices, etc.

Planning the report layout

The format for most reports is similar to that shown in Figure 6.2. This was taken from the program Dbase 4, which is very similar to the report design screen of Microsoft Access.

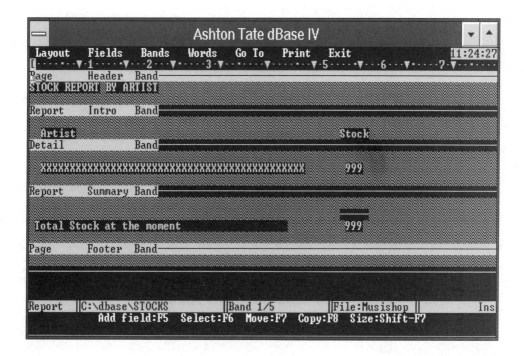

Figure 6.2 A simple report template

Each page of the report is made up of various sections or bands:

- The page header, which appears at the top of every page
- The report intro, which usually contains the titles for the data in the columns below
- The detail, which contains the selected data from the database
- The report summary, which may contain calculations from columns of figures
- The page footer, which may contain information such as the date and time the report was printed.

Some databases also allow extra sections for a report header and report footer, which are printed at the beginning and the end of the complete report.

The example shown in Figure 6.2 shows the report title to be STOCK REPORT BY ARTIST in the 'Page header' band.

The titles for each of the columns of the report ('Artist' and 'Stock') are in the 'Report intro' band. The line of Xs under 'Detail band' shows the maximum width allowed for the data in that field. The '999' entry indicates a numeric field. This is the place where all the information from the database will be inserted when the report is compiled, so it can result in many lines of printing. Above and below each line in the 'Detail' band there is a blank line so that the entries will be spaced out. If space is not required, the blank lines can be omitted in the template.

Next, the 'Report summary' has a closing line and a total for the sum of all the stock items.

Not all of the sections must be present – if they are omitted the report is simply printed without them. This can lead to many different layouts for a report. It is also possible to place boxes round various parts of the report or to underline sections for greater emphasis.

Printing the report

Once the template has been designed, it is normal to save it with its own name for future use. The report can be then printed using the data from the current database. Most systems have the option of viewing the report on screen before it is printed. This is always a good idea – checking a report on screen before printing it will probably save a lot of time printing a report that is not quite right. It will also save a lot of scrap paper.

Reports with groups

One of the benefits of a report from a database is that it can group the data in whatever categories are required to provide the most useful information. The groups are decided at the design stage as part of the template. Each group in the report has its own header, detail band and footer, to retain maximum flexibility. The contents of these sections are part of the report template, as shown in Figure 6.4

The template that produced the report in Figure 6.1 is shown in Figure 6.4. Here the groups on the report are the categories of food. The 'Page header' contains the headings for each of the columns on the report. The 'Category name header' has the title for each section, which is the name of category of food in the group. This is then followed by the 'Detail' where each of the database fields to be printed is entered.

STOCK REPORT BY ARTIST

Artist	Stock
Andrew Lloyd Webber	5
Beatles	1
Andrew Lloyd Webber	3
Mehta	10
Ismal Fernandez de la Cuesta	1
Glen Miller	2
Various	6
Original Cast	2
James Galway	1
Total Stock at the moment	31

Figure 6.3 Report printed from the template in Figure 6.2

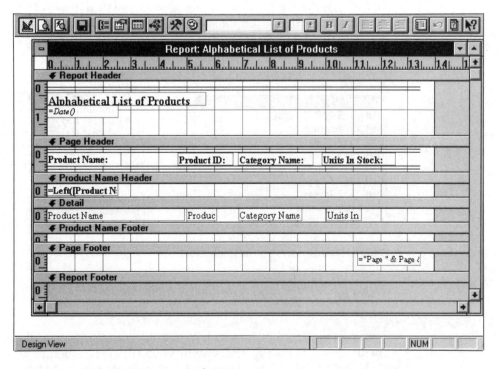

Figure 6.4 Template for a grouped report

Printing labels from a database

The reason for keeping many databases is to allow information to be sent to the people whose name it contains. There are two main ways to do this. One way is to extract the information and use it to customise a letter or a form created by a word processor. This is known as 'mail-merging' the data.

The second method is to create address labels for envelopes directly from the database software. With large databases, this is easier than transferring all of the information to a word processor.

The choice of whether to use mail-merge or labels depends upon the individual circumstances. Printing labels automatically creates an extra task of sticking them on the envelopes, which may be very time consuming.

Label formats

There are several formats for labels, depending upon the supplier and the type of printer to be used.

Labels for dot matrix printers generally come on a continuous sheet designed for a sprocket feed system. The basic page is often A4 sized, but on it there may be labels in a number of different sizes. Some are very small, with three or more across the width of the sheet, while other are much larger, with only one across the sheet.

Laser printer labels also come in many different sizes but each of them is based on an A4 sheet so that they feed through most printers easily. Some of the possible sizes are illustrated in Figure 6.5. Of course, labels do not all have to used for envelopes – they can easily be stuck on folders, video boxes, name badges, files, or anything that needs labelling.

In many ways the production of a mailing label is almost the same as creating a report. The basic format for the template has to be designed, then the data from fields in the database are added to the template to customise each label.

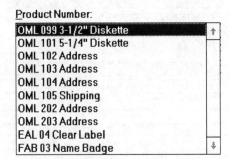

Product Numbers for Avery Dot Matrix Label: Product Numbers for Avery Laser Printer Labels.

Figure 6.5 Various sizes of mailing label that are available

Different database programs have slightly different ways of designing the label format, so it is best to check with your supervisor before attempting the task. The label has to be linked with a database so that the field names can be allocated a position on the label. In DOS-based systems like Dbase 4, the label may not show the data until it is actually printed or previewed on screen. In the label design only a series of Xs is shown to indicate the maximum size of the field on the label. The names of each field are shown at the foot of the screen.

Windows-based systems can show the data on screen as it will be printed both at the design stage and as a print preview display.

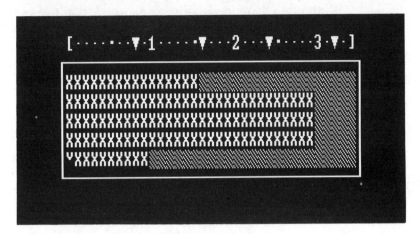

Figure 6.6 Label design screen from Dbase 4

Creating mailing labels

The first task in the design of a label is to decide which database it will be attached to. The database will provide a list of the possible fields that may be placed on the label.

Next, choose a label size. This has to be exactly the same size as the labels in the printer. Any miscalculations will result in the printing starting at different places on each label – and this will become steadily worse as more labels are printed. If possible, use one of the pre-defined label sizes that most databases now contain. However, if none of these fits your stock, you will have to design your own format. This means that the number of lines per label and the spacing between labels must be correctly specified.

Then lay out the design on the template by placing the selected fields on the empty label. Most labels will simply contain the name, address and postcode fields from the database but it may also be possible to add extra information or text. For example, it may be necessary to add 'For the attention of' as a first line on every label.

When the label design is complete, save it for future use. You are then ready to print the labels. It is a good idea to check them on screen first make sure that everything is correct. After that, check that the printer is ready and begin printing.

Problems with label printing

If anything is likely to go wrong, it will probably be related to the printing of labels. The first set of problems relates to the label size. Although it is possible to obtain labels of the exact size specified on the screen, more often than not those supplied seem to be slightly different.

The printer has to be precisely aligned so that the first line printed appears the correct distance from the top of the label. On some dot matrix printers this is a matter of trial and error. On laser printers it is a matter of ensuring that the top margin for the sheet is exactly right.

The next problem is to make sure that the position of the paper in the printer allows the printing to start the correct distance from the left hand edge. Allowance has to be made for the sprocket holes if a dot matrix printer is used. With more than one label per line, check that the second label also starts in the right place.

All of these matters should be decided automatically by the software, but it is frequently less than satisfactory. Proceed with care! A little care can result in perfect labels.

Progress check

Try the following questions before going on with the rest of this chapter. They cover the work so far, and are designed to ensure that you understand the basic ideas. In addition, if you have access to some database software, try the exercises at the end of the chapter. They will help you to put the theory into practice. Alternatively, any similar tasks to do as part of your GNVQ could be done instead.

1. What is the purpose of a 'Report' from a database? Give some examples of reports that may be derived from a database of students in a school or college.

2. Why might a set of reports be supplied as part of a large database system?

3. Briefly describe the main stages in producing a report from a database. In particular, explain why it is necessary to link the report to a database.

4. What is the purpose of the following sections of a database report?
   • The page header
   • The report detail
   • The report summary

5. Describe a typical database that you have used or created which could be the subject of a report. Explain its purpose and the main fields. In what ways would it be useful to group the records on a report?

6. Mailing labels can be produced by both a word processor and a database. What are the advantages and disadvantages of each method?

7. What types of printer are suitable for A4 sheets of labels without sprocket holes?

8. List at least four uses for different types of label.

9. What precautions would you take when printing a series of 250 labels from a database?

Exporting data to a word processor

There are two reasons why you may want to send data from a database to a word processor. The most probable is to allow you to include the data in a merged letter or document, but it is sometimes necessary to include data in a report compiled on a word processor. The procedures are similar in both cases.

If you are not using an integrated package such as Microsoft Works, or a Windows-based system, you are likely to have to create an intermediate file containing the data to be transferred between the database and the word processor. This is known as 'exporting the data to a file'.

Merging database information into a form letters

Creating customised letters with a word processor was dealt with in some detail in Chapter 4. The process involves the creation of the 'form' letter to be sent to each person on the database. This contains special blank entries, sometimes known as 'place holders', for the data fields to be inserted. Each one generally contains the name of the field from the database to be inserted.

The data to be inserted, such as the name and address information, is usually contained in a separate file. This data file can be created by almost any database software.

The most usual format is known as a 'comma delimited' file, which means that the file contains all of its entries within quotation marks and separated by commas. This would appear in the file as shown in Figure 6.7. The first line of the file may also contain the field names in the same order as the data on the following lines. This line is known as the 'data header'.

```
1001,"ADULT","MISS","HILARY","FRANKLIN","GRAY STOKE COTTAGES","FITNESS"
1002,"STUDENT","MR","DONALD","WATERSTONE","12 THE STREET","SQUASH"
1003,"ADULT","MR","ERIC","SNAITH","3 SIMPSON STREET","SWIMMING"
1004,"STUDENT","MR","LEONARD","BIRCH","FLAT 2, MANSION HOUSE","BADMINTON"
1005,"ADULT","MRS","JACKIE","ABBOT","1 HOWARDS WAY","SWIMMING"
1006,"ADULT","MR","DANIEL","ABBOTT","1 HOWARDS WAY","BADMINTON"
1007,"SENIIOR","DOCTOR","FRANK","LETHBRIDGE","OLD MILL HOUSE","SWIMMING"
1008,"CONCESSION","MRS","ALICE","ROWNTREE","17 WINDERMERE PLACE","SWIMMING"
1009,"ADULT","MISS","JOAN","RIVERS","","FITNESS"
```

Figure 6.7 Comma delimited file

Use the database's 'export' or 'copy' command to create the comma delimited file containing the fields to be transferred. This will need a new file name to distinguish it from the database file. Once the file has been saved on disk, it can be used as often as required, to merge with different documents or letters.

The command to merge the document and the data is normally in the 'File' menu of the word processor. The system will ask for the file names of the template and the data file before the merging process can take place. It is also likely to ask if you wish to view the records on screen before they are printed. This is always a good idea – it can save a lot of wasted paper.

Including data in a word processed report

Data from a database is sometimes needed in a word processed report. In this case, the format of the file exported from the database needs to be carefully considered. The data fields can be separated with spaces or tabs instead of commas before the file is created. Alternatively, fixed length fields which are the same length as the data in the database can be created. This may prove easier to manipulate than a comma delimited file.

Use the word processor commands to insert the file at the point required in the new document. By careful selection of the format of the data to be transferred, minimum adjustments will be necessary in the final layout. This could be very important if there is a lot of data to insert.

Data transfer with Windows-based systems

For Windows-based systems the process of data transfer is much more simple using the 'Cut' and 'Paste' commands. These allow data to be transferred easily from a database directly to a word processor or a spreadsheet. This can be useful for a quick transfer, but the results may not be exactly as expected. Some additional formatting may be required in the application receiving the data.

For example, to transfer a database from Microsoft Access into Word or Ami-Pro, highlight the information to be transferred in the database and select 'Copy'. Then switch to the word processor and 'Paste' the information onto the page in the required position. The word processor will automatically create a table for the data, but it may need reformatting using commands in the 'Table' menu before it looks exactly correct in its new location.

The data can be transferred into a spreadsheet in the same way, but the reformatting may be more difficult because the column widths may need to be changed to accommodate all of the information in the database records.

Relational databases

Many databases are simple enough to keep all of their information in a single table. The rows of the table represent the records in the database, while the columns are the fields for each record. This type of database has many applications, from address lists to inventories and product information. They are often called 'flat' databases.

If many of the entries in such a database would contain the same information, it may be more efficient to arrange it in two or more tables.

For example, consider the case of a company who keep the names and addresses of all their suppliers together with the products purchased from them. The same supplier may be used for many different products, so the name and address could be entered many times. This would waste a lot of storage space on disk as well as a lot of time in typing the data.

Product	Product Name	Supplier Name	Supplier Address	Phone Number
G87	Gel seat cover black	Johnson Bikes	16 Gower Place, Cardiff	(2) 121-6678
H411	Brakes adjustor	Wilson Brakes Parts	Old Mews Works, Bristol	(3) 422-3675
A124	Lever brakes front - alloy	Wilson Brakes Parts	Old Mews Works, Bristol	(3) 422-3675
A134	Lever brakes rear - alloy	Wilson Brakes Parts	Old Mews Works, Bristol	(3) 422-3675
B135	Brake block set small	Great Chains	55 High Wayside, Brighton	(67) 735-1886
B155	Brake block set large	Great Chains	55 High Wayside, Brighton	(67) 735-1886
B934	Handlebar tape - red	Johnson Bikes	16 Gower Place, Cardiff	(2) 121-6678
B935	Handlebar tape - blue	Johnson Bikes	16 Gower Place, Cardiff	(2) 121-6678
G99	Gel seat cover grey/patterned	Johnson Bikes	16 Gower Place, Cardiff	(2) 121-6678
K321	Spanner set - plastic case	Great Chains	55 High Wayside, Brighton	(67) 735-1886
K344	Spanner set - steel boxed	Great Chains	55 High Wayside, Brighton	(67) 735-1886

Figure 6.8 Inefficiencies of a simple database

A much more efficient way of storing the same information is to store it in two separate tables which form part of the same database. One table could contain all of the suppliers, with their reference numbers, names, addresses, telephone numbers, fax numbers, contact names, etc., while the other could contain details of the products such as the product reference number, a description, size, supplier, etc.

Linked tables

The two tables can be linked together if one of the fields in each table is related in some way. In the example above, this would probably mean that the supplier reference number would be repeated in both tables, as shown in Figure 6.9.

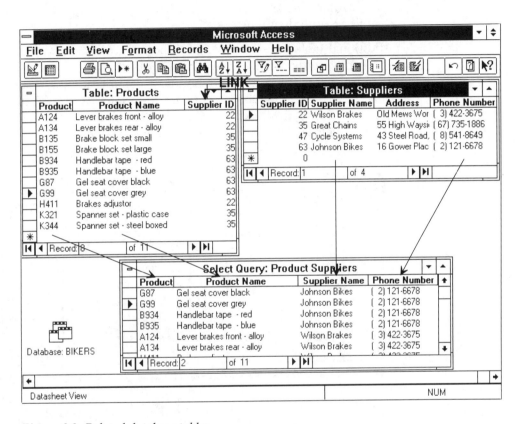

Figure 6.9 Related database tables

The product information in the first table has a supplier's reference number, 'Supplier ID', in each entry, so that the full supplier data can be found in the other related table. To find that information, the 'Supplier ID' is looked up in the second table until a match is found. This then provides the complete set of information. The advantage of the system is that the supplier's name and address are held only once, but can be used many times.

This type of system is known as a 'relational' database. Relational databases form the majority of databases found in industry and commerce because they are so efficient and flexible. Relational databases have multiple data tables that are linked or related to each other in some way.

Complex linking

Most relational databases have many more than two tables. Some have hundreds, and the links between them can be very complex. A diagram is often needed so that the users have a picture of the links between the many tables.

It is easy to see how the system in the example above could be extended. If each product was purchased on a company order form another database table could hold the details of the order reference number and the products purchased. It may also include any discount calculations. Instead of the supplier name and address being stored with each order, it could be obtained from the suppliers' data table using a simple reference number. The product details could be identified in the same way, with a reference number rather than the complete specification. The only extra information needed for the order would be the quantity required and the price.

Additional tables could be added to hold information on the salesperson who handled the order, such as the personal information for the sales staff, including a payroll reference, so that any bonus or commission payments could be made directly. Some of the tables from such a system are shown in Figure 6.10. The diagram shows the links between the tables. Note that the link takes place between fields of the same name in two of the tables.

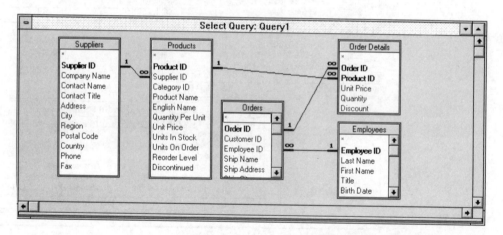

Figure 6.10 Linked tables in a relational database

Automatic database operation

When a database has been established and is in frequent use, it is likely that the same actions will have to take place regularly. For example, a typical operation may involve transferring data to a spreadsheet or copying records between database tables. These actions can be undertaken manually each time, but it is much more efficient to make the computer perform the actions automatically at the press of a mouse button or key.

Fortunately, most databases, apart from the most basic, have a built-in programming feature that makes this automation possible. The programs created are called 'macros'.

Macros

In early databases, writing the commands to make the database perform even simple functions required some programming skill. However, with more modern databases, a lot of the programming has been eliminated so that it is possible to create macros simply by selecting commands from a menu. Once the macros have been written, they must be thoroughly tested to ensure that they perform exactly as expected under all conditions. It is quite common for the whole operation of a large database to be controlled by a series of macros. The users need not know anything about the database software – they can simply follow the commands on the screen and operate the system by clicking the mouse button on screen icons.

The commands shown in Figure 6.11 form part of a simple macro that runs on a company sales database. It allows the manager to see quickly the performance of the sales team by viewing the orders generated by each one. The macro contains only two commands. The first opens the employee database, the second displays the data on a pre-designed 'Order review' form. The two commands could be entered manually, but by making them into a macro they can be executed much more easily by any user. The macro avoids the need to understand the database operation.

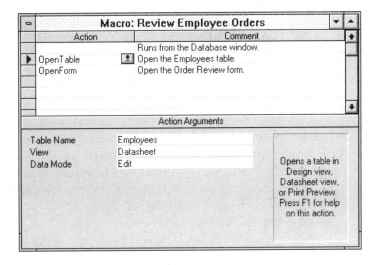

Figure 6.11 Simple macro from a company sales database

Databases on CD-ROM

One of the most powerful sources of large volumes of information is the CD-ROM. This relatively new technology has made it possible to store vast quantities of data in a very cheap and easily accessible form. Most fairly new computers can have a CD-ROM drive fitted for a few hundred pounds.

Data CDs look exactly like music CDs but they can contain text, music, video and computer programs. Since a CD can store up to about 650 MBytes of data, the complete text of a 25-volume set of encyclopaedias would occupy only a quarter of the space. The same disc can also store the pictures, diagrams and photographs in the encyclopaedia. To bring some of the reference material to life, it is also possible to store video clips. Suppliers like CD-ROMs because, unlike floppy disks, they are almost impossible to copy.

CD-ROM databases exist for many different applications. Some of the most common examples that illustrate the range available are

- *Book Bank*, the complete list of books in print – often used in libraries and book shops to check information
- *The Complete Oxford Dictionary* – not just the shorter version – complete with over 2,400,000 quotations, all on one disk
- *The Times*, *Daily Telegraph* and *Guardian* newspapers for a whole year – extremely valuable source material for scholars and historians, each on a single disk
- *Ecctis 2000*, a complete national database of all the courses on offer at 700 universities and colleges throughout the UK – a good starting point when looking for a university place
- *Languages of the World* – dictionaries in 12 languages, cross-referenced for easy translation
- *The Pill Book*, data on 1500 of the most commonly prescribed drugs – a valuable reference source for doctors
- *Film Index International* – a catalogue and details of over 90,000 films released up to 1991.
- *Renaissance Masters* – colour pictures of about 1300 great works of art on a single disk.
- *Information Finder* – text and tables from a 22-volume encyclopaedia

Search facilities

One of the most important aspects of a data CD is the ability to search for particular information. Most CDs have a set of built in programs that make the searching process very easy.

For example, it would be very difficult to have to look through all the newspapers for a year to find a particular article. With a search facility, a single word or phrase can be entered, and the system will search its comprehensive indexes for each occurrence. This normally results in a report showing the number of times the word or words appear. If there are only a few, you can then choose to browse each one of them to see if they are of interest. If there are a large number of occurrences, you may need to refine the search by adding extra conditions. Most systems index every word except 'the', 'and', 'but', etc.

Suppose you were looking for information about the effects on the environment of oil spillage. Searching for the word 'environment' would result in thousands of references, since everything related to the environment would be included. The search could be refined further by adding a second word, 'oil' and another, 'spill'. This would restrict the number of articles to those which contained all three words in their titles.

Multimedia database systems

'Multimedia' refers to systems that can include text, graphics, sound, and video. Modern databases are not only limited to text. Many now store high resolution pictures and some can store video clips. Both pictures and video take up a large amount of storage space, so a CD-ROM is the only portable storage medium that has enough capacity. However, video compression techniques are becoming much better, so that it is possible to store enough video for a 100 minute show on one CD-ROM.

Figure 6.12 Search screen from a CD-ROM database

Storing pictures

Typical applications for this type of system include the use of pictures to illustrate the database information. One system already in use can store pictures of people along with their personal details. If a person is a member of an organisation where security is important, they could be checked by security staff from their picture stored on the computer system. The same digital picture can be printed on any security badges that may be issued.

This type of system has many different applications and will probably become widespread in the near future. Already many clubs and organisations use the technique for their membership cards. It has been proposed that credit cards should also contain pictures.

Video

Video clips can help to illustrate many types of information. Encyclopaedias on CD-ROM are much more interesting than their paper equivalent because they can include video with the facts. For example, historic events such as the first moon walk can be shown in video whenever the subject is being studied. As with any video, sound is included as part of the information, so the commentary can provide yet more information. Unfortunately, the systems available at the moment are rather restricted in quality, but this is likely to be a temporary problem. As computer systems become ever more sophisticated, they will be able to provide television quality video images with many types of information.

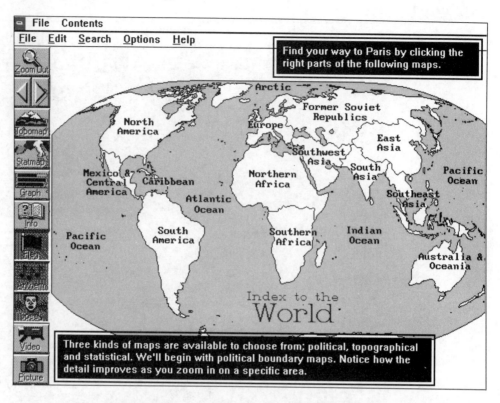

Figure 6.13 Screen display from a multimedia CD-ROM

Remote databases

With a computer and a telephone, it is not only possible to have access to databases on the computers hard disk or CD-ROM, but it is also possible to connect to databases anywhere in the world. Access to the world-wide network of computers first requires a modem to convert the computer signals to telephone signals. It also requires some communications software to both send and display information in the right format. To connect to a remote database, you will also need telephone numbers for the systems you wish to use and, usually, an account number on the destination computer, although many allow general access.

Once equipped with the necessary equipment and accounts, it is possible to tap into almost unlimited information of both a highly specialist and general nature. All of the computers in the major universities are connected together so that research students can share information. This linking also provides a very comprehensive electronic mail facility between students and staff.

The Internet

The Internet is a network of thousands of computers which are all linked together over the 'Information Superhighway'. This is a high speed communications network which extends around the world. Initially it linked up research and academic institutions, but now it includes both companies and individuals who have connected to it.

The Internet contains information on just about everything.

Anyone can join the network by linking up with an information provider (IP) who is already connected. The simplest type of access is via a modem and a telephone line, with an arrangement similar to that shown in Figure 6.14. Large organisations may have their own direct connections.

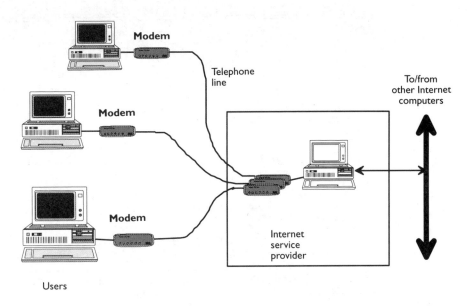

Figure 6.14 Connection to the Internet

The IP supplies the telephone number of an access point or point of presence (POP) and a user password for each person. They can also set up an individual account so that they can work out the billing and provide each user with an electronic mail box. This enables each user to send and receive electronic mail, or e-mail. Information providers may also provide the software necessary to access the system. E-mail is a good way of transferring data around the world at low cost.

The World Wide Web (WWW)

There are many different ways of accessing the data on other computers, but the most useful is a system called the World Wide Web, WWW or 'Web' for short. Information on computers all over the world can be accessed with software known as a 'Web browser'. Once connected to one computer, the browser can download both text and pictures. However, the beauty of the system is that it can also link the user automatically to many other computers where specific information can be found. The operation is entirely transparent to the user. One minute, the information may be coming from a computer in London, and the next it may be coming from a computer in New York. There is no noticeable speed difference, so it is hard to tell where the information originates.

Extracting data from the Web pages is usually similar to using a copy and paste operation. In addition, specific files can be stored for insertion later into other documents.

Most Web pages are free, but you may have to pay for others in addition to the cost of the telephone connection time. A typical Web page is shown in Figure 6.15.

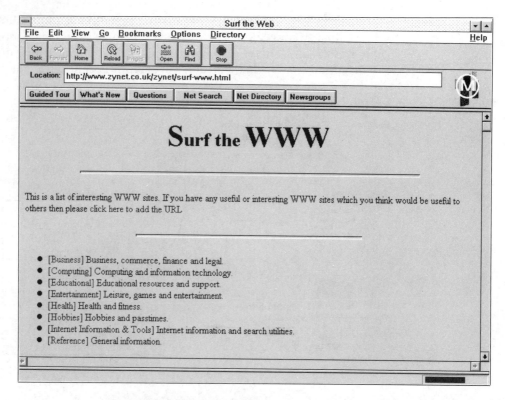

Figure 6.15 A page on the World Wide Web

The Internet also provides a range of other services, such as Gopher, FTP (file transfer protocol) and electronic mail, each of which have special functions. They allow the retrieval of text files, remote logging on the other computer systems and the transfer of world-wide e-mail. However, not all information providers provide the complete range of services, and additional software is required for each one.

Many individuals and organisations also operate their own databases or 'bulletin boards'. These range from dating agencies to the enormous Compuserve database that holds the latest technical information from major suppliers, specialist bulletin boards, general interest databases and many others.

Prestel

Prestel was one of the first remote database systems. It was originally run by British Telecom but is now operated as a separate business. It has around 10,000 subscribers, who are mainly business users. Within the service there are many specialist groups in the finance, travel and insurance sectors.

Some examples of the types of information available through the Prestel system include:
• Travel information and booking services
• Regional and local tourist information
• Share prices from the Stock Exchange, updated every few minutes
• Electronic mail
• On-line *Yellow Pages*
• National telephone directories.

With all remote databases, there are likely to be charges for the information supplied. These may include:

- *Telephone time,* normally charged at the standard rate, depending upon whether the call is local or not. Once a call is connected, the line charge may continue to be at local rates even though the data may be coming from the other side of the world.
- *Access time.* The time connected to the computer may be charged at a fixed rate, although with many systems this is free – particularly at off-peak times.
- *Data charge.* There may be a charge for the amount of data transferred to your terminal or for each page of information. In the Prestel system, charges are made only for certain pages which carry real information and not for the pages of menus that you may need to go through to get at what you want.

Review questions

When you are happy that you have understood most of the ideas so far, try the questions below. They are based on the work from the second part of the chapter. It is best to relate the questions on databases to the other work you may be doing in your GNVQ studies. When you have completed the questions you can put some of the concepts into practice by undertaking the exercises that follow.

1. Why might you want to transfer information from a database to a word processor? Think of at least two reasons.

2. Check the database software you normally use. Are there any commands that allow data to be transferred to other application programs? If so, what are they?

3. What advantages are there in using an 'Integrated' IT package rather than separate word processing, database and spreadsheet packages? What are the disadvantages?

4. What makes a 'relational' database different from a 'flat' database?

5. Briefly explain why a relational database is the preferred method of storing large amounts of complex data.

6. Think of an application that you have come across, such as a stock control system, a library, a business sales system or a college student record system, which could be based on a relational database. Write down the names and contents of some of the possible tables in the system.

7. What is the function of a 'macro' in a database system?

8. Go to your library or Learning Resources Centre and find out what databases are available on CD-ROM. For the six most useful, give a brief description of their function.

9. Why are CD-ROM database systems likely to become much more important in future?

10. What type of information is available in your Learning Resource Centre or other IT service, from a remote database? Give the name and type of information that any specific databases you can access contain.

11. What equipment is needed to access a remote database?

12. What might be stored on a multimedia CD?

13. What charges may be incurred if you want to retrieve information from a database in the USA?

Exercises

Try the following exercises using your normal database software if you need to gain some practice in its operation. Some exercises may be very simple with certain systems, but could prove to be quite time consuming with others. You may need to check with you supervisor whether the system you use can perform the required functions very easily.

1. The following information about holiday homes to rent in France is held in the database of a tour operator. Create a similar database using the same fields and data. The field sizes are indicated but some are characters and others numeric.

Fields:

TOWN	(12)	town
REG	(12)	region
CAP	(2)	sleeping capacity
RENT	(3)	weekly rental in pounds (high season)
SHOP	(2)	distance to nearest supermarket (km)
BEACH	(2)	distance to nearest beach (km)
TEN	(2)	distance to nearest tennis (km)
GOLF	(2)	distance to nearest golf course (km)
HORSE	(2)	distance to nearest horse-riding (km)

TOWN	REG	CAP	RENT	SHOP	BEACH	TEN	GOLF	HORSE
Chalais	Charente	10	1260	2	30	3	40	7
Quillan	Aude	10	610	1	10	0	55	3
Menton	Alpes	6	425	8	8	8	25	50
Eymet	Dordogne	4	230	4	1	3	5	5
Sarlat	Dordogne	16	1150	10	10	10	25	20
Hautefort	Dordogne	12	950	3	10	4	25	3
Valence	Gers	4	220	8	10	1	26	10
Villebois	Charente	12	550	2	30	0	30	10
Duras	Lot	2	175	6	2	2	10	2
Cancon	Lot	12	800	2	9	1	10	12
Bauge	Maine	9	740	2	8	0	18	0
Duras	Lot	7	500	17	5	5	10	2
Baud	Morbihan	8	400	5	38	1	10	8
Pontivy	Morbihan	7	575	2	35	2	10	10
Figeau	Lot	8	690	7	4	0	70	7
Lucon	Vendee	6	325	15	35	15	15	15
Civray	Vienne	2	130	5	3	3	45	3
Poitiers	Vienne	9	2500	15	15	0	15	1
Les Sables	Vendee	6	405	1	2	1	15	20
Mareuil	Vendee	9	260	5	30	3	10	15

When the database has been created, carry out the exercises below.

(a) Produce a report from the database information for a customer who wants a list of all properties with a capacity of more than seven in any area. Print all the data in a table for those which meet the criteria in any order. Use the report header to indicate how the selection has been made.

(b) Produce a second report for another customer who wants to know all of the properties within 5 km of a beach.

(c) Produce a third report for a customer who wants a property within 25 km of a golf course.

2. Using the database you created for Question 1, create a report with a group subsection for each region. In each one, list the properties in the region with all their details, in alphabetical order of their town name.

3. Modify the report created in Question 2 to show the properties in their regions but in descending order of cost, i.e. the most expensive first.

4. The database has to be used to create some labels that will be stuck to files for each property. The fields to be included are: Region, Town, Capacity and Price, each with the field name displayed first.

   Using your database software, create a label template with the four fields displayed on rows 2 to 5 of the label. The first row of each label should read 'Summer bookings only'. Choose whatever label stationery format you have available.

5. The same database is to be used to customise letters to potential customers. The template letter is given below, with the field names from the database where required.

   Type the letter using your usual word processor but arrange to link it to the database so that the information can be added automatically with the 'mail-merge' facility. In place of the field names in angle brackets, insert the field place-holder from the linked database.

   ```
   Dear . . . . . . . . . . . . ,

   Thank you for enquiry about the property in <TOWN>. The
   region of <REG> is one of the most popular this year,
   and I am sure that you will find that it has all the
   amenities you need. The nearest beach is <BEACH> km
   away, with golf and horse riding, <GOLF> km and <HORSE>
   km away respectively.

   The property has all modern conveniences and can
   accommodate <CAP> people easily. With the high season
   cost at only £<RENT>, I am sure that you will agree that
   it is good value for money.

   If you would like to make a firm booking, please return
   the enclosed booking form as soon as possible since I
   know that there are a number of other people interested
   in booking at the moment.

   Yours sincerely,
   ```

   When you are happy with the letter template, try to create one letter for each of the properties on the database. It is always a good idea to view the letters on screen before printing them, just in case there are any problems.

Assignment I starts on the next page

Assignment 1
Choosing an application to analyse data

This assignment could provide evidence for the following Performance Criteria of the GNVQ Core Skills:

Element 2.1	PCs 1 to 4
Element 2.2	PCs 1 to 6
Element 2.3	PCs 1 to 5
Element 2.4	PCs 1 to 4
Element 3.1	PCs 1 to 5
Element 3.2	PCs 1 to 7
Element 3.3	PCs 1 to 6
Element 3.4	PCs 1 to 5

Introduction

A team of researchers has been gathering public opinion outside a new art gallery in the town. They are trying to discover if the types of paintings on display are the most appropriate for the area. At the same time, they are trying to find out what additional facilities the gallery could provide which would be of most value.

They have interviewed 200 people and asked them the following questions.

1. How often do you visit art galleries?   Rarely/Occasionally/Often

2. Are you involved in any 'creative' activities?   Rarely/Occasionally/Often

3. Did you find your visit to the gallery an enjoyable experience?   Not at all/Quite enjoyable/Very enjoyable

4. Would you come again to another exhibition with paintings of the same type?   No/Possibly/Yes

5. Would you like more explanations of the works?   No/Some of them/Yes

6. Would you come to another exhibition if the paintings were very different? No/Possibly/Yes

7. If the gallery provided talks about the artists featured, would you come to one?   No/Possibly/Yes

8. If the gallery provided more literature would this be useful? No/Possibly/Yes

Your task

You have been asked to analyse the data from the survey. All you have are the 200 forms with a series of answers which have been ticked.

The questions which need to be answered are:

- Do most people find the visit to the gallery enjoyable?
- Of those who find it enjoyable, how many would possibly or definitely come to another exhibition of very different paintings?
- How many people who were not involved in 'creative' activities found the visit enjoyable?
- How many people would like either more literature or more explanation of the works?

The task can be broken down as follows.

1. Decide whether the analysis is best undertaken using a spreadsheet or a database.

2. Next, design a suitable layout for the data using the chosen application. If it is a spreadsheet, choose suitable column headings. If it is a database, choose suitable field names and then in either case, choose the acceptable entries for each field.

3. Enter a reasonable number of responses covering a range of opinions.

4. Design four queries that will provide answers to the questions being asked. These may be either in the form of a report or a set of data extracted from the system.

5. Write down the conclusions of your sample of visitors to the questions being asked.

6. What other information could be gathered from the questionnaires? List at least three examples.

Present your findings in a short report compiled using a word processor and containing the extracted information from either a spreadsheet or a database. Justify your selection of either a spreadsheet or a database to carry out the task. Explain the effects of any problems that occurred in use.

Assignment 2
Designing labels for a mailshot

This assignment could provide evidence for the following Performance Criteria of the GNVQ Core Skills:

Element 2.1	PCs 1 to 4
Element 2.2	PCs 1, 2, 4 and 5
Element 2.3	PCs 1, 2, 3 and 5
Element 2.4	PCs 1 to 4
Element 3.1	PCs 1 to 5
Element 3.2	PCs 1, 2, 4,5 and 7
Element 3.3	PCs 1, 2, 3, 4 and 6
Element 3.4	PCs 1 to 5

Introduction

You need to collect some product information from a number of suppliers as part of a major project, so you decide that the most efficient way to do this will be to send a mailshot. The same letter can be sent to each one, so only the label needs to contain the firm's name and address. They need to be addressed to 'The Sales Manager' in each case.

The list of suppliers is as follows:

Jones Suppliers Ltd, 3 North Hill, Bloomsbury, London EC1 4DT
Schooner Products, 23 Lakeside, Wellcome Bridge, Stafford
Hills Ltd, 15 Brake Rd, Hillingdon Ridge, Gateshead,
Butcher Wholesalers, Green Estate, Sunderland, Tyne & Wear
Flowers Product Supplies, 4 High St, Exeter, Devon
A to Z Supplies, James St Mews, Kensington, London SW7 6TT
JJ Components, Acre Estate, Littleover, Derby

Your task

1. Start by entering the supplier names and addresses into a simple database. Add some more entries of your own to bring the total to about 20.

2. Select the most appropriate size of mailing label from those available.

3. Design the layout of your label using the facilities available in the software you normally use and save the design with its own name. This will allow it to be used again.

4. Produce the labels for each of the companies in the database, ensuring that they each are addressed to 'The Sales Manager'. Ensure that the printer is correctly loaded before printing.

Write down the pros and cons of using a database package rather than the database facility of a word processor to undertake this task. Include a list of Dos and Don'ts for other people who may have to create labels after you. Be sure to explain what to do in the case of a paper jam in your printer during the production of the labels. Include some sample labels in your portfolio, along with a printout of the fields from the database containing the records which created them.

Assignment 3
Collecting selected information from different sources

This assignment could provide evidence for the following Performance Criteria of the GNVQ Core Skills:

Element 2.1   PCs 1 to 4
Element 2.2   PCs 1, 2, 4, 5 and 6
Element 2.3   PCs 1 to 5
Element 2.4   PCs 1 to 4
Element 3.1   PCs 1 to 4
Element 3.2   PCs 1, 2, 4, 5 and 6
Element 3.3   PCs 1 to 6
Element 3.4   PCs 1 to 5

Introduction

You need to collect information for a major research project from a number of different sources. These include CD-ROM and remote databases. The information has to be compiled into a short report, which also explains the way in which the data has been collected.

Your task

1. First choose the type of information that you need to collect. Ideally this should be related to the work you are doing at the moment in your GNVQ.

   The information could be on the manufacture of a product, a scientific process or the design of buildings. It could be on the availability of leisure or social services in an area, or population data for marketing purposes. It may be technical details on how something works or a list of books on a given subject.

   Clearly specify the information you need.

2. The next task is to discover the most appropriate sources for the information you need. Find out if it is available on any CD-ROMs you have access to, or if it can be found on a remote database. You may need to do a considerable amount of searching. Try to use both local and remote sources of data so that you can compare the value of the information, speed of access and the techniques required for each method.

3. If possible, save the information from your searches electronically in files on a floppy disk. Otherwise, make sure that you have printouts. It is sometimes possible to print to a file on disk rather than directly onto paper.

Produce a summary report on the type of data found from the various sources, illustrating it with examples. If possible, insert the data saved on your disk with your report, but make sure that the format is consistent throughout. Comment on the ease or difficulty you have experienced in obtaining, then combining, the data from different sources. Write a list of instructions for your colleagues on how to access a remote database which you have found useful.

CHAPTER 7

Introduction to spreadsheets

Objectives

When you have finished this chapter you should be able to:
- Understand the basic functions of a spreadsheet
- Understand how to enter text, numbers and formulae into a spreadsheet using a typical software package
- Understand simple terminology such as cell, column, row, active cell, range
- Use a spreadsheet command to change the format of a cell
- Understand how to enter a formula into a spreadsheet
- Appreciate how to print part or all of a spreadsheet

This chapter covers the Performance Criteria and Range from all of the IT Core Skills Elements at levels 2 and 3 related to the preparation, processing and presentation of numbers in spreadsheets, and the use of automated templates.

What is a spreadsheet?

A spreadsheet works like a collection of calculators. Instead of working out just one calculation at a time, a spreadsheet can work out hundreds. It makes all sorts of mathematical problems in business and technology very simple.

On a computer screen, a spreadsheet looks like a sheet of paper which has been ruled into a grid of columns and rows. One is shown in Figure 7.1. The grid is made up of number of **cells** and in each one you can type numbers or normal text. The whole sheet can be treated as a blank piece of paper, like the page of a word processor.

Calculations are performed by entering formulae into the cells, as well as numbers and text. This is what makes the spreadsheet so powerful. The formulae perform your calculations in a fraction of a second and so they provide almost instantaneous answers to mathematical problems. The formulae themselves are hidden so that they are invisible on the printed sheet. All you see on the spreadsheet itself are the answers for each of the calculations.

Where are spreadsheets used?

Whenever numbers have to be manipulated in a business, the use of a spreadsheet is likely to improve both the efficiency and the accuracy of the calculations. In addition, since the results can be saved on a computer disk, the same calculation can be stored for future use. It can be modified later if small changes have to be made.

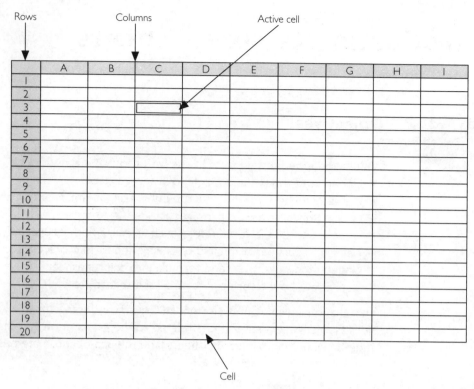

Figure 7.1 Typical spreadsheet

Engineering calculations

Many engineering design problems involve a number of related calculations. Checking the forces on the suspension of a car, or working out the power of an amplifier can both be done with a calculator. However, with a spreadsheet the calculations can be made much more easily.

Manufacturing

The cost of manufacturing a component in a factory depends upon many factors, such as the materials, assembly time, cost of labour and overheads. These can all be entered into the spreadsheet calculation so that the cost of manufacturing many different parts can be worked out simply by changing the numbers slightly.

Survey processing

By using a spreadsheet to process the results of a survey, the answers can easily be turned into charts that show graphically the various replies. Calculations to find out averages and percentages are very straightforward.

Marketing

The cost of conducting a market survey or the promotional costs for a product can all be kept on a spreadsheet. This allows the effect of changes to be easily seen. For example, the cost of changing from a black and white brochure to one in full colour can be calculated for different print runs just by changing a few figures.

Small business cash flow

Daily income and expenditure can have a dramatic effect upon the profitability of a small business. A spreadsheet allows the business manager to see the effect of late payments or bad debts upon the cash flow. This may be a way of avoiding problems and deciding when to see the bank manager.

Budgeting

All companies have budgets that have to be calculated and then checked. Even though some records may be kept on large computer systems, many managers keep their records on a simple spreadsheet. This helps them to get early warning when the budget is being overspent or underspent for any reason. It also allows them to find out what would happen if they took certain actions. They can put the numbers into the spreadsheet and find out very quickly what the effect would be. This is sometimes called a 'what-if?' calculation.

Accounting

Accountants were the first group of people who used spreadsheets in their work. The ability of the spreadsheet to add and subtract numbers and perform all sorts of calculations saves hours of work with a calculator. It also eliminates many of the errors that can creep into long calculations using a calculator.

These examples give only a brief idea of all the possible ways in which a spreadsheet can be used. There are very few types of business in which a spreadsheet would not be applicable.

Spreadsheets not only make calculations of all types both quick and easy, they also allow charts and graphs to be drawn from the numbers on the spreadsheet. Many different kinds of chart can be drawn from the same set of numbers, so it is possible to select one which displays the data in the most convenient way. Axes, titles, grids and other information can be added to the chart to improve its layout and ensure that it is easy to interpret.

Basic principles

Think of a spreadsheet as a very large grid of many **rows** and **columns**. Part of one is shown in Figure 7.1.

The rows are normally numbered, starting at 1 in the top left-hand corner, and can go down as far as 16384. The columns are normally given letters, going from A on the left through to Z, then AA, AB, AC, etc. to IV on the right. There are usually 256 columns, although some spreadsheets are bigger than others.

Each row and column meet at a **cell**. The cells are given the number of the column and row that they are in. The cell illustrated in Figure 7.1 is cell C3. The highlighted cell is known as the 'active' cell and it is here that information can be entered. Its contents are normally shown at the top of the screen. Groups of cells are often referred to as a **range** of cells.

Moving around a spreadsheet

Because the computer screen is so small it cannot possibly show all of the spreadsheet at once. By using the cursor keys on the keyboard it is possible to move the screen 'window' around the spreadsheet and look at other parts of it. This can have the effect of moving the active cell at the same time.

Windows-based spreadsheets, such as Microsoft Excel and Microsoft Works, can also be operated with a mouse. In these spreadsheets, the active cell can also be changed simply by clicking the mouse button while pointing to the required cell. Dragging the mouse over the spreadsheet or using the scroll bars moves the screen window to a different part of the sheet.

What can go on a spreadsheet?

A spreadsheet should be treated like a piece of paper ruled in a grid. There are three main types of entry that can be made in any of the cells – text, numbers and, for the calculations, formulae.

Text and numbers

Text or numbers can be entered into each cell in exactly the same way as on a sheet of paper. Labels, such as Total, Cost price, are given to column headings to illustrate what the numbers mean. The precise layout of text and numbers within a cell can be adjusted in most spreadsheets to allow a very professional appearance to be achieved. When you are designing your own spreadsheet, always choose a layout that looks neat.

Formulae

Formulae can be placed in cells where calculations are needed. These appear at the top of the computer screen as they are entered, but do not appear on the spreadsheet – instead, the *result* of the calculation performed by the formula appears on the spreadsheet. If a formula is entered which adds a column of numbers, the total would appear in the cell containing the formula. Formulae use cell references, such as A3 and F64, in the calculations. For example, the formula

    =D6+D7

means 'add the contents of cell D6 and D7, and place the results in this cell'.

Typical small spreadsheet

An example of a small spreadsheet as it would appear on a computer screen is shown in Figure 7.2. This figure illustrates how it is possible to calculate the cost of a series of driving lessons and a driving test.

The title of the spreadsheet appears at the top so that when it is printed its purpose is clearly stated. The title is in a slightly larger font than the rest of the spreadsheet for greater impact. Each column is given its own title, which in this case have been printed in italics.

Down the left-hand side of the sheet the various items that make up the total are listed simply by typing the text into the appropriate cells. Pressing the down arrow key or the return key completes the entry in each cell.

Column B contains the number of each of the items that are being counted, and column C shows the cost of each one.

The 'Total' column contains a formula in each cell from E6 to E11. These

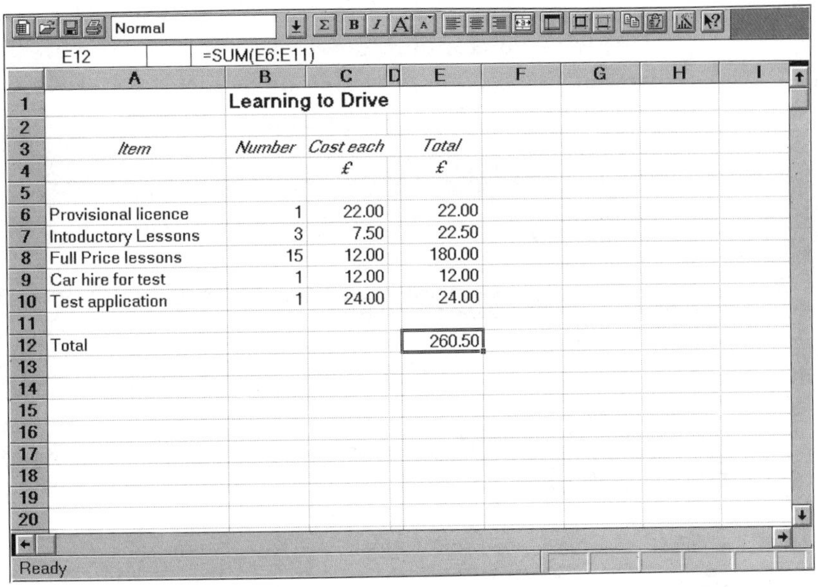

Normal

E12 =SUM(E6:E11)

	A	B	C	D	E
1		Learning to Drive			
2					
3	*Item*	*Number*	*Cost each*		*Total*
4			£		£
5					
6	Provisional licence	1	22.00		22.00
7	Intoductory Lessons	3	7.50		22.50
8	Full Price lessons	15	12.00		180.00
9	Car hire for test	1	12.00		12.00
10	Test application	1	24.00		24.00
11					
12	Total				260.50

Ready

Figure 7.2 Calculating the costs of learning to drive

multiply the number in column B by the number in column C, and puts the answer in column E.

Finally, the grand total is calculated in cell E12 by another formula that adds up all of the figures in the column above it.

Although the calculations done by the spreadsheet could easily be done on a calculator, they would take some time. The real advantage of the spreadsheet can be seen if any of the figures have to be changed. For example, if less than 15 full price lessons are needed, by changing the figure in cells B8 to 12 the new total can be seen instantly. If the price of a lesson is different or any other changes are entered, the spreadsheet automatically recalculates the new total.

Commercial spreadsheets

There are many commercial spreadsheets on the market, and they can all do all the operations required for this course. They differ mostly in size, the number of special functions they include, their ability to be programmed for automatic operation, and the range of graphics they have available. All of them perform basic mathematical functions such as addition, subtraction, multiplication, division, sines, cosines, powers of numbers, square roots, etc. Naturally, their commands are slightly different, but once you understand the basic principles of a spreadsheet these differences are very small.

Case study – Microsoft Excel

Excel is a Windows-based spreadsheet which has a range of features similar to a number of others, such as Lotus 1–2-3 for Windows and Borland Quattro Pro. It has a standard Windows 'feel', and is easily learned by anyone who is familiar with the mouse and icon principles. The pull-down menus give access to the commands available, and the icons on the tool bar provide a quick method of activating the most common of them. There are also a number of 'short-cuts' which make common tasks much simpler. Figure 7.3 shows Excel's opening screen. Special 'Help' menus are available for all the commands.

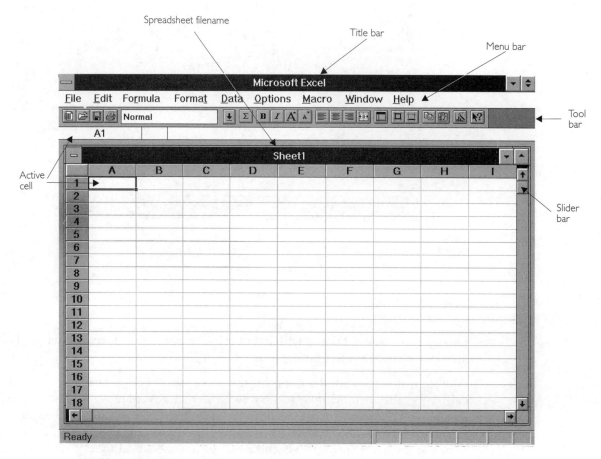

Figure 7.3 Microsoft Excel opening screen

The screen has typical Windows layout, with a title bar at the top and the usual maximise and minimise buttons. The right side and bottom of the screen have the slider bars to move the spreadsheet area visible on the screen and help to change the active cell location.

Below the title is the menu bar, with a series of pull-down menus that are activated either by clicking the mouse on them or by using the Alt key and underlined letter.

The tool bar shows a set of icons that represent the most frequently used operations, such as 'Open file', 'Save file', 'Sum', 'Bold', 'Italic' or 'Borders'. These are very useful. Different sets of icons can be placed on the tool bar for different tasks.

Below the tool bar, the active cell reference is shown together with its contents. In Figure 7.3 cell A1 is the active cell, but it is blank. As information is entered into a cell it appears on this line and can be edited or corrected before the return key is pressed.

'Help' is a menu option for all Windows software. Click the menu bar then choose the subject on which you need help. 'Help' also includes a tutorial program that contains all of the basic instructions in a series of short lessons. Try to work through the tutorial which comes with the software. It is usually the quickest way to become familiar with the basic operation of the commands.

Moving around and entering data

You can use the cursor keys or point and click with the mouse to move the active cell around the sheet. Groups of cells are selected by dragging the mouse from the top left to the bottom right corners of the group or vice versa. Text, numbers or formulae can be entered by typing the information directly into the active cell. Whatever you type appears at the top of the spreadsheet first so that it can be edited using the backspace or cursor keys, and it is then fixed in the cell when the return key is pressed.

A quick way of moving to a particular cell in Excel is to use the 'Goto' function or by pressing Function key F5. This allows a cell number or name to be entered and when 'OK' is selected the active cell moves directly to the cell chosen. This is best used for very long moves.

Formulae are started in Excel with a special symbol, =. Other spreadsheets, such as Lotus 1-2-3, use + or @ instead. For example, to enter a formula which 'adds cells B3 and C3', type

    =B3+C3

in the active cell.

Saving the spreadsheet contents

Saving information regularly is very important with any software and spreadsheets are no exception. It is best to save the sheet every few minutes while information is being entered. Check the information on screen very carefully by comparing it with the original each time. Regular checking will avoid many mistakes that could lead to very strange results, particularly if they are in formulae which are not visible on a normal spreadsheet screen.

When you are happy that a spreadsheet is complete, don't forget to make a backup copy by saving it onto another floppy disk. This is a wise precaution with all files. The Excel spreadsheet and other Windows software has a 'Save as' command which allows you to enter a new name or a new disk drive letter to make a backup. Computer disks (and operators!) have a habit of going wrong at the most inconvenient times.

Worked example ———————————————————————————

Doing some 'What-if?' calculations on a spreadsheet

There are many occasions in business and commerce when a decision has to be made about the purchase of a new piece of equipment. The cost of the purchase normally has to be recovered by improvements in the service or increased productivity over a period of two or three years. As long as the equipment purchased lasts longer than it takes to pay for itself, the business will have made a profit from its investment.

PROBLEM

A company supplies the small photographic booths used to take passport style photographs. It already has a number of booths in a town centre, but they believe that more business could be generated if another booth was set up near the railway station. The booths cost £15,000 each, but this cost can be spread over three years. Each set of photographs cost an average of £0.25 for materials. Maintenance of the machine costs £800 per year in wages and parts.

Use the spreadsheet set out in Figure 7.4 to work out the answers to the businessman's questions.

	A	B	C	D	E
1		PHOTO BOOTH - Profit calculations			
2					
3	INCOME				
4	Customers	Customers	Price		Total
5	per day	per year			
6	10	=A6*365	2.00		=C6*B6
7					
8	EXPENDITURE				
9	Purchase (per year)		5000.00		=C9
10	Materials (per photo)		0.25		=C10*B6
11	Maintenance (per year)		800.00		=C11
12					
13	PROFIT				=E6-E9-E10-E11

Figure 7.4 *'What-if?' calculations on a spreadsheet*

QUESTIONS

1. If it takes three years to pay off the cost of the booth, and an average of ten customers use it per day, each paying £2.00, will it make a profit? If so, how much per year?

2. What would the profit be if the price was increased to £2.50 if there was still an average of ten customers per day?

3. If the price is £2.50 per set of photographs, what is the smallest number of customers needed per day, on average, to make a profit?

4. What profit would be made in the fourth year, when the cost of the booth has reduced to zero, if the price of a set of photos is still £2.50, and ten customers use it per day?

SOLUTION

The answers to each of the questions can be found by entering different values into the spreadsheet. The known values are entered into the sheet, as shown in Figure 7.4. Each of the formulae required are shown in the figure, but on the actual spreadsheet these are displayed as numbers.

Notice how the number of customers per year is automatically calculated from the average number of customers per day. Also, the cost of the materials used, is the cost per customer multiplied by the number of customers. The profit is the total income, minus all of the expenditure.

1. The result of the first calculation is shown in Figure 7.5. Here, the known values have been entered, and the result is shown on the bottom line. It indicates a profit of £587.50 in the first year.

2. By changing some of the values on the spreadsheet, the answers to the other questions can be calculated easily. Change the price cell to £2.50, and the profit immediately increases to £2412.50.

3. If the number of customers per day is reduced to seven, the booth makes a loss of £51.25.

4. In the fourth year, when the cost of purchase is changed to zero, the booth makes a profit of £7412.50 as long as an average of ten customers per day keep using it.

	A	B	C	D	E
1		PHOTO BOOTH - Profit calculations			
2					
3	INCOME				
4	Customers	Customers	Price		Total
5	per day	per year			
6	10	3650	2.00		7300.00
7					
8	EXPENDITURE				
9	Purchase (per year)		5000.00		5000.00
10	Materials (per photo)		0.25		912.50
11	Maintenance (per year)		800.00		800.00
12					
13	PROFIT				587.50

Figure 7.5 Results of the 'What-if?' calculation

Note: If you would like to try the questions for yourself, enter the spreadsheet exactly as it is shown in Figure 7.4 onto the spreadsheet you normally use. In a cell containing a formula, enter it as shown if you're using Excel. If you are using Lotus 1-2-3, change the = sign to a + sign.

Good layout

The layout is probably more important for a spreadsheet than for many other kinds of document. This is because columns of figures can take on completely new meanings if they are in the wrong place in a calculation. If numerical information is not very easy to read, it can be very difficult to make any calculations based on it.

Spreadsheets naturally encourage good layout because they have a grid of rows and columns. It can be tempting, when first using a spreadsheet, to cram everything into the top corner of the sheet. This looks very poor and can be difficult to interpret. Treat the screen as a blank sheet, approximately the width of an A4 piece of paper. If you spread out the columns across the page and use as many lines as necessary to include all of the data, the layout will immediately improve.

Column width

Data in a spreadsheet cell spills over into the next cell on the right only if it is empty – look at cell B1 in Figure 7.5. If other cells are not wide enough to contain all of the required information their width must be increased. In some spreadsheets this is simply a matter of dragging the cell border. In others, the column width must be set from the menu by choosing a fixed number of characters.

Item	No.	Cost	Total
Blue roset	2	£2.50	£5.00
Scarves w	5	£9.99	£49.95
Stickers (1	3	£1.25	£3.75

Item	No.	Cost	Total
Blue rosettes (large)	2	£2.50	£5.00
Scarves with stripes	5	£9.99	£49.95
Stickers (12 per box)	3	£1.25	£3.75

Figure 7.6 Changing column widths

Select the most appropriate width for each of the columns on your spreadsheet to improve the presentation. Some columns can be made very narrow, as shown in column D in Figure 7.5, so that a small margin is left between columns of figures.

Number format

Spreadsheets must be able to display numbers in many different ways. Although the calculations are done to an accuracy of many decimal places, the actual presentation on screen can be selected from a range of options. For example, you may want numbers with no decimal places, or with two decimals, you may want to use scientific or engineering notation, you may want percentages or currency notation. All of these are possible if 'Format' for a cell or a group of cells is chosen. Figure 7.7 gives a few examples of the many ways in which most spreadsheets can display numbers.

57	no decimal places
57.123	fixed number of decimals
–57.123	negative
(57.12)	negative numbers shown in accounts
57.12%	percentage
5.71E+00	scientific
£57.12	currency

Figure 7.7 Numbers in a spreadsheet may be presented in different formats

Positioning in cells

Numbers are normally moved as far to the right as possible in a spreadsheet cell. This is so that the smallest numbers line up with each other. Text, however, normally starts on the left. This is so that all of the words begin in the same place in each column.

Sometimes you may wish to change these positions to improve the presentation of the spreadsheet. For example, the headings of wide columns may not line up with the numbers below them. In this case it would be best to right-justify the text for the headings. In some spreadsheets, the headings may look best if they are centred. It all depends upon column width and the rest of the layout of the sheet.

Text style

Most Windows-based spreadsheets can include various fonts to improve the appeal of the text. Stick to two or three at most, or a spreadsheet may look rather messy. The text size can be increased for headings or any numbers you wish to highlight.

	Text	LEFT	CENTRE	RIGHT	
	Numbers	123.4	123.4	123.4	
		3.4	4.4	5.4	

Figure 7.8 Various ways of aligning text and numbers

Add emphasis to the important parts of a sheet by using italic or bold text. For example, make column headings italic capitals.

Different text styles can be found on the menu bar at the top of most spreadsheets. First, highlight the cells which need to be emphasised, then select the style required from the 'Character format' menu or directly from an icon. It is also possible to pre-format large areas of a sheet before anything is entered, so that it automatically appears in the right style.

Borders and highlights

Layouts can often be improved if the main areas that contain related information are enclosed in boxes. The commands which do this vary between spreadsheets, but they are worth investigating. Borders round the spreadsheet or between columns can mean the difference between a poor presentation and a good one.

In some systems special cells can also be highlighted with a background shade or colour. This is also a very good way to improve the appearance of the spreadsheet and make it easier to use.

Adding and removing columns and rows

Often the layout of a spreadsheet can be improved by adding or removing a number of rows or columns. Use extra columns to separate data and make the spreadsheet easier to read. This is normally achieved with the 'Insert' command. Remove columns or rows to prevent the information being too far apart, or if the sheet contains a lot of unwanted data. This is done with the 'Delete' command.

Most software contains the commands to add or remove sections of the spreadsheet in the 'Edit' menu. Take care to highlight the section to be removed, or the place where new cells are required, then execute the command.

Progress check

Quite a lot of information about spreadsheets has been covered in the chapter so far. It would be a good idea to try to recap on some of the main ideas by trying a few simple questions. Try to answer them without looking back at the previous pages unless you are really stuck. Some of the questions are quite general. Think about the work you are doing at the moment, or are likely to be doing soon in the GNVQ you are studying, as you answer them.

1. What is the basic purpose of a spreadsheet? Give three possible applications for a spreadsheet drawn from your own experience.

2. What is meant by the following terms when referring to a spreadsheet?
   (a) Cell
   (b) Active cell
   (c) Range
   (d) Row
   (e) Formula

3. Give three methods of moving from cell B1 to cell D1266 on your spreadsheet. Which would be the quickest?

4. If the contents of cell C12 always have to be the same as the contents of cell A17, what formula would you enter in cell C12 to make this happen automatically?

5. Why is it important to make sure that a spreadsheet has a good layout? Give two examples of what this means in practice.

6. Why do the numbers in some columns of a spreadsheet not line up with the column headings?

7. What is the maximum size of spreadsheet that can be accommodated with the software you normally use? How large would this be on paper if each cell measures 3 cm $\times$ 1 cm?

8. In what way is the efficiency of an office improved if the computer is equipped with a spreadsheet?

Now try Exercises 1, 2, 3, and 4 at the end of the chapter to give you some practice in the use of a spreadsheet. You will be able to do them with any spreadsheet software although the commands may be slightly different for each one.

Creating a new spreadsheet

Simple spreadsheets can often be designed on a computer screen and can provide the results to calculations quite quickly. However, for more complicated spreadsheets, the layout can be very important, so that the printed version can be easily understood. It is no good getting the right answer if the way in which it was calculated is not clear.

Orientation

The first problem with a spreadsheet design is to decide whether it will be in landscape or portrait format. For small sheets, it makes very little difference but if the design needs more columns than comfortably fit across the width of a screen a landscape format might be better. This makes the page wider than it is long.

If the spreadsheet will have more rows than columns, then a portrait format is likely to be best. This is the usual setting for most systems.

It is usual to design the spreadsheet so that the fixed data or known information appears somewhere near the top or on the left-hand side of the sheet. The calculations and the answers then appear on the right. This is not a fixed rule, but it does help the layout appear logical to anyone looking at the sheet for the first time. Spreadsheets which work in reverse can be very confusing.

Size

Some spreadsheets can be enormous. They need many sheets of paper to print them out completely. The problems this creates are only obvious when all of the sheets have to be stuck together with sticky tape so that the whole thing can be seen at once.

It is better, if possible, to print summary sheets with all of the incidental information removed or hidden instead of large spreadsheets. Some systems allow this to be done automatically so that only the results of calculations are shown. It may also be possible to compress the printing of a sheet so that it can be squeezed onto one page.

Calculations

All types of calculations can be made very easy by employing a spreadsheet. The skill in designing a spreadsheet is in working out the formulae needed to give the right answer in each cell.

Most spreadsheets contain only simple calculations such as addition, subtraction, multiplication and division. These operations are the same for all spreadsheets, and use the +, −, * and / symbols respectively. These symbols are known as 'mathematical operators'.

Functions

For more advanced calculations most spreadsheets also contain a large number of **functions**. These cover special applications such as finance, trigonometry, statistics, engineering and database operation.

The 'Sum' function is probably the most common, and is used to add columns of numbers. The references of the cells to be added are contained in brackets as shown below. These formulae could be used in an Excel or Works spreadsheet.

`=SUM(A1+A2+A3)`	adds the numbers in A1, A2 and A3
`=SUM(A1:A25)`	adds the numbers in A1, A2, A3 up to A25
`=SUM(A3+B7+J20)`	adds the numbers in A3, B7 and J20
`=SUM(5+A5+SUM(B3:B7)`	adds 5 to the number in A5 and the sum of B3 to B7

In Lotus 1-2-3 the 'Sum' function is very similar to that in Excel, but is written as
`@SUM(A1..A25)`

to add together cells A1 to A25, for example.

Other functions

Many different functions are available on all spreadsheets. They make some types of calculation very simple. In Excel, for example, 'Mod()' returns the remainder from a division calculation in the brackets, 'Round()' rounds a number in the brackets to a fixed number of decimal places and 'Int()' rounds a number down to the nearest whole number. The Microsoft Excel spreadsheet has over 200 different functions. Two of the more useful functions will be covered in the next chapter.

Worked example

The cost of mail order

INTRODUCTION

You have just set up an agency for a mail order catalogue and decide that working out all of the orders on a spreadsheet will help to avoid errors and ensure that you have a record of all of the orders. In addition, the spreadsheet will help you to work out the customer discount and your commission very easily.

The spreadsheet needs to record the following information for each item: item reference number, quantity, price each, discount percentage, total price and commission.

There is a discount for customers of 5% if they buy more than two of any one item. Your commission is 10% of the total price before postage is added. Each order costs £4.50 in postage and packing.

PROBLEM

1. Design a spreadsheet that will calculate all of the values mentioned above. It will need a suitable title and column headings. All of the calculations need to be automatic as soon as an item, the quantity and price each and discount have been entered.

2. Enter a list of up to five items in various quantities to test the operation of the spreadsheet design.

3. Use the highlighting and border drawing facilities of the spreadsheet to improve its appearance. Print the finished version on an A4 page.

4. Save the spreadsheet in a suitable directory on a disk, and give it a suitable filename.

SOLUTION

1. The first task is to do a rough layout on paper. This shows that you will need seven columns. As well as those listed in the introduction, one called 'Price before discount' would help to make the calculations easier. The top of the page also needs some basic information such as the order number, your name and address, and the date.

2. The layout chosen is shown in Figure 7.9. Since the orders could be of any length, it was decided to use the portrait layout and try to squeeze all of the columns across the page.

3. The header information at the top was entered first with the title of the spreadsheet and the other basic order information. The column headings are quite long so these were spaced over three rows to improve their appearance. The column widths were adjusted as necessary to fit in all the words.

4. The formulae on each line are shown in Figure 7.9, although these would not normally be visible. Each line is similar apart from the reference to the row in each case.

5. Each column can be formatted even though they are empty. The columns for the quantity and the discount percentage for example, have been centred. The amounts have been given a 'Currency' format so that a £ sign and two decimal places are automatically added.

6. The layout was improved by adding borders to the different sections of the form. All of the order itself is enclosed in a box with the final amount due highlighted at the bottom.

	A	B	C	D	E	F	G	H
1		MAIL ORDER - THE HOME DELIVERY SPECIALISTS						
2								
3	ORDER NO.			NAME				
4	DATE			ADDRESS				
5								
6								
7								
8	Item	Quantity	Price	Discount	Price before	Total after	Commission	
9	Reference		each	percentage	discount	discount	due	
10	Number			%				
11	VN1298-98	1	£17.99	0	=B11*C11	=E11-D11%	=F11*10%	
12	GG2892-12	4	£5.50	5	=B12*C12	=E12-D12%	=F12*10%	
13	BJ2093-90	1	£32.79	0	=B13*C13	=E13-D13%	=F13*10%	
14								
15								
16								
17								
18								
19								
20								
21								
22								
23								
24								
25	TOTAL					=SUM(F11:F24)	=SUM(G11:G24)	
26								
27	Postage and Packing					£4.50		
28								
29	Amount Due					=F27+F25		
30								
31								
32								
33								

Figure 7.9 Order spreadsheet

7. The file was then saved in an 'Orders' directory on drive C: with a filename of BLANKORD.XLS

Note: Although Figure 7.9 shows the cell names at the top and the left-hand side, and the cell grid lines, these would not normally be visible when the sheet is printed.

Copying cell contents

If you look at the formulae in each column in Figure 7.9, you can see that they are all very similar. The only difference is the row number. Each one performs the same calculation as the one above. For example, the formula in G11 (=F11*10%) means 'multiply the number in the cell on the left by 10%'. This is the same as the formula for all the cells in the column. 'The cell on the left' is known as a 'relative cell reference'.

An easy way of entering the formula into all the cells in the row is simply to copy them. The row number is adjusted automatically as the formula is copied. Each spreadsheet manufacturer has a slightly different method of copying the cell contents, so it is best to check in the manual or with your lecturer. Windows-based systems generally have 'Copy' and 'Paste' icons on the menu bar.

> **Remember:**
> 'Relative cells' are those related in the same way to any active cell, e.g. one above, on the left, two below, etc.

Some systems allow cells to be copied simply by dragging them to the new locations.

Copying formulae is a very powerful spreadsheet technique that can save many hours of laborious typing. Spreadsheets always use *relative* cell references unless told to do otherwise, so that if any formula is copied its cell references will change.

Groups of cells or ranges can also be copied – this increases the speed at which complex spreadsheets can be created. One cell may be copied as many times as required.

Absolute cell references

Sometimes, when formulae are copied, it is necessary for cell references to stay the same and not be changed automatically by the software. Telling the spreadsheet not to change the cell reference is simply a matter of indicating this in the formula. This can be achieved by adding a dollar sign ($) before the row and column reference. For example, A3 would fix the cell reference as A3; $A3 would fix the column as A, but when the formula is copied the row number may be changed to A4, A5, A6 etc.

The spreadsheet in Figure 7.9 could be changed to that shown in Figure 7.10. Here the percentage commission has been placed in cell G10. The formulae in the column have been changed so that they use the value placed there. One advantage in this arrangement is that the rate of commission can be changed without having to alter all of the formulae in the column.

	A	B	C	D	E	F	G
7							
8	Item	Quantity	Price	Discount	Price before	Total after	Commission
9	Reference		each	percentage	discount	discount	at
10	Number			%			10%
11	VN1298-98	1	£17.99	0	=B11*C11	=E11-D11%	=F11*G10
12	GG2892-12	4	£5.50	5	=B12*C12	=E12-D12%	=F12*G10
13	BJ2093-90	1	£32.79	0	=B13*C13	=E13-D13%	=F13*G10
14							
15							

Figure 7.10 Formulae with 'absolute' cell references

Naming cells

Even on very small spreadsheets the formulae can become very complicated. If you have to work on a spreadsheet created by someone else, it is almost impossible to work out all of the formulae. After a few months, the formulae on your own spreadsheets will also seem a little strange. One way to overcome the problem is to give the cells names. This means that the cell references in all the formulae can include names instead of numbers. The headings of the columns are often the best names since they appear on the spreadsheet and are easy to remember.

In Figure 7.10, the columns could be named Quantity, Price, Discount, Commission, etc. This allows the formulae in the cells in column E, for example, to be entered as: =Price*Quantity.

Finding cells

On large spreadsheets it can be very difficult to locate particular cells. To help users, most spreadsheets have a 'Goto' function, which is often just a matter of pressing a function key. For example, in Microsoft Excel, Lotus 1-2-3 or the Microsoft Works Function Key 5 (F5) is the 'Goto' key. Whenever F5 is pressed the system asks for a cell reference or a named cell. When a cell reference or name is entered this immediately becomes the active cell and the screen moves to show the area around it.

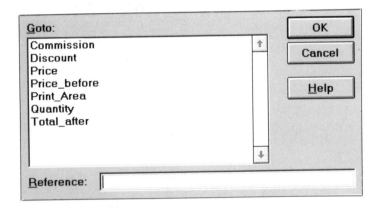

Figure 7.11 Finding named cells in Excel using the 'Goto' function

Protecting cells

Spreadsheets are often used by people who did not design them and who may not understand them properly. This means that an inexperienced user may change the formula in a cell by mistake and ruin the operation of the whole spreadsheet.

To protect important information in spreadsheets, most of them include security features.

Cell protection allows individual cells to be marked so that when the protection is applied their contents cannot be changed – data can only be entered into or changed in unprotected cells. In addition, passwords can be added to individual spreadsheets so that the cell protection cannot be switched off except by an authorised person.

Hidden cells can also be an added security device. If cells are marked as hidden, their formula cannot be seen. The value calculated by the formula still appears in the normal way. This prevents unauthorised users from copying the spreadsheet contents, which may be secret or of some commercial value.

Printing a spreadsheet

Printing a spreadsheet is not quite as easy as printing a document from a word processor because the spreadsheet may be too large to fit on a normal sheet of paper. If your spreadsheet is less than about eight columns by 50 rows, with standard width columns, it should fit on a single sheet of A4 paper. If it is larger than this, the software will divide it up into pages so that it can be joined together later. The way in which this occurs is shown in Figure 7.12.

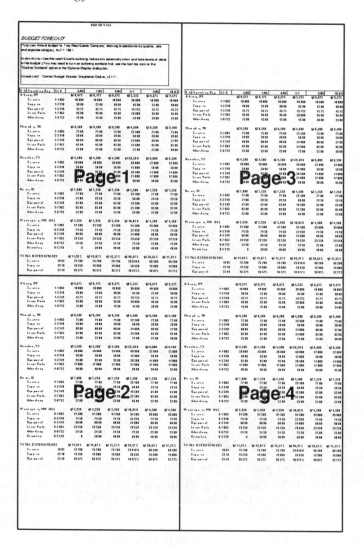

Figure 7.12 Dividing a large spreadsheet into pages for printing

The software first checks the printer settings for the size of the paper and the width of the margins, then works out how many characters can be fitted on each line. If large fonts or wide cells are used, the amount on each line will be reduced. Most software then shows dotted lines on the spreadsheet to indicate the page breaks.

Fitting the paper

If the page breaks prove to be inconvenient, perhaps because one column is put onto a second page, there are a few tricks that can be used to correct the problem.

The first is to ensure that all of the columns are reduced to their minimum width for the data they hold. This reduces the overall width of the sheet.

If that fails, reduce the left margin slightly and try again.

The third option is not available with all software, but it may be possible to scale the whole spreadsheet as it is printed. The software asks how many pages you wish the spreadsheet to cover, then tries to reduce the font size so that it all fits. Unfortunately, this sometimes means that the print is too small to read.

As a last resort, print the spreadsheet on larger paper. This may involve changing to a printer that will accept A3 paper or the standard 'music score' computer paper which is $14\frac{7}{8}''$ wide by 11" long. Take care not to reduce the margins so much that the spreadsheet goes over the perforations between sheets.

Page preview

Before printing the spreadsheet, it always a good idea to look at a preview on the computer screen. This is a feature of most Windows-based software and can save a lot of time and paper.

It is surprising how many faults on a spreadsheet can be spotted by looking at the page preview. Things that are not obvious on the spreadsheet, like missing lines or badly aligned text, show up very clearly. Always use the facility if your software has it, before the final printing.

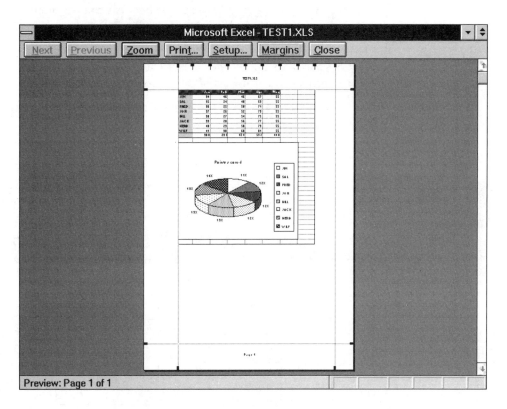

Figure 7.13 'Page preview' facility in Excel

Print area

It is not always necessary to print the whole spreadsheet. If only part if it is required, highlight that part and choose the 'Print area' menu option. Only the selected area will then be printed. However, if you need to print the whole spreadsheet later, you will have to reset the print area.

Review questions

Now you have finished the chapter, see if you can answer the following questions. They cover the work from the second part of the chapter and in particular how it relates to the work of your GNVQ.

1. What could you do if the spreadsheet you need to create is likely to be larger than the size of the paper available? Think of at least two solutions to the difficulty.

2. What is the purpose of a 'Function' in a spreadsheet? Give three examples.

3. How would you copy cell F5 to cells F7 and F8 with the software you normally use?

4. What happens to the cell references when a cell is copied within a spreadsheet?

5. Give two advantages of naming the cells in a spreadsheet? Find out if your software supports this facility and, if it does, how to do it.

6. What is the purpose of cell protection? Give an example of when it might be useful in a spreadsheet you have seen or created yourself.

7. If a small section of a very large spreadsheet has to be printed, what steps are needed to achieve this with your software?

8. Think of a spreadsheet you have already created or may need to create soon as part of your study for another unit. Write down the reason for using a spreadsheet rather than any other means of calculation.

Now complete the exercises in this chapter to make sure you are familiar with the operation of your spreadsheet software.

Exercises

If you have access to some spreadsheet software, the following exercises will give you practice in the main operations required to use it. You also can invent your own exercises and do those related to the work in your GNVQ subjects.

1. Set up the simple spreadsheet shown in Figure 7.14. It represents some of the basic costs of living in a flat while studying at college.

	A	B	C	D
1		Living in a flat		
2				
3	Item		Cost per week	
4				
5	Rent		35	
6	Gas		3.5	
7	Water		2	
8	Electricity		3	
9				
10	Food		19	
11	Clothes		8	
12	Entertainment		9	
13	Books etc.		2	
14	Transport		11	
15				
16	Total		92.5	

Figure 7.14 Calculating the costs of living in a flat

Enter the spreadsheet exactly as it is shown in the figure. The entries are all either text or simple numbers, apart from the one in cell C16, which is a formula. This adds together all of the numbers above it. Enter the formula `=C5+C6+C7+C8+C10+C11+C12+C13+C14`.

If your spreadsheet is Lotus 1-2-3 or something similar you may need to replace the = sign with a + sign.

Now change some of the figures in the list and check that the total changes accordingly.

2. Using the spreadsheet from Question 1, add two of your own lines by adding two extra rows between 8 and 10. Use the 'Insert row' command from the 'Edit' menu while you are highlighting a cell in row 9. The total should now be in row 18.

    Modify the formula in the last line to make it easier to understand. Change it to `=SUM(C5:C17)`. Note that Lotus 1-2-3 and some other spreadsheets will use `@SUM(C5..C17)` instead.

3. The presentation of the spreadsheet can be improved with a few changes. Carry out the following tasks.
    (a) Make the title in cell B1 bold text.
    (b) Change the column headings to italics in row 3.
    (c) All of the numbers in column C represent money, so they can be displayed with two decimal places. Highlight the column from row 5 down and change all the numbers to a format with two decimal places.

4. Add another column to the spreadsheet you used in Question 3. In column D put the title 'Cost per month'. The width of column C may have to be adjusted to ensure that the title can be seen.

    Now add a formula in each cell from D5 down which multiplies the value in the cell on its left by four. For example, in Excel the formula in cell D5 would be `=4*C5`.

5. Enter the spreadsheet in Figure 7.15 into the computer you normally use. It shows the cost of manufacturing a small item from a number of other parts.

	A	B	C	D	E
1		The cost of an assembled item			
2					
3	Part number	Item	Quantity	Price each	Total
4	14452	Box - plastic	1	2.25	2.25
5	17639	Base plate	2	0.33	0.66
6	18634	Screw - 3mm by 12mm	12	0.02	0.24
7	12775	Nut 3mm	10	0.01	0.10
8	14463	Plastic insert	3	0.09	0.27
9	14533	Tube - steel	1	0.21	0.21
10	16680	Tube 82mm plastic	5	0.19	0.95
11	12776	Washers - 3mm	12	0.01	0.12
12	13365	Valve	2	3.66	7.32
13					
14		Total			12.12

Figure 7.15 The cost of an assembled item

Try to produce a neat display as you are entering the information. Use bold and italic text for emphasis. Centre words above columns or place them on the right so that the format looks good. Make sure that all of the numbers have the correct number of decimal places. Change the column widths to fit the widest entry.

Work out the formula to place in the cells in column E so that all of the total costs are calculated automatically. Use a formula to calculate the final total.

6. Using the spreadsheet you created in Question 5, calculate the new cost of the assembly if the prices for everything except the valves increase by 10%.

7. Add three extra rows to your spreadsheet from Question 6, inserting them after row 12. Copy the appropriate formulae into the new cells in column E. Enter some additional parts in the new rows and check that the formula for the total has changed to give the right answer.

8. What formulae would you use for the following calculations?
   (a) Add the numbers in cells B7 and B10
   (b) Add the numbers in cells G3, G5 and G7
   (c) Subtract cell C22 from the sum of cells D5 and D6
   (d) Multiply the contents of cell G4 by 33%
   (e) Divide the contents of cell E6 by the number in cell E12
   (f) Sum all of the cells from G2 to G88

9. Write down the sequence of commands required to print cells D1 to H33 from a much larger spreadsheet.

10. Use the column headings as the name of each of the columns on the spreadsheet. When this is done, how would it change the formulae in the 'Total' column?

Assignment 1
Break-even analysis for a new product

This assignment could provide evidence for the following Performance Criteria of the GNVQ Core Skills:

Element 2.1	PCs 1 to 4
Element 2.2	PCs 1 to 5
Element 2.3	PCs 1, 2, 3 and 5
Element 2.4	PC 4
Element 3.1	PCs 1 to 5
Element 3.2	PCs 1, 2, 3, 4, 5 and 7
Element 3.3	PCs 1,2 , 3, 4 and 6
Element 3.4	PC 5

Introduction

The company you work for have produced two designs for a new type of chair, but they are not sure which one to put into production. The first design costs £40 in material and £25 in labour costs to produce. In addition, the machine to make them costs £9000. The marketing department estimate that the chairs will sell for £85 each.

The second design costs £20 in materials and £18 in labour to produce, but the machine to make it costs £20,350. The marketing people guess that these chairs could sell for £75.

The indirect costs, such as the overheads, advertising and administration, will be the same for both products and can be ignored.

Your task

1. Using your usual software, create a spreadsheet that looks similar to the one in Figure 7.16. The exact format can be varied slightly, and it may be improved with highlighting, etc. All of the entries are either text or numbers, apart from the formulae in cells E10 and E11. The formula in E10 is =B10*(E8-E6-E5)-E4. Work out the correct formula to put in cell E11.

	A	B	C	D	E	F
1		Break-even Analysis				
2						
3					Chair A	Chair B
4	Fixed cost - machine				9000	20350
5	Materials per chair				40	20
6	Labour per chair				25	18
7						
8	Sales income per chair				85	75
9						
10	Sales	0		Profit	-9000	-20350

Figure 7.16 Break-even analysis

Design the layout of your spreadsheet so that it looks neat on the computer screen by using whatever highlights you feel are necessary. Change the text font sizes if you wish.

2. Check the data on your spreadsheet carefully against the original. Now use the spreadsheet to calculate how many of each type of chair should be produced to break even on the investment in the equipment.

3. Find the cell with the number of chairs in it, then work out what would be the profit for each chair if 600 chairs were sold.

4. What would the profit be on each chair if 1000 were sold?

5. How many chairs would need to be sold if each design were to make the same profit?

6. If possible, extend the spreadsheet to create a table showing the profit generated by each design for sales of 100, 200, 300, etc. up to 1000 chairs.

7. Save a copy of the spreadsheet in a suitable directory with a file name of your choice. Make a backup of the file in case the first is lost or damaged.

8. Print the spreadsheet onto A4 paper with a 2.5 cm margin all round it. Do not print any row or column headings, but include grid lines. Check it carefully on screen first to avoid unnecessary printing. Highlight any special features.

9. In your comments list the problems you had while creating the spreadsheet and explain how you overcame them.

Assignment 2
Budget forecast

This assignment could provide evidence for the following Performance Criteria of the GNVQ Core Skills:

Element 2.1	PCs 1 to 4
Element 2.2	PCs 1 to 5
Element 2.3	PCs 1, 2, 3 and 5
Element 2.4	PCs 3 and 4
Element 3.1	PCs 1 to 5
Element 3.2	PCs 1, 2, 3, 4, 5 and 7
Element 3.3	PCs 1, 2, 3, 4 and 6
Element 3.4	PCs 3, 4 and 5

Introduction

A new business has been asked by their bank to provide a cash flow forecast as part of their business plan. This is an indication of when the main income and expenses will occur during the year. It will allow them to predict when their bank account will be in credit and when it will be overdrawn, if everything goes according to plan.

Your task

You have been asked to design a spreadsheet for the business based on the example shown in Figure 7.17. This shows the months of April, May and June but the forecast is required for the whole year.

The following figures are the best estimates at the moment.

Monthly expenses:

Staff salaries	£2100
Rent on premises	£400
Advertising	£200 each in June, September, December and January
Cost of production	£1800 per month, but only £1000 in August
Loan repayments	£900 per month

Monthly income:

Sales	£4000 in April, rising by £400 per month throughout the year, except August, which is expected to be the same as July.

1. Use the spreadsheet in Figure 7.17 as the basis for the design of your own. The basic entries are continued for each of the 12 months of the financial year.

    The figure carried forward to each month is the previous month's balance.

2. Add extra emphasis to the headings and some of the columns to make the important figures stand out.

3. Copy the formulae wherever possible to make the creation of the spreadsheet very

	A	B	C	D	E
1			Cash Flow Forecast		
2			April	May	June
3	INCOME				
4	Carried forward			-1200	-800
5	Sales		4000	4400	4800
6					
7	EXPENDITURE				
8	Staff salaries		2100	2100	2100
9	Rent on Premises		400	400	400
10	Advertising				200
11	Cost of production		1800	1800	1800
12	Loan repayments		900	900	900
13					
14	Total Expenditure		5200	5200	5400
15					
16	BALANCE		-1200	-800	-600
17					

Figure 7.17 Cash flow forecast

simple and less prone to error. When you are happy that the sheet is correct, save it on disk with a suitable filename.

4. Use the spreadsheet to calculate the final balance for the business at the end of March.

5. Calculate the minimum monthly sales in April that will result in a zero balance at the end of the year. Assume that the sales increase by £400 per month except in August as before.

6. Print a copy of the complete spreadsheet. Since it is likely to be too wide to fit on a sheet of A4 paper in portrait mode, print it in landscape mode if possible. Alternatively, find another way of fitting it onto one sheet. Check it carefully on screen before printing it.

7. When the spreadsheet is complete and functioning correctly, save it again and make a backup copy with a different file name on a different disk.

8. Since this could be sensitive information for a business, find out if your software will allow you to protect it with a password. If the facility exists, use it.

Comment on the effects on the efficiency of a business which has its budget forecast on a spreadsheet.

How would the use of a spreadsheet affect the day to day working of the budget holder? Do you think a password facility is necessary? If so, why?

Include a copy of your spreadsheet in your portfolio and find a way of displaying the formulae used. Print these on a separate sheet. Include a directory listing to show the file names used.

CHAPTER 8

Advanced spreadsheets

Objectives

When you have finished this chapter you should be able to:
- Appreciate the use of more advanced spreadsheet functions
- Create a chart from spreadsheet data
- Choose the most appropriate type of chart for different types of information
- Include a chart and numerical data on the same page
- Transfer information between a spreadsheet and a word processor
- Understand the function of a 'macro' used to automate spreadsheet operation
- Correct simple spreadsheet errors

This chapter covers the Performance Criteria and Range from all of the IT Core Skills Elements at levels 2 and 3 related to the preparation, processing and presentation of numbers in spreadsheets, the creation of automated routines, the combination of data from different sources and an evaluation of the techniques used.

Advanced functions

Many spreadsheets need nothing more complicated than addition, subtraction, multiplication and division to do all of their calculations. Even sheets that look very complicated can have a simple underlying structure.

However, there are times when you want to perform an operation with a spreadsheet that cannot be done with basic mathematics. The most common of these occurs when you want to choose between two or more alternatives. This is where the 'IF' function is very useful. Including functions like this where appropriate helps to make spreadsheets more useful and improves their value to a business.

The 'IF' function

Consider the problem for a supplier who produces all the invoices for customers on a spreadsheet. There is a 10% discount for quantities over 20, but no discount for smaller amounts. Part of the invoice spreadsheet is shown in Figure 8.1

The formula that calculates the discount uses an 'IF' function to apply the right deduction. Its format is:

IF(condition, action if condition met, action if not met)

The commas between the condition and the actions are very important.

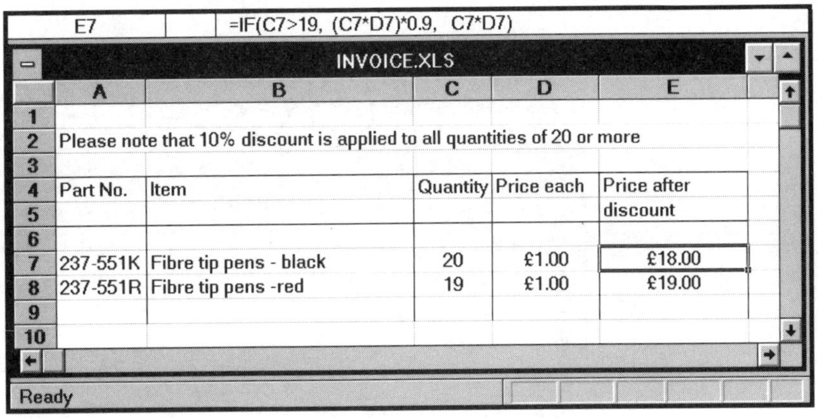

Figure 8.1 Part of an invoice spreadsheet

In cell E7, the formula

```
IF(C7>19, (C7*D7)*0.9, C7*D7)
```

means that if the quantity in cell C7 is over 19, the total price is multiplied by 0.9 to give a 10% discount. If the quantity is not greater than 19 (i.e. is 19 or less) the total price is just the quantity multiplied by the price per item. This means that the same formula can be copied to all the cells in the price column knowing that the correct discount will be applied automatically.

In its basic form, the 'IF' function has many applications where decisions have to be made based upon the values on the sheet. The values may be those entered directly, as in the example above, but they may also be the results of other calculations.

More advanced use of the command can be made if there is more than one choice to be made. The action taken after the first condition can itself be another 'IF' statement. This can lead to some very complicated alternatives. Consider the formula below, which prints the words 'Too high', 'Twenty' or 'Too low', depending upon whether the value in cell G4 is above, equal to or below 20.

```
=IF(G4=20,"Twenty",IF(G4>20,"Too high","Too low"))
```

The 'CHOOSE' function

When more than one alternative is needed, the 'CHOOSE' function can often help to simplify the spreadsheet formulae. This allows one of a number of alternative actions to be taken depending upon the index number in a cell. Its format is as follows:

```
CHOOSE (index number, value 1, value 2, value 3, etc.)
```

The index number must be 1,2,3,4, etc., and the values which result can be cell references, numbers, or text. The index number determines which of the values is chosen. If the index number is 1, the first value is chosen. If the index number is 2, the second value is chosen, etc. For example, if cell B3 contains the number 2, the result of the formula

```
CHOOSE(B3, 12, 20, 50)
```

would be 20. If cell B3 changed to 3, the result would be 50.

Example
Part of a spreadsheet is shown in Figure 8.2. The amount of VAT added to a bill depends upon the type of goods and its VAT rating. These ratings are given the

D7		=CHOOSE(C7, 0, 0.08, 0.175)					

RECEIPT.XLS

	A	B	C	D	E	F	G
1							
2	Electricity Showroom Sales						
3							
4	Quantity	Item	VAT	VAT	Price	VAT	
5			Code	Rate			
6							
7	1	Electric kettle	3	17.5%	£125.00	£21.88	
8	1	"Safe use of electricity" - book	1	0%	£3.50	£0.00	
9							

Figure 8.2 Choosing the correct VAT to add

codes 1, 2, 3 to represent 0%, 8% and 17.5%. When the code is added in the 'VAT Code' column, the correct calculation is carried out automatically. It places the VAT rate in column D, which is then used in the calculation in column F.

Charts from spreadsheet data

Numbers on spreadsheets can often be very difficult to interpret, particularly if you are looking for trends or averages. Sometimes, the actual numbers themselves may not be very important, such as in the results of a survey. The important factor is the percentage of each response compared with the rest.

Consider the following results from a survey:

	Strongly agree	Agree	Disagree	Strongly disagree
Question 1	1205	1497	874	332
Question 2	455	1229	1400	179
Question 3	1019	801	328	795

Each line of figures can be interpreted to see roughly where the peak of the opinion lies, but they do not convey a very accurate impression. This is made worse because different numbers of people have answered each question.

By producing a chart from each of the sets of data, you can get an immediate idea of the results of each question. This is shown in Figure 8.3. A simple line chart has been chosen so that the peak for each question can be easily seen.

It shows, for example, that, although the opinion is fairly strongly in favour of question 1, question 2 has a very balanced response and question 3 has strongly divided opinions. None of these shows up clearly from the figures alone.

Types of chart

Most spreadsheet software includes the facilities to create a wide range of charts from numerical data. The more modern the spreadsheet, the greater the range of charts there is likely to be.

Choosing the best type of chart depends upon:

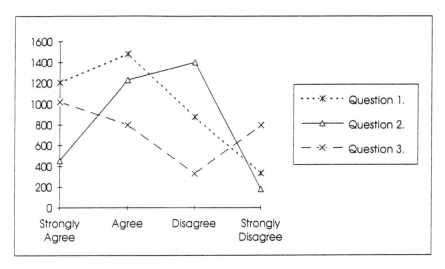

Figure 8.3 Chart prepared from survey results

- the number of sets of values which need to be displayed
- the type of information being displayed
- the capabilities of the software
- personal preference

Although the same data can be displayed in different ways, some charts are much better than others for certain kinds of data. There are many variations of each chart type – bar charts, column charts, pie charts, straight line charts. The main ones are shown in Figure 8.4. Each type may be available as a three-dimensional version showing the same information with some spreadsheets.

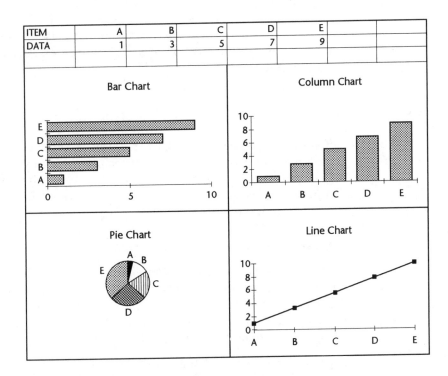

Figure 8.4 Different types of chart available in a spreadsheet

Bar charts and column charts

Bar charts and column charts have a wide range of applications because they can show both the magnitude of each item and the relationship between them. The values of each item in the charts in Figure 8.4 are clearly gradually increasing, and the highest number is about 10. Exact values can be obtained from the charts if a grid is added, or if the exact magnitude is added as a number on the chart.

Pie charts

Pie charts are intended to show the relative values between each item. To plot the chart, the computer adds up all the values, then works out the percentage of the total that each one is. It then divides the circle into the correct percentages. It is impossible to see from the pie chart in Figure 8.4 that the values are 1, 3, 5, 7 and 9 – they could just as easily represent 10, 30, 50, 70 and 90.

Line charts

Line charts can show trends in numbers as well as the exact values. They are more frequently used in mathematical and engineering disciplines although they can be useful in others. If data has to be interpreted mathematically, such as to find out where a line meets the axis, the line chart is the best choice.

Line charts are best for showing the relationship between two quantities. They can be appropriate when a number of quantities have to be displayed together as long as the chart is not overcrowded.

Three-dimensional charts

Three-dimensional charts are available with some systems and may fulfil one of two purposes. They may simply be a more impressive picture of the same set of data as a two-dimensional chart but they may also show on one chart the relationship between three sets of figures or quantities. An example of this is shown in Figure 8.6.

Creating a chart

Different spreadsheet software has slightly different methods of creating a chart, so you may need to check the exact technique with your supervisor. However, the general principles are the same for all systems. If your software supports it, you may find an automatic chart facility called a 'Chart wizard' that will guide you through the steps.

Prepare the data

All spreadsheets expect the data for charts to be held in adjacent cells. Although it is possible to include data from other parts of a sheet, it is much easier to bring the data together, into a separate part of the sheet if necessary. Rather than simply copy the data, use a formula such as '=B6' to copy the data from, for example, cell B6 to the required cell.

Labels for the axes and the values themselves can be plotted automatically if they are in the cells immediately surrounding the data. The x-axis is normally horizontal, and the y-axis is vertical. A 'Series' or row on the spreadsheet creates one line or one set of bars. This format is shown in Figure 8.5. Once the data area has been arranged, it can be highlighted then the command entered to open a new chart.

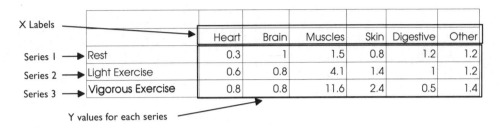

	Heart	Brain	Muscles	Skin	Digestive	Other
Rest	0.3	1	1.5	0.8	1.2	1.2
Light Exercise	0.6	0.8	4.1	1.4	1	1.2
Vigorous Exercise	0.8	0.8	11.6	2.4	0.5	1.4

Figure 8.5 Preferred spreadsheet layout for chart creation

Select the chart type

When a new chart has been opened, the next step is to choose the most appropriate kind of chart for the data. Some of the possibilities are given above but your spreadsheet software may have others, such as Scatter, Radar, and X-Y, etc. It is best to keep the chart as simple as possible so that it is easy to interpret.

The best way to choose the right chart type is to see what each one looks like. Work your way through the 'Gallery' of different types of chart until you find the one that looks best. Remember that some of the charts will be inappropriate because they are not capable of displaying the data in the right form.

Add the title, labels and legend

All charts need some text to explain them to people who see them for the first time. As a minimum, every chart needs a title, but in addition, it is also likely to need labels for the axes. A legend or key may also be helpful to explain what each of the lines or bars represents.

It is very important to add the title and the labels for the axes when the type of chart has been chosen. Without them most charts are meaningless.

If there are a number of lines on the same chart, they will probably need a legend or key to explain what each one represents. If exact values are to be calculated from the chart, it is also a good idea to add some grid lines.

Extra highlights

Some systems allow extra features to be added to a chart for extra emphasis such as text for each data point, arrows to highlight certain features or special colour schemes. If it is appropriate, add these to the chart as a last step.

The chart shown in Figure 8.6 was created from the data in Figure 8.5. Some of the features listed above have been added.

By turning the chart round, other information can be provided, as shown in Figure 8.7.

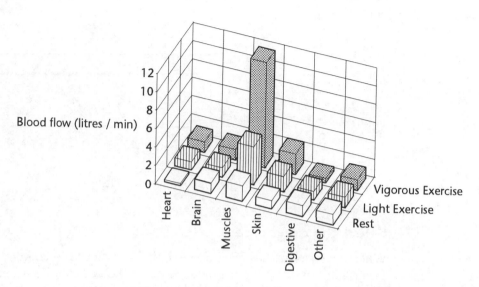

Figure 8.6 Three-dimensional chart prepared from the data in Figure 8.5

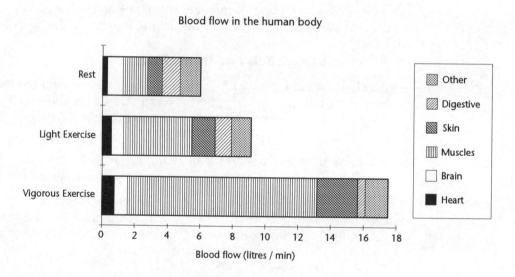

Figure 8.7 Alternative chart from the same data

Placing a chart on a spreadsheet

Since most charts are created from spreadsheet data, it is common to include them on the sheet with the numbers. Some are created automatically. The task is made very simple with Windows-based applications and integrated packages but DOS-based spreadsheets vary in their ability to accept data such as charts from different sources. You may find therefore that they cannot perform this function unless they are very recent versions.

With a Windows-based system, if a chart was created as a separate file, it can be placed on a spreadsheet by opening the chart file and then using the 'Copy' command. This places the chart on the Windows clipboard. From there, the chart can be 'Pasted' onto the required place in the spreadsheet where it can be used to illustrate the data. An example was shown in Figure 8.4.

The advantage of having the chart alongside the data that it represents is that any change in data is immediately shown on the chart. A simple example is shown in Figure 8.8, where the chart represents a relationship between the voltage and current in a transistor. The spreadsheet has been printed without any grid lines between the data and the chart so that each part of the page can be seen clearly.

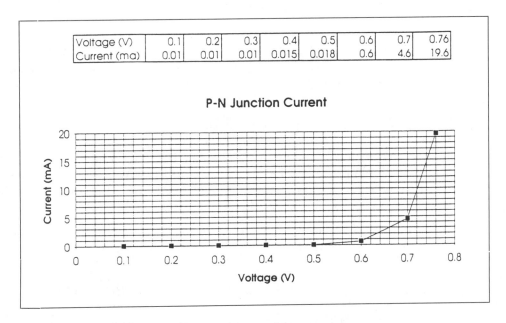

Voltage (V)	0.1	0.2	0.3	0.4	0.5	0.6	0.7	0.76
Current (ma)	0.01	0.01	0.01	0.015	0.018	0.6	4.6	19.6

Figure 8.8 A chart included as part of a spreadsheet

Progress check

Try the following questions before progressing further. They will help you to discover whether you have understood the ideas presented so far in this chapter. They will also prompt you to think about the applications of the techniques to the GNVQ you are studying.

1. What functions are available in the spreadsheet you normally use which allow you to perform calculations based on the time and date? List at least three.

2. Write down at least one example from your own study area of a spreadsheet which may require an 'IF' function.

3. In a pie chart, how many data series can be represented?

4. What would be the most appropriate type of chart for the following types of information?
   (a) The results of an opinion poll, question by question
   (b) The change in the price of a product over a period of time
   (c) The cash flow in a small business.

5. Under what circumstances would you consider using a three-dimensional chart?

6. What is the best way to prepare the data on a spreadsheet if you intend to create a chart based on it?

7. With the spreadsheet you normally use, find out if you can place a chart directly under the spreadsheet data that it is based on. If so, write down the basic commands for future reference.

If you wish to try out some of the techniques described so far in this chapter, turn to the exercises at the end and try the first three questions. You may have some of your own projects you wish to use or some others to do as part of your programme.

Using a spreadsheet as a word processor

Although spreadsheets are not designed to have all the features of a word processor, they can be made to perform some basic text processing. This feature is intended only for the occasions when a paragraph of text would be useful to explain part of a spreadsheet or a chart.

Normally, the text in a cell will spill over into the next empty cell. If a large amount of text is entered, it will simply continue to fill the same row. However, there may be a limit of 250 characters per cell. To make the text appear as a paragraph, the area it has to cover must be highlighted, then it has to be formatted with the 'Justify' command. This breaks up the text into a number of lines and places it on the spreadsheet.

Basic features such as changing the font size may be available, but they are likely to be very limited when compared with a full word processor.

Copying a spreadsheet to a word processed document

If spreadsheet data has to be included as part of a word processed report, it is always best to try and transfer the data rather than enter it manually. This should avoid any transcription errors.

DOS-based systems

It may be difficult to transfer data from some DOS-based spreadsheets such as Lotus 1-2-3 into a word processor. The basic task is to 'export' the information from the required cells into a file which the word processor can read. Lotus has a built-in translation program that can convert files for different types of system. Other software also has similar features, but you will need to check them carefully with your supervisor before attempting to use them.

With a DOS-based word processor it is important to prepare the document in advance. Set up the tabs in the document to the correct width for each of the cell entries on the spreadsheet. It is unlikely that the exact formatting of each cell will transfer with the data but the numbers and text should be accurate. Ensure that the spreadsheet data has tabs between the columns so that it will align correctly with the document tabs. For the best results, use right-justified tabs in the document.

When the document has been prepared, position the cursor, then read the file containing the spreadsheet data into the document at that point.

Integrated packages such as Microsoft Works have all of the links built in to allow transfers between the spreadsheet and the word processor. It is not necessary to create a separate file. However, it is still a good idea to prepare the document before the data is transferred by ensuring that the insertion point is in the right place.

The same principles apply when transferring data to other applications such as desktop publishing packages. It is vital to set up the tabs on the page to receive the data before it is transferred otherwise some very unpredictable results may occur.

Windows-based systems

It is a very simple matter to transfer data between different Windows-based packages. However, the precise formatting of a spreadsheet may not always be transferred to a word processor.

For example, in a spreadsheet the text in a cell spills into the next empty cell on the right. When the same information is transferred to a document the text in each cell will probably form a few lines. The exact format varies between different word processors. This problem was highlighted in Chapter 4.

Placing a chart in a document

Charts can illustrate some types of report far better than a lot of numerical information. They can save a lot of writing if they can be included in the body of a report. Unfortunately, some of the more common software packages do not make the process of including charts all that easy.

It is almost impossible to place a chart created by a spreadsheet into a document produced with a DOS-based word processor. The easiest way is to print the chart and glue it in a suitable space later! Even with some versions of integrated packages such as Microsoft Works, the word processor only shows a 'place holder' where the chart will appear instead of the chart itself. This means that it is impossible to see what size the chart will be and how the complete page will look.

Fortunately, in a Windows-based system the process is much easier, but it is still not without problems. In some word processors, such as Ami-Pro, it is best to create a frame for the chart to go in first. The chart then appears in the document exactly as it will appear on the page when printed. Its size and position can be adjusted if necessary.

With other word processors, a chart may appear only as a 'place holder' in the document, which can be seen only if the page preview facility is used.

The chart can be transformed within Windows either through the 'Copy' and 'Paste' method or by the 'Insert object' function. The advantage of inserting an 'object' is that it can be linked to the spreadsheet data that created it. For example, if a standard sales report is required every month, the chart in the document can be linked directly to the spreadsheet. This means that when the data for the spreadsheet changes, the chart in the document changes with it.

Worked example

Illustrating the costs in a business

INTRODUCTION

A small business starts the year with stock worth £38,000. The following projections for the business sales and costs over the next 12 months have been made:

Sales   £108,000
Purchases   £60,000
Closing Stock   £50,000
Direct Labour   £32,000
Overheads   £10,360

The business profit can be calculated from the following relationships:
  (a) Cost of goods sold = purchases + direct labour + (opening stock – closing stock)
  (b) Gross profit = sales – cost of goods sold
  (c) Net profit = gross profit – overheads.

PROBLEM

You have been asked to illustrate the figures above with a small pie chart showing the cost of goods sold, the overheads and the net profit. These should add up to the same value as the total sales.

1. First, produce a simple spreadsheet that includes each of the figures above and the correct formulae to calculate the others.

2. From the spreadsheet, plot a pie chart with any additional annotation you consider necessary.

3. Use the chart to illustrate a report on the business profitability.

SOLUTION

1. The first task is to enter the values into a spreadsheet. This is illustrated in Figure 8.9, where the formulae have been shown which calculate the required information.

	A	B	C
1	Business Projections - April to March		
2			
3	Sales	£108,000	
4			
5	Opening stock	£38,000	
6	Closing Stock	£50,000	
7	Purchases	£60,000	
8	Direct Labour	£32,000	
9			
10	Cost of goods sold	=B7+B8+(B5-B6)	
11	Overheads	£10,360	
12	Gross profit	=B3-B10	
13	Net Profit	=B12-B11	

Figure 8.9 Business calculations using a spreadsheet

2. The data needed for the pie chart has been arranged in a block to make it easy to plot the chart automatically. First highlight the data, then choose 'New chart' from

the menu. Some spreadsheets may include a 'Chart wizard' to guide you through the steps required.

Select a chart from the menu and check that it contains all the required information. Add a title and a legend if one is not created automatically.

3. Once the chart has been produced, it must be included in the report document. The document can be created with a word processor, preferably Windows based, and the chart can then be placed on the page in the right place using one of the methods described above.

The easiest method is to select the complete chart, then choose 'Copy' from the 'Edit' menu. This stores the chart on the windows clipboard. Change to the word processor and open the document required if it is not already open. Move the insertion point to the required place, then select 'Paste' from the 'Edit' menu. This transfers the chart to the page of the document.

Part of the completed page is shown in Figure 8.10.

PROJECTIONS FOR YEAR 2
The projected sales for the second year of trading look reasonably healthy taking into account the difficult trading conditions and the new products under development.

The following chart illustrates the projected business costs and profits.

Business costs

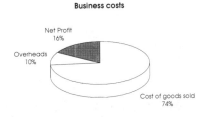

The gross profit at 26% should provide a good return for the investments made as long as the projected volume can be maintained. Overheads are estimated to be 10% of income and will need to be kept under control if the expansion is to be maintained without undue erosion of profits.

Figure 8.10 Report from a spreadsheet including a chart

Using a spreadsheet as a database

A database and a spreadsheet are very similar in many ways. A database can easily be laid out as a table, so that the rows each contain one of the database records. The columns represent the fields of the database. If each one has a heading, this can be used for the field name. Look at the example in Figure 8.11.

The information in the figure is part of a database of personnel records which has been created on a spreadsheet. Each row contains the record for one person, while the columns represent the various fields. One disadvantage of this simple

	A	B	C	D	E	F
1	Employee	Last Name	First Name	Title	Birth Date	Hire Date
2	1	Davolio	Nancy	Sales Representative	08-Dec-48	29-Mar-91
3	2	Fuller	Andrew	Vice President, Sales	19-Feb-42	12-Jul-91
4	3	Leverling	Janet	Sales Representative	30-Aug-63	27-Feb-91
5	4	Peacock	Margaret	Sales Representative	19-Sep-37	30-Mar-92
6	5	Buchanan	Steven	Sales Manager	04-Mar-55	13-Sep-92
7	6	Suyama	Michael	Sales Representative	02-Jul-63	13-Sep-92
8	7	King	Robert	Sales Representative	29-May-60	29-Nov-92
9	8	Callahan	Laura	Inside Sales Coordinator	09-Jan-58	30-Jan-93
10	9	Dodsworth	Anne	Sales Representative	27-Jan-66	12-Oct-93
11	10	Hellstern	Albert	Business Manager	13-Mar-60	01-Mar-93
12	11	Smith	Tim	Mail Clerk	06-Jun-73	15-Jan-93
13	12	Patterson	Caroline	Receptionist	11-Sep-72	15-May-93
14	13	Brid	Justin	Marketing Director	08-Oct-62	01-Jan-94
15	14	Martin	Xavier	Marketing Associate	30-Nov-60	15-Jan-94
16	15	Pereira	Laurent	Advertising Specialist	09-Dec-65	01-Feb-94

Figure 8.11 A spreadsheet being used as a database

system is that only a few fields can be seen on the screen at once. Each field may also be limited to 250 characters.

Database commands

Spreadsheets usually include several commands that allow the data in the rows to be manipulated as a database. However, before they can be used, the area that the database covers on the spreadsheet has to be defined. It is normal to define the database area by highlighting it, including all of the column names, then selecting the 'Set database' command.

Extracting data

Once the database is defined it can be used to perform some basic operations such as selecting data to meet certain criteria. This is achieved by creating a new area of the spreadsheet with selection criteria under the selected field names. The data to be extracted from the database appears in another area of the spreadsheet, called the 'Extract' area. This technique is sometimes called 'Query by example' or 'QBE'.

An example is shown in Figure 8.12, where all of the employees with names beginning with P and Birth date after 1-Jan-1960 have been selected from the database.

Rows 19 and 20 have been set up as the 'Set criteria' rows.
The two criteria can be seen in cells B20 and E20.

The data extracted as a result of the query is given in rows 26 to 28.

Other features

The use of a spreadsheet as a database has many practical applications, particularly where most of the data being stored is numeric, but some vital fields contain characters. Most spreadsheets allow other operations to be performed, such as sorting the records into alphabetic or numeric order. They also allow easy finding and deleting of data.

	A	B	C	D	E
1	Employee ID	Last Name	First Name	Title	Birth Date
2	1	Davolio	Nancy	Sales Representative	08-Dec-48
3	2	Fuller	Andrew	Vice President, Sales	19-Feb-42
4	3	Leverling	Janet	Sales Representative	30-Aug-63
5	4	Peacock	Margaret	Sales Representative	19-Sep-37
6	5	Buchanan	Steven	Sales Manager	04-Mar-55
7	6	Suyama	Michael	Sales Representative	02-Jul-63
8	7	King	Robert	Sales Representative	29-May-60
9	8	Callahan	Laura	Inside Sales Coordinator	09-Jan-58
10	9	Dodsworth	Anne	Sales Representative	27-Jan-66
11	10	Hellstern	Albert	Business Manager	13-Mar-60
12	11	Smith	Tim	Mail Clerk	06-Jun-73
13	12	Patterson	Caroline	Receptionist	11-Sep-72
14	13	Brid	Justin	Marketing Director	08-Oct-62
15	14	Martin	Xavier	Marketing Associate	30-Nov-60
16	15	Pereira	Laurent	Advertising Specialist	09-Dec-65
17					
18					
19	Employee ID	Last Name	First Name	Title	Birth Date
20		P			>1-jan-60
21					
22	Employee ID	Last Name	First Name	Title	Birth Date
23	12	Patterson	Caroline	Receptionist	11-Sep-72
24	15	Pereira	Laurent	Advertising Specialist	09-Dec-65

Figure 8.12 Data extracted from a spreadsheet database

The database facility can be particularly useful if data needs to be looked up in a table. The database can contain all of the reference information and selected records can be taken from it for other parts of the spreadsheet. These may then be used in calculations.

For example, the prices for a range of goods could be kept in a spreadsheet. When the name of an item is entered, it is first looked up in the database, then its price can be transferred automatically to an order form.

Automatic operations

Some spreadsheets and other types of software have a built-in programming language. This means that advanced users can write routines that make the spreadsheet perform certain operations automatically. The program is generally known as a 'macro'.

For example, one of the regular tasks for a business manager may be to collect the monthly information on sales figures and compile them into a report for a meeting. The task may involve opening a number of other spreadsheets to collect the right data. If the figures are arranged in the same format each month the whole process can be automated, so saving a lot of time.

It may not even be necessary to write a special macro to do it. Some systems allow a sequence of actions to be 'recorded' and the software then writes the program itself. This means that people without any programming experience can automate common tasks.

Simple macros

A macro can be treated as a separate but related spreadsheet that contains a list of commands for the system. The commands can often be started by pressing a sequence of keys, known as the 'hot keys'.

The macro shown in Figure 8.13 was written for the Microsoft Excel spreadsheet. Its function is to select part of a spreadsheet for printing, then print it. All of the lines were written by the system as the actions to be repeated were recorded. The comments on the right were added later. Each line of the macro is the equivalent of a command, so when the 'hot keys' are pressed each one is executed in turn. When it is finished, the last macro command returns the user to whatever operation was being done when the macro started. The 'hot key' in this case is 'Control + A'. Whenever these keys are pressed the macro runs.

Print table (a)	- The MACRO name and Hot Key (Ctrl + a)
=OPEN("C:\EXCEL\BREAKEVN.XLS")	- Opens the required spreadsheet
=SELECT("R12C4:R26C6")	- Select Row 12, Column 4 to Row 26, Column 6
=SET.PRINT.AREA()	- Set the Print Area
=PRINT(1,,,1,FALSE,FALSE,1,FALSE,1)	- Print data (each entry in ( ) is a menu option)
=SAVE()	- Save the file
=FILE.CLOSE()	- Close the file
=RETURN()	- Return to the previous operation

Figure 8.13 Macro, which, when run, will print part of a spreadsheet

Correcting errors

Complicated spreadsheets are quite likely to contain errors if they have not been properly checked and tested. Simple mistakes in presentation can easily be corrected by careful observation, but it is surprising how many spreadsheets still have problems.

Formatting

Check the formatting and alignment of both text and numbers in cells, and the numbers of decimal places displayed. These are often the cause of poor presentation.

Check formulae

The main cause of numerical errors is the fact that the formulae are invisible so only their results can be seen. If the results are not obviously incorrect, errors can go undetected for a long time.

Keep the formulae as simple as possible. Most systems will not allow an incomplete formula to be entered, but they cannot check that the results are what were intended. By double clicking the mouse on a cell, some systems highlight the cells involved in formula. This makes checking much easier.

Use test data

It is always a good idea to test any spreadsheet which you create by inserting known data first. This may be numbers which can be easily checked, such as 1, 10 or 100. If choices are made in certain cells, put in numbers which will force different choices to be made.

Circular references

If a formula depends upon a number in another cell, which in turn depends upon the first number, it is said to be a 'circular reference'. The spreadsheet software normally cannot calculate such formulae. Most cases are not as simple as only two cells. There may be a very complex relationship between many different formulae on the same sheet. The usual way to resolve such problems is to slowly work backwards from one cell, carefully checking all of the formulae until the error is located.

Copying cells

Always take special care when copying cells. If a formula is copied, the cell references will change unless 'absolute' cell references are used. Check that a $ sign is placed before any cell reference which must stay the same wherever the formula happens to be on the spreadsheet.

Printing problems

Most small spreadsheets are easy to print, but as the size increases so do the problems. Be prepared to stick pages together if a large sheet has to be printed. Alternatively, use the reduction feature available in some systems to reduce the print size and squeeze it all on one sheet. Always try to use the 'Page preview' feature to check a sheet before printing. This can save a lot of wasted time. Sometimes altering the page margins may help to fit a few extra lines or characters on a page, but the sheet will look untidy if the margins are too small.

Review questions

These questions are intended to cover the last part of the chapter and relate the use of a spreadsheet to the other work you are doing at the moment.

1. A spreadsheet can be used as both a database and a word processor. How would you choose the most appropriate piece of applications software for a certain task?

2. What limitations does your normal spreadsheet have when creating blocks of text?

3. How would you include a large section of text created by a word processor into a spreadsheet, using your normal software?

4. In a DOS-based system, what limitations are you likely to encounter when trying to transfer a spreadsheet into a word processed document? How might these be overcome?

5. A report which covers several pages has to be typed and needs a chart on page 5. Briefly describe which of your normal software packages you would need to achieve this, and how you would go about it.

6. Think of at least three ways in which a spreadsheet could improve the efficiency of the work in a small business related to your area of study. How might it be used to save time, reduce costs or improve accuracy?

7. Complete the following by choosing one of the answers below. The columns in a spreadsheet can be thought of as:
   (a) the records of a database
   (b) the data of a database
   (c) the fields of a database
   (d) the data types in a database.

8. What database features can you find in the spreadsheet software you have access to?

9. What is the function of a 'macro' and why might it be useful? Give some examples of how a macro may be used.

10. What could be done to fit a spreadsheet onto an A4 sheet of paper if it is slightly too large?

Exercises

These exercises are designed to provide a means of practising some of the techniques described in the chapter. Use the software available on your usual computer as far as possible. It may not be possible to all of the exercises with every software package. The assignments require more investigation and application of the principles to the work of your GNVQ.

1. Look at the information on the spreadsheet in Figure 8.14. The first two columns are figures that have been entered directly. The third column is the greater of the first two numbers. The fourth column is the sum of the first three.

	A	B	C	D
1	Number A	Number B	Greatest	SUM
2	12.5	12.6	12.6	37.7
3	3.0	2.6	3.0	8.6
4	18.0	17.0	18.0	53.0
5	22.0	24.0	24.0	70.0
6	8890.0	8890.0	8890.0	26670.0
7	34.0	30.0	34.0	98.0

Figure 8.14 Simple spreadsheet

Work out the correct formulae to place in the third and fourth columns to ensure that all of the entries are exactly as shown. Make sure the number of decimal places is set to the same value and that the column headings are highlighted in the same way. Enter your own numbers to test the system.

2. The figures in Figure 8.15 represent the data on the destinations from a course in a college. It shows the number of students who progress to higher education, those who get jobs, those who are unemployed and those whose destination is unknown. Produce a simple pie chart from the figures to show this data more graphically. Add a suitable title and ensure that the percentage figures for each sector are calculated.

If your software allows it, include the chart just below the data on the spreadsheet itself.

Course destinations			
HE	Job	Unemployed	Unknown
17	12	4	3

Figure 8.15 Destinations of students graduating from a course

Try a three-dimensional chart using the same data.

3. The data in Figure 8.16 has been collected after a science experiment on cooling using different surfaces. Plot the results on a chart clearly showing the three separate lines on the same axes. Include a legend to identify each one.

Time (sec)	Temperature		
	A	B	C
0	150.0	150.0	150.0
20	97.5	90.0	80.7
40	49.4	54.0	44.5
60	33.1	39.0	32.3
80	24.8	34.9	26.1
100	19.9	31.9	22.4
120	16.6	30.0	19.9
140	14.2	28.5	18.2
160	12.5	27.5	16.8
180	11.1	26.6	15.8
200	10.0	26.0	15.0
220	9.1	25.4	14.3
240	8.3	25.0	13.7
260	7.7	24.6	13.3
280	7.1	24.3	12.8
300	6.7	24.0	12.5
320	6.2	23.7	12.2
340	5.9	23.5	11.9
360	5.5	23.3	11.7

Figure 8.16 Experimental results

4. Use the chart created for Question 3 to illustrate a report on the cooling of different materials. The report consists of an opening paragraph as given below, followed by the table of results and the chart.

    Introduction
    The temperature of each of the three samples A, B, and C, was raised to 150 degrees by immersing it in an oil bath for about 15 minutes. When a stable temperature had been reached, the samples were removed and allowed to cool in a temperature controlled chamber held at 4 degrees. Readings of the sample temperature were taken every 20 seconds for a period of 6 minutes.

    Results

    (Insert table and chart from Question 3 here.)

5. Enter the data from the spreadsheet in Figure 8.11 into your own computer. Add some extra names or simplify the data if you would like to. Make sure that there are at least ten entries.

(a) Use the database facilities of your software to rearrange all of the entries into alphabetical order. This may require you to highlight the whole data block then use the 'Sort' command.

(b) Set up a 'selection criteria' area similar to that shown in Figure 8.12. Copy the headings, then highlight them and select the 'Set criteria' command or its equivalent.

(c) Set up an area to receive the extracted data below the 'criteria' by copying the headings and using the 'Set extract' command or its equivalent.

(d) Extract the records which meet the following criteria:
   (i) Last name beginning with B
   (ii) Born before 1-Jan-1960
   (iii) Sales representative hired after 1-Jan-1992.

6. Use your normal word processor to enter the following paragraph, then extract the data from the spreadsheet in Question 5 to include in the report. There is no need to copy all of the spreadsheet, just the records selected as part of the selection criteria for part (d) (ii).

```
The Sales representatives who are under the age of 35
tend to achieve better results. They seem to have more
drive, although the experience of the older staff can in
some circumstances make up for the lack of energy. They
know a few of the short cuts to making a quick sale,
learned from years of trial and error. If we choose one
of the older staff for promotion, the following
candidates should be considered
```

(Enter the data on staff born before 1960 here.)

7. One of the regular office tasks requires the sales figures for a couple of branch offices to be assembled into a single spreadsheet. Because the task has to be done every week, it is a good application for a 'macro'.

Create a simple macro, using the 'Macro recording' feature of your spreadsheet, if it has one, to copy the data from each of the spreadsheets shown below onto a new one automatically. The new sheet, called 'Region', automatically adds together the results from the other two spreadsheets and places the result below the two other entries.

	A	B	C	D	E
1	York				
2		Week 1	Week 2	Week 3	Week 4
3	Art materials	560	412	690	512
4	Books	200	185	300	98
5	Frames	750	900	200	310
6	Prints	1200	954	233	490
7	Originals	380	790	430	1390
8		3090	3241	1853	2800

	A	B	C	D	E
1	Leeds				
2		Week 1	Week 2	Week 3	Week 4
3	Art materials	450	278	390	600
4	Books	177	59	280	184
5	Frames	390	700	850	400
6	Prints	990	277	1230	760
7	Originals	700	500	399	750
8		2707	1814	3149	2694

Figure 8.17 Sales spreadsheets

Assignment 1
Choosing the best type of chart

This assignment could provide evidence for the following Performance Criteria of the GNVQ Core Skills:

Element 2.1   PCs 1 to 4

Element 2.2   PCs 1 to 6

Element 2.3   PCs 1 to 5

Element 2.4   PCs 2 and 3

Element 3.1   PCs 1 to 5

Element 3.2   PCs 1 to 7

Element 3.3   PCs 1 to 6

Element 3.4   PCs 2 to 4

Introduction

Prices for most products vary throughout the year, but only by looking at a chart showing the variations can the trends be easily seen.

Most spreadsheets can create a number of different types of chart for the same data. However, some charts are better than others for displaying certain types of data clearly. There is not always a right and wrong choice for a chart.

Your task

The data from the spreadsheet in Figure 8.18 has to be displayed in the best possible way, in a chart complete with a title, labelled axes and a key. However, a chart can only be chosen once all the possibilities have been investigated.

1. Enter the data from the figure into your own spreadsheet. Check it carefully against the original for accuracy and correct any mistakes.

2. Create at least three different types of chart from the same data and save them all on disk. Make sure that the axes are labelled, that there is a title and that there is a key. Print out each chart on a separate sheet of paper. Before doing so, make sure that the page formatting is correct by using the 'Page preview' facility if it is available with your software.

Briefly write under each chart what you think are the good and bad points about the type of chart chosen. From your comments draw your own conclusions about which is the best choice for the data. Comment briefly on how the same results could have been obtained by alternative means.

Price variation over a year											
Jan	Feb	Mar	Apr	May	Jun	Jul	Aug	Sep	Oct	Nov	Dec
17.5	18.9	24.5	22.1	18.4	29.9	48.7	63.9	61.3	50.4	61.9	53.5

Figure 8.18 Chart data

Assignment 2
Compiling a report with a table and charts

This assignment could provide evidence for the following Performance Criteria of the GNVQ Core Skills:

Element 2.1	PCs 1 to 4
Element 2.2	PCs 1 to 6
Element 2.3	PCs 1 to 5
Element 2.4	PCs 1 to 3
Element 3.1	PCs 1 to 5
Element 3.2	PCs 1 to 7
Element 3.3	PCs 1 to 6
Element 3.4	PCs 1 to 5

Introduction

The customers at a new theme park have been asked their opinions in a questionnaire about each of the features of the park. The results have been analysed into a table by the park manager who has asked you to help produce a report for the directors of the company. The report has to include both the table and a series of charts to illustrate the figures.

The results of the survey are given in Figure 8.19.

Results of the theme park customer survey

Ride	Loved it	Liked it	OK	Disliked it	Hated it
Monster Looper	231	180	117	65	70
High Rapids	50	212	359	87	99
House of Horrors	38	75	191	226	164
Round and About	126	316	267	71	20

Figure 8.19 Results of the theme park customer survey

Your task

1. The report for the directors must include a short explanation of the way in which the survey was conducted. This must be written on a word processor but needs only to be a few paragraphs long. It should contain your ideas on how to perform such a survey. Use you usual word processor to write the introductory paragraphs.

   Note the font and its size so that the same style can be used in the rest of the document.

2. Use a spreadsheet to enter the data from the survey data. This will be used to create the charts.

3. Find the appropriate cells, then transfer the data from the spreadsheet table to the

word processor. Place it into the final report after the introductory paragraphs. If your word processor has a built-in table feature, this could also be used for the data but it may be more difficult to create the charts.

4. Create four bar charts, one for each of the features in the table. Each one needs its own title. They can be saved with different file names if necessary.

5. Include the four charts in the report so that they each occupy about a quarter of a page.

6. Check that the format of the text, table and charts is similar. Save, then print the final report. Choose the most appropriate orientation and page size for the type of presentation chosen.

7. Discuss ways in which the presentation of the data could be improved. What limitations were the result of the software packages that were used? List any errors which occurred and how you corrected them.

Assignment 3
Designing a cash flow forecast spreadsheet

This assignment could provide evidence for the following Performance Criteria of the GNVQ Core Skills:

Element 2.1	PCs 1 to 4
Element 2.2	PCs 1 to 6
Element 2.3	PCs 1, 2, 3 and 5
Element 2.4	PCs 1 to 4
Element 3.1	PCs 1 to 5
Element 3.2	PCs 1 to 7
Element 3.3	PCs 1, 2, 3, 4 and 6
Element 3.4	PCs 1 to 5

Introduction

In business, it is very important to plan income and expenditure as far as possible at the start of a financial year. Every month a check can be made to see how much progress has been made towards the business objectives and whether or not the budget is being met. The normal method of doing this is to prepare a budget spreadsheet with columns for 'Budget' and 'Actual' income and expenditure each month. An example for the first few months of a financial year is shown in Figure 8.20

Your task

1. Copy the spreadsheet from Figure 8.20 into a new file using your usual software. It will need to be extended later to cover all of the months of the year, but you should be able to do this by copying the column for the first month.

Cash flow forecast

Month	April		May	
	Budget	*Actual*	*Budget*	*Actual*
Receipts				
Sales (inc VAT)				
Other income				
Loans received				
Capital introduced				
Total Receipts	0	0	0	0
Payments				
Cash Purchases				
Wages/Salaries				
PAYE				
Capital items				
Rent/Rates				
Loan repayments				
Bank charges				
Advertising				
VAT				
Dividends				
Total Payments	0	0	0	0
Net Cash flow	0	0	0	0
Opening Bank Balance			0	0
Closing Bank Balance	0	0	0	0

Figure 8.20 Spreadsheet for forecasting cash flow

2. Work out what formulae are required in the 'Total receipts', 'Total payments', and 'Net cash flow' rows. The 'Opening bank balance' row represents the cash available at the start of the month, and 'Closing balance' is the 'Opening balance' plus or minus the 'Net cash flow'. The closing balance for one month is of course the opening balance for the next.

3. Enter all of the formulae into the 'April' column on the spreadsheet. Format the cells as required for currency, with no decimal places, right-justified data and with borders.

4. When the first column is correctly formatted, copy the contents across the spreadsheet to create 13 columns altogether, one for each month and one for the totals.

5. In the last two columns, a formula is required on each row, to add together each monthly entry for the 'Budget' or 'Actual' columns.

6. When the whole blank spreadsheet is complete, save it as a new file so that it could be used again if necessary. Then enter some test figures into the cells. Choose simple numbers. The actual values are not important, but the correct results are. For example, if only one entry is made for income in the first month, this should be seen to affect all of the 'Bank balance' figures throughout the year. Thoroughly test the spreadsheet by placing test figures in all of the areas that will result in other changes. Make sure that everything works correctly.

7. When you have entered a number of figures throughout the spreadsheet, print it in the most appropriate way. It may be necessary to use a page in landscape format or

reduce it to fit it on one page. Alternatively, print it on two or more pages and stick them together.

Comment on the benefits and the problems of using a spreadsheet for this type of activity. If there are any efficiency gains through the use of IT, explain what they are. Include your spreadsheet in a report showing at least two sets of numbers which give different cash flow projections throughout the year.

CHAPTER 9

Graphics

Objectives

When you have finished this chapter you should be able to:
- Appreciate the importance of graphics in business
- Appreciate the range of graphics available
- Use a graphics package to create a simple image
- Understand how to use graphic tools to draw lines, circles, rectangles, and fill them as required
- Know how to create more complex images by using the computer facilities to mirror, scale and copy images
- Appreciate the range of images available commercially via line art libraries
- Understand the need for specialist graphics packages in various businesses
- Understand how to include a graphic image to a document
- Appreciate the value of a scanner to import images for processing
- Understand the benefits of a desktop publishing package
- Compare the advantages of IT-based graphics systems with traditional methods

This chapter covers the Performance Criteria and Range from all of the IT Core Skills Elements at levels 2 and 3 related to the preparation, processing and presentation of graphic images, their creation and manipulation, the combination with other types of data and an evaluation of the systems used.

Graphics in business

We are surrounded by pictures in many different forms. Television, newspapers, magazines, books, computer graphics, notices, and advertisements all carry many pictures which are designed to catch our attention. Because pictures are so good at conveying ideas and impressions, it is almost as important to be able to use them effectively as it is to be able to write clearly. One illustration can save a lot of words.

Computers have now become powerful enough to be able to process pictures almost as quickly as text. With modern software, all sorts of graphics can be included in documents, databases and spreadsheets. Special programs can display three-dimensional drawings, colour photographs, and even video or television pictures on a computer screen. Many businesses rely upon the ability of a computer to mix text and graphics.

Commercial applications

Some of the ways in which graphics are used in business are:

- *Company logos* for an immediately recognisable identity – think of Pepsi, Banks, British Telecom, etc.
- *Product packaging* to give a brand identity or simply to draw attention to the product
- *Advertising material* printed adverts in magazines, newspapers, buses, tube trains, carrier bags
- *Notices* graphical instructions are easier to follow than written ones
- *Technical illustrations* plans and drawings of technical objects are vital in many businesses.

Graphics help to break up pages of text to make them easier to read and therefore keep the reader's attention. They also serve a very important function of communicating information that is not easy to convey with words alone. For example, a chart can display the relationship between two or more quantities which may be very difficult to describe. The graphics in the advertisements of a company may convey a message which is never written down.

Graphics packages

Until recently, it was difficult to process graphic images on a desktop computer. The computer power needed for graphics meant that they could be processed only very slowly. However, modern computers allow complex pictures to be processed very quickly. Generally, graphics have to be created with special applications programs, which have a range of special 'tools' to deal with pictures. These pictures can then be combined with text using a word processor or a desktop publishing package.

Many of the most recent word processors now include a graphics system so that images can be added to documents more easily. They can either be created as part of the document or imported from one of the many graphics systems available.

Types of graphics

Many types of image are referred to as 'graphics', and they each have certain applications. The most common types are line art, photographs, diagrams, charts, technical drawings and video images.

Line art

Some examples of line art are shown in Figure 9.1. Line images are pictures drawn with a basic drawing package, and can be used in all types of basic illustration. Although many examples of line art are in black and white, they can be full colour illustrations. One of the advantages of basic line art is that if the image is not quite right for the job in hand, it can be modified slightly to make it better, with some types of software.

Line art libraries are often provided with a word processor package, and they can also be supplied on CD-ROM. A single CD-ROM can hold thousands of line art images which can be added to documents to make them more interesting. Images can be used in newspaper articles as cartoons, in advertising material, as illustrations in presentations to add some interest, and in many other ways.

Figure 9.1 Examples of line art

Photographs

Photographs have been processed electronically by newspapers for many years, but now that desktop computers have become very fast they have the necessary speed to be able to manipulate photographic images. Photographs have to be converted into digital format before they can be processed by computer software. This may be achieved with an optical scanner, with a special digital camera or with a video capture system.

For most users, the usual way of converting a photograph to a suitable digital form is to use a scanner. Some scanners are basic hand-held devices little larger than a mouse, but others are desktop versions which can scan the whole of an A4 page at once. They need special software to drive them, such as Micrografix Picture Publisher or Adobe PhotoShop, which provides the facilities to manipulate the images once they have been captured.

One problem with the use of photographs is the size of the files which they generate. The more complex the picture, and the higher the resolution, the larger the file is likely to be. Simple black and white photographs can occupy up to about 1 MByte, while full colour pictures may be 30 MBytes or more. This means that only computers with very large memories and fast processors can manipulate them quickly. Others have to manipulate the image by writing parts of it to disk, which can be a very slow process. The same problems occur if the photograph has to be inserted into a document. The process can be very slow.

The best advice when dealing with photographs is to keep them small, and to use the fastest computer you can, with the largest amount of memory possible.

Figure 9.2 A photograph after scanning

Diagrams

Basic diagrams are required for many purposes, and can be created either with the built-in facilities of a word processor or with a special drawing package. The graphics feature of word processors is sufficient for most drawings such as flow diagrams, structure charts, simple mechanical drawings, building layouts and instructions.

Figure 9.3 shows the drawing facilities that are built into the Ami-Pro word processor.

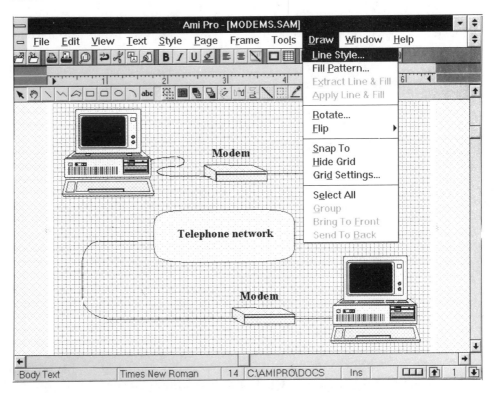

Figure 9.3 Drawing a diagram within a word processor

The menu of special features needed for drawing appears as soon as the 'Drawing' icon is clicked. The main items are designed to help with basic drawings using boxes and circles rather than the freehand artistic type of drawing (although these are possible). Careful use of the features allows diagrams to be created with various line types, text of various sizes, colour and fill patterns. They can be added over the top of text on a page if necessary. If lines have to be in fixed places on a page, so that they all line up for example, a grid can be added which makes all the lines snap into place.

Charts

Charts or graphs are generally used to illustrate sets of figures. They can be created within some word processing packages, but most often they are created by spreadsheet software. Modern spreadsheets are capable of a wide variety of different types of chart – these were covered in Chapter 8.

Some charts can be enhanced with special charting software such as Corel Chart. This adds enhanced graphics to the basic chart format so that the images can be made more relevant. For example, a chart showing CD sales might be made from stacks of CDs.

Technical drawings

Companies in engineering, construction and manufacture all depend upon computer aided design (CAD) systems to create vital technical drawings. This may be electrical diagrams, mechanical engineering drawings of components, architects' drawings of a new building, factory layouts, maintenance schedules, etc. Very few engineering businesses can now work without needing a technical drawing facility.

The most widely used CAD software is called AutoCad. It can be used to draw virtually anything in two or three dimensions. Its popularity stems from the fact that it can be customised by specialist companies for certain applications. For example, special systems exist to make it easy to design buildings, boats, structural steel work, drainage systems, maps, etc.

One of the newest features of CAD systems is their ability to draw in three dimensions. All of the lines in a diagram are positioned in space, even though only two dimensions appear when they are printed on paper. This feature allows a solid model to be built up in the computer memory. Each surface can have colour and texture added to it so that it appears just as it will in the finished product. If a series of views are created from slightly different angles, then shown as a video sequence, it can be possible to seem to walk inside a building or any other object. This is known as 'virtual reality'.

Video images

With a fast computer, it is now possible to manipulate video images at their normal speed. The pictures themselves can be captured from a video recorder, a camera or a broadcast and stored on a computer disk. The computer system converts them immediately into digital format. The size of video files is enormous, and they have to be compressed so that they can be stored efficiently. Multimedia computers are specially equipped to display video clips on screen directly from a CD-ROM. In addition, special TV cards can be fitted to computers so that they operate as normal TV sets when required.

Video pictures can also be placed in documents in the same way as a still picture. When the document is opened, the text and the opening picture of the video clip is displayed. When the mouse is clicked on the picture, the complete video clip can be replayed.

Graphics files

There are two basic types of computer graphics – these are known as 'bit mapped' and 'vector' graphics. Bit mapped graphics are usually used in systems where the end product is a picture, a photograph or some other form of art. Vector graphics are normally used in technical drawing packages.

Bit mapped graphics

Pictures are made up of thousands of tiny picture elements called 'pixels'. A pixel is the smallest part of an image. Each one can be a different colour, and when they are viewed together they create the image we see on screen. The number of colours is determined by the number of bits (binary digits) allocated to a pixel by the computer hardware or software. Many modern computer systems use 24 bits for each picture element, giving the possibility of more than 16 million different colours on screen. With resolutions as high as this, the screen image is of photographic quality.

The only real problem with these images is that they are so detailed they take up enormous amounts of memory and disk space. The computer that has to manipulate them also has to be particularly fast so that the user is not left waiting while the computer changes the image on screen. Fortunately the latest generation of computers can manipulate images of this size almost instantaneously.

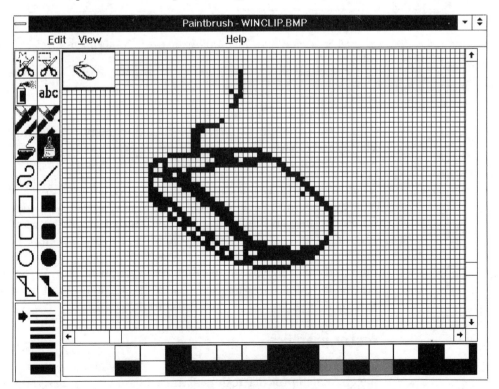

Figure 9.4 Creating a bit mapped image within a paint package

More advanced bit mapped drawing systems manipulate much finer detail by working with images containing thousands more pixels than the example shown in Figure 9.4. These handle photographs and professional designs and provide all of the special effects that graphic artists require. An example is shown in Figure 9.5

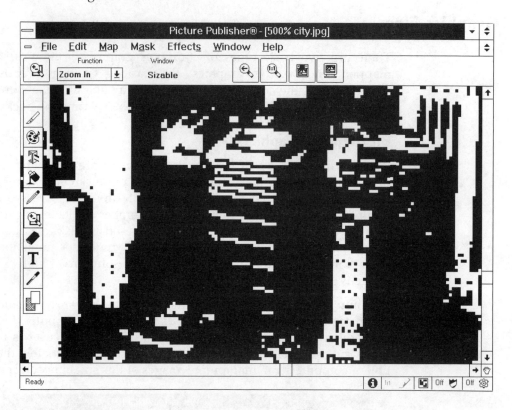

Figure 9.5 High resolution graphics picture of skyscrapers

Screen dumps

One of the most common bit mapped images is a picture of a computer screen printed on paper or as part of another document. These are useful to illustrate what may be happening in a computer system at any time. Most of the illustrations in this book were created in this way.

Capturing the image of the computer screen at any time is very easy with the Windows operating system. When the image is exactly as required, simply press the 'Prt Sc' key on the keyboard. This stands for 'print screen', and the image is transferred to the Windows clipboard. From there it may be viewed with the 'Clipboard Viewer' program or pasted into a document. To do this, open a document and place the insertion point at the required spot. Some systems may need a frame for the illustration. Choose the 'Paste' command from the menu and the previous screen image is transferred to the page.

Vector graphics

Vector graphics are usually used for CAD systems such as AutoCad and Auto Sketch, which produce technical drawings. They are based on mathematical representations of the picture as a series of lines or shapes. The pictures themselves on the screen of a computer are represented by a series of dots, but the positions of these dots are calculated from the underlying formulae for the lines and shapes in the image. Changes in the images such as sizing and scaling can be done mathematically, maintaining the accuracy of the data. In addition, calculations such as the distance between lines and the areas of parts of the drawing can be easily made.

The real difference is in the size of the data files created. The files created by a CAD package are relatively small and depend upon the size of the drawing they represent. In a bit mapped system, most of the graphics are about the same size and the files can be very large. These take up a lot of space on a computer disk and the files are frequently larger than a floppy disk can hold.

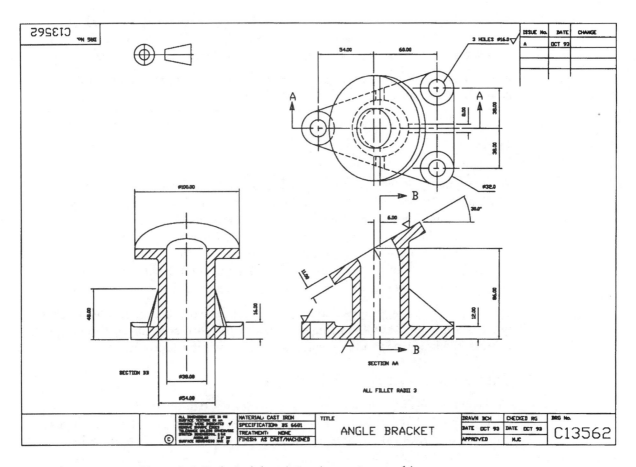

Figure 9.6 Technical drawing using vector graphics

Progress check

The following questions are designed to check your understanding of the concepts covered in the chapter so far. If you have any difficulty in answering them, refer to the text again rather than looking at the answers. Think about the graphics you have come across on a computer, and ask yourself how they were created.

1. Write down three examples of where you would find both text and graphics combined in a business or commercial setting.

2. What are the special features of a computer which make it possible to manipulate graphic images easily?

3. Give four examples of the types of image which may be handled by a computer.

4. What features of a CD-ROM make it suitable for storing pictures?

5. What must happen to video clips before they can be stored on a computer disk?

6. Explain the difference between vector and bit mapped graphics and give examples of the use of each one.

7. What is a 'screen dump'?

8. What is the difference between a high resolution picture and a low resolution picture?

9. Think of two illustrations that you will have to create as part of your vocational course. What software do you intend to use to create them? How do you plan to integrate them into other work in a consistent fashion?

If you would like to try to create some graphics using a word processor's drawing facility, try Assignment I at the end of this chapter now.

Creating graphics

There are many different graphics packages available – from the most basic such as Windows Paintbrush, PC Paint and IBM Drawing Assistant to very advanced types such as Corel Draw. Most word processors also have a built-in drawing package similar to those found in Ami-Pro and Microsoft Word. They are all relatively easy to use if only simple drawings are needed, but some of the more advanced features may take a lot of practice to master. Like all artistic tools, they need a good deal of practice before their use becomes second nature.

Not all packages have the same range of features, so it is a good idea to check what is available before starting to create a masterpiece. Check the range of colours, the line types and the features such as mirror, rotate and text.

Case Study – Windows Paintbrush

All Windows users will have access to Windows Paintbrush because it is supplied as part of the system. It can be used to create many different types of graphics which can then be inserted into any other Windows application, so it can be extremely useful.

The screen layout of Paintbrush is shown in Figure 9.7, with a drawing of a simple electronic circuit.

The screen layout is very similar to other Windows format screens, with a title bar at the top and a menu bar just below it. This contains the basic menu items 'File', 'Edit', 'View', 'Text', 'Pick', 'Options' and 'Help'. These each activate pull-down menus with the main commands.

To the left of the screen is the tool bar containing all of the basic drawing tools. These can be selected one at a time to create the drawing. The colour can be selected from the range at the bottom of the screen .

The drawing page itself contains a large number of tiny dots known as pixels.

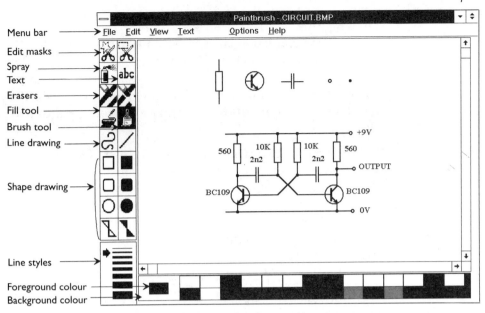

Menu bar
Edit masks
Spray
Text
Erasers
Fill tool
Brush tool
Line drawing
Shape drawing
Line styles
Foreground colour
Background colour

Figure 9.7 Screen layout in Windows Paintbrush

On the normal-sized page there are 800 × 545 or 436,000 pixels, although not all of them can be seen on screen at the same time.

Drawing tools on the tool bar

At the top of the tool bar there are two edit masks that allow parts of the picture to be selected for special treatment. For example, when part of the drawing has to be copied, it is first selected with the edit mask, and then the shift key is pressed once to copy it. Parts of the drawing can be moved just by surrounding them with the box and sliding them into the required place. The two edit tools allow different types of masks to be drawn, one with any shape, and the other a rectangle.

The spray can or airbrush is a painting tool which 'sprays' the 'active' colour, selected from the palette at the bottom onto the screen, in a series of dots. The more the spray is used, the thicker the colour becomes.

Text can be added to any picture with the text tool. All of the available Windows fonts are also available in this package, although this may not be true of other painting software. The text can be positioned anywhere on the screen and can be of many different sizes. More advanced graphics packages allow a much greater range of options with text. For example, Corel Draw allows text to be added to follow a curve or change in size as though it were disappearing into the distance.

Erasers are provided to correct mistakes. These can erase either everything or only a selected colour. Colour filling can be achieved using the roller. The active colour is used to fill enclosed areas of the drawing. Care must be taken when using this tool that there is no gap in the border of the shape or the fill colour will spill out and fill the whole page.

Most freehand drawing can be done using the brush. Its shape and size can be varied from a line to a circle and from a small dot to a large circle. It always paints in the 'active' colour, so this must be selected before the brush tool is selected.

Drawing tips

Line diagrams and similar objects can be drawn more easily with the line and shape drawing tools. These allow straight lines, rectangles, rounded rectangles, circles, ellipses and polygons to be drawn with ease. Each one can be drawn already filled with the active colour if required. If the shift key is pressed while the shapes are being drawn, rectangles become squares and ovals become circles.

By combining the drawing tools with the extra facilities in each of the menus, a very powerful set of drawing tools is available. Some of these features include, for example, the ability to shrink and magnify selected parts of a drawing. Larger versions of parts of a drawing can be added to give the impression of distance or three dimensions. Objects can be inverted or mirrored so that complex drawings that are symmetrical can be created by drawing only one half or even only a quarter of it.

Look again at the drawing in Figure 9.7. The simple electronic circuit was drawn with only the five shapes above it. Each one was drawn carefully, and then copied as often as necessary. The whole of the left part of the drawing was mirrored with the 'flip horizontal' command so it was an exact mirror image of the right-hand side. Once the drawing was complete, the lettering was added and these were moved carefully into exactly the right positions.

By careful use of the filled box tools, with either square or rounded corners, complex images can be built up by overlaying one box on top of another. Circles and filled polygon shapes can be used if rectangles are not sufficient for certain objects. Choose the foreground and background colours before drawing each shape so that the shapes which need a border have one in the appropriate colour.

Scanned pictures

More complex pictures can be scanned from other documents or photographs using a hand-held or desktop scanner. A hand-held scanner has a row of photosensitive devices inside it. It has to be used with some special software which translates the light from the scanner into a standard computer image. When the software is started, the scanner can be drawn over the surface of the image it has to capture. As it moves, the picture on the screen is built up into a complete image.

Some types of scanner software are very sophisticated and can allow a number of passes of the scanner over the same image. These can then be combined or 'stitched' into a much larger picture.

Hand-held scanners

A hand-held scanner is shown in Figure 9.8. The main advantages of these over desktop scanners are their price and ease of use, but they also have a number of disadvantages. They are best at scanning small pictures and have difficulties with anything the size of an A4 sheet of paper. They are not very good for scanning a lot of pages.

Figure 9.8 A hand-held scanner

Desktop scanners

Desktop scanners can be quite expensive, depending upon the resolution required. Some are capable of scanning colour images at a resolution of 1200 dots per inch. The only problems with this are that it is quite a slow process, the files created are enormous, and the scanner is very expensive.

Modestly priced desktop scanners can provide good quality pictures in full colour at a resolution of up to 600 dots per inch. Scanning an A4 page takes about a minute, but with the right software a high quality image can be produced. The process of capturing an image is simply a matter of laying the picture on the scanner glass, just like a photocopier, then selecting 'Scan' from the software controlling it. The scanner is controlled by the computer and the image is created in its memory automatically.

If you have access to a scanner and want to try it out now, have a go at Assignment 2 at the end of this chapter.

Optical character recognition (OCR)

One of the most useful features of a scanner is its ability to transfer the picture of a page of text into the computer in a matter of seconds. Unfortunately, the image is just a series of dots and can only be treated as a picture. However, some types of software can take the picture from the computer memory and attempt to recognise any letters or numbers from their shapes. This is called 'optical character recognition' (OCR) and is now so sophisticated that if a good quality typed document is scanned into the computer, the OCR software will recognise almost every letter perfectly. This can save hours of retyping – as long as there are not too many errors in the OCR.

Graphic file types

Unfortunately, as the technology of computer graphics has developed, many different ways of saving the images on disk have also been invented. Each method produces files which have a special extension for the file name, and each is used for different purposes. Some of them are:

.TIF   Tagged Image Format
.BMP   Bit map
.GIF   Graphics Image Format
.JPG   Joint Photographics Expert Group (JPEG)
.EPS   Encapsulated PostScript
.PCX   PC Paintbrush

Because all of the file types are different, they are incompatible with each other. This means that not all types can be read by every graphics program. When scanning a file with scanner software there is often a choice of file formats available since some programs can change one file type to another. Before scanning the picture, decide which file type you want by checking the types accepted by the destination program.

For example, if you wish to scan a picture to put into a document created with Word for Windows version 2, it would be best to have a file with a .PCX or .TIF extension. There would be no point asking the scanner to create a .JPG format file because it could not be read by that version of the software.

File sizes

Graphics images can be very large, particularly if they are in colour. This means that the computer will take a long time to process them unless it is a very high speed machine. It is possible to speed up graphics processing by observing a number of precautions.

- Try to keep the size of the image as small as possible.
- Only use colour if the final version will be printed in colour, otherwise change it to black and white as soon as possible.
- Use a scanning resolution which will be the same as the printed resolution. There is no need to scan at 300 dots per inch if the printer is only capable of printing 120 dots per inch.

With a smaller file, not only will the processing be much faster, but the amount of disk space taken up will also be reduced.

Printing pictures

The image on a computer screen and the picture on a sheet of paper when it is printed are not always exactly the same. The printed image depends very much upon the capabilities of the printer. No matter how good a picture may be, if it is printed on a poor quality printer the results will be disappointing.

Different types of printer were dealt with in detail in Chapter 1, but their main features as far as graphics are concerned are summarised below.

For pictures in black and white, the best quality can be obtained from a laser printer, followed closely by some of the modern ink jet printers. Dot matrix printers do not produce such high quality. However, they are popular because they are quite cheap and can produce some reasonable pictures with the right software. They can also use more types of paper than the other printers.

Colour pictures produced on colour ink jet printers are generally of acceptable quality, and are certainly better than those obtainable from most colour dot matrix printers. However, if price is no object, a colour laser printer will produce very high quality pictures. In some cases these are almost as good as the original photographs.

Dot matrix printers

Dot matrix printers were the most popular types of printer before the invention of the laser printer. They work by pressing a ribbon against the paper in a series of vertical dots as the print head moves across the paper. Many are still in every-day use because:
- they are relatively cheap
- they are able to print on cut sheet paper, fan fold wide music score computer paper, envelopes etc.
- they can print on NCR paper ('no carbon required') to give multiple copies of a printed document without the need for photocopying
- they are quite fast
- they can use a variety of fonts and also print graphics
- they can print on sticky labels.

However, the quality of graphics from dot matrix printers depends upon the number of dots used. Since these are limited by the size of the print needles, they are never likely to be as fine as the dots from an ink jet printer. Dot matrix printers can also be very noisy.

Ink jet printers

Monochrome ink jet printers are about as cheap as dot matrix printers and can produce near laser quality images and text. They work by squirting a series of tiny ink dots at the paper under computer control to form the letters and pictures. The mechanism can be made so small that ink jet printers can now be found built into lap top computers. They may be slightly slow, but this is balanced by the output quality. Ink jet printers:
- are relatively cheap
- can produce high quality text and graphics
- use A4 paper (although some can print on A3 and envelopes)
- print on sheets of labels
- are quiet in operation
- can print on transparencies.

Laser printers

The quality of the images and text from a laser printer is the best available on a desktop printer, and almost as good as the quality of some commercial printing machines. They work by attracting ink or toner onto the surface of a drum using a laser beam under computer control. It is then fused onto the paper as it passes through the printer. Laser printers have the following advantages:
- they produce very high quality printing
- they print largely on A4 paper (although some can use A3 and envelopes)
- quiet operation

- they can print on sheets of labels
- they can print on transparencies
- however, they are also the most expensive printers to buy and run.

Colour ink jet printers

The cheapest way of producing a colour image is to use a colour ink jet printer. These work in the same way as the black and white version, but have colour cartridges as well. They squirt dots of black, yellow, cyan and magenta ink at the paper. These coloured inks are combined in different proportions to make all of the other colours.

Unfortunately, the limitations of the printing process means that it is not always possible to create exactly the same colour on the paper as that seen on the computer screen. Special paper is needed for the best colour images, but normal paper can also be used.

Colour ink jet printers are particularly useful for presentations since they can produce very effective colour transparencies.

Colour laser printers

Although colour laser printers are very expensive, their price is bound to fall as they become more popular. They can produce colour pictures with almost photographic quality although this is a relatively slow process (typically four pages per minute). Inside they work like four laser printers. The paper passes through three different printing processes, one for each colour of yellow, cyan, magenta and black.

Problems with printers

If anything goes wrong with a computer system, it will probably be with the printer. This seems to be particularly true when printing a large graphics file. Before printing anything, always try to do two things:
- Check that the correct printer is selected
- Use the 'Print preview' facility, if one is available.

Most computers can be attached to different printers from a range of manufacturers. Unfortunately, they all require slightly different instructions to control them. This is the job of a program called a 'printer driver', which is found either as part of the application program or as part of the operating system. If you select the wrong printer from the list of those available, the wrong driver will be selected – with very unpredictable results!

If the printers are similar, this may only cause a few of the functions to work incorrectly but, in the worst case, totally meaningless rubbish will be printed. Some laser printers use a set of codes called 'PostScript' and you must be careful to choose a 'PostScript' printer driver in these cases.

Whatever you intend to print, it is always a good idea to choose a print preview on screen if possible. This can save a lot of time and paper. It can also remind you to check that the page orientation is correct. If you have selected a portrait format when the particular page is in landscape format, it can be very frustrating to get only half a picture printed.

Progress check

The following questions are designed to check your understanding of the last concepts covered. If you have any difficulty in answering them, refer to the text again rather than looking at the answers.

1. Investigate the software available on your computer system. Write down the names of the applications programs which will allow you to create graphics images. If you have a word processor, find out whether it can be used to create a drawing as part of a document.

2. What file types can be created with the graphics packages which you have available? Write down each three-letter extension which can be created as a default by the system.

3. What are the advantages of a hand-held scanner over a desktop version?

4. Why do graphics files tend to have many different formats?

5. If you wish to impress your audience with a colour transparency for a presentation, which type of printer would you choose?

6. In a simple graphics package such as Windows Paintbrush, how would you ensure that all the little mistakes, such as lines not quite meeting, were corrected?

7. What is the function of the 'grid' available in most drawing packages?

8. Why is a dot matrix printer preferable to a laser printer for some types of printing?

9. Why is it good idea to keep file sizes as small as possible when processing pictures on a computer?

10. What is the function of a 'printer driver'? Write down the names of the printers to which your computer may be connected by looking at the 'Print setup' menu.

If you would like to try some practical activities which will show your graphical abilities, and give you some practice with the software, try some of the exercises or assignments at the end of the chapter now.

Desktop publishing

Desktop publishing (DTP) is the term used to describe software which can produce documents ready for publishing on a desktop computer. Hundreds of documents are published every day, from simple publicity brochures to newspapers, magazines and books. Very few are created using the old methods, which involve typesetting the text and then sticking the illustrations in place on the pages. Most are now created on computer systems which are equally good at combining text, graphics, pictures and any other type of visual material.

These computers use DTP software which combines all of the features of the manual printer and typesetter with the convenience of computer technology. It could be more accurately described as 'page makeup and layout software'. The special features of DTP systems include:
- the ability to have any number of columns of text on a page
- the use of many different fonts and font sizes at any angle
- the ability to overlay text and graphics
- the ability to wrap text round graphics of any shape

- special bullets and highlights
- the use of transparent images
- colour separation for direct printing
- precision placement of all objects on a page
- the ability to deal with large documents.

DTP software

There are a number of special DTP software packages available, such as Aldus PageMaker, Serif Pageplus and QuarkXpress. Each of these has all of the features listed above and will produce professional quality page layout in the hands of an expert. Their basic features can be learned fairly easily, however, and so it is possible for most people to create a reasonable page layout with minimum tuition. Their more advanced features may take a long time to learn.

The opening screen of a typical package is shown in Figure 9.9

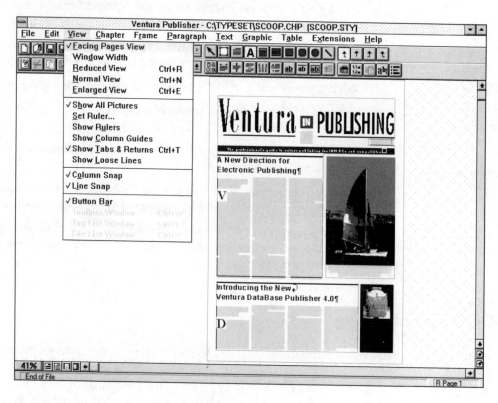

Figure 9.9 Ventura Publisher – a DTP package

Many of the most common features of DTP software are now incorporated in modern word processors. They allow multi-column work, can include pictures from many different sources and have a wide variety of fonts available. This has meant that for basic publishing, which does not require the sophistication of a complete DTP system, the work can often be done on a word processor.

If the exact page layout you require for your special project cannot be created with your word processor, you may need to try out a DTP package. It should allow you to combine text and graphics from almost any source and make up a professional looking page.

Transferring pictures to other applications

With DOS-based applications software it is very difficult to transfer pictures from one application to another. This is because they are mainly text based and only those specially designed to do so handle pictures very well. This is why DTP systems are the only real way of combining text and graphics in DOS-based computers.

Windows, and the Apple Macintosh, are designed around graphics instead of text, and so they can easily combine text and graphics in most applications. It is possible to include a picture in a database record, in a document or on a spreadsheet and they can be sent from one computer to another as easily as sending electronic mail.

When combining pictures with other files, be careful that the extra size of the picture does not slow down the application so much that it becomes unusable. If possible, arrange the settings so that pictures are not displayed on screen unless they are specifically required. This means that you can work with their outline box, but can ignore them until they are ready to be printed. It is always worth making at least one check to see that they are exactly as expected, however.

Frames and borders

If possible, include your pictures in a frame. This will allow you to alter the size and position of the picture very easily by repositioning its frame. Check the properties of the frame before the picture is added if possible. using a frame will also allow you to 'crop' the picture by cutting off any unwanted edges.

Borders do not have to be visible. They can often be selected to add emphasis to a picture, but in many cases the picture does not need an extra border so it can be switched off.

Why use graphics software?

Before computers could manipulate and print graphics easily, most pictures had to be created by hand then stuck in place on the page for display. It was almost impossible to create two colour copies of a picture without photography.

Now, with the ability of computers to scan, manipulate and print colour pictures just as easily as plain text, there is bound to be a boom in the use of illustrations in documents.

There are, however, some serious problems which mean that it is not always as easy as it is supposed to be. Some of these are:
- Many computers are still too slow to handle large graphic images quickly
- Very large computer memories are required, which can be expensive
- Exact colour matching between scanners, computers and printers requires very careful setting up and sophisticated equipment
- Photographic quality printing is very expensive
- The more specialised graphics software is quite difficult to learn.

Even with all these limitations, the advantages of using computers can still outweigh conventional techniques.

High speed publishing

An advertising brochure produced without a computer requires the text to be typeset on a special machine and then carefully placed in exactly the right position on a master page. Any colour images have to be produced as 'colour separations' which are versions of the picture used for the four ink colours (cyan, magenta, yellow and black). Colour information has to be supplied to the printer so that the exact colour ink can be used for each part of the brochure. The whole process may take several days.

In contrast, if a computer is used, the master can be created with DTP software in full colour on screen. The layout can be created very precisely so that there is no need for manual 'cut and paste' operations. If only a few copies of the brochure are needed they can be printed immediately. However, for a large run, the disk can be sent to the printer where it is used to control the printing process. The most up to date printers use electronic mail facilities to transfer the complete file over a telephone system direct to their office. This is how many of the books printed in the Far East are transferred around the world.

The main advantage of the electronic system is that there are great time savings, and this means the cost is also lower. Some of the cost savings are swallowed up in the price of the equipment, however. The speed of data transfer and manipulation mean that the computer based system is much more efficient than alternative methods. However, they do depend on reliable data transmission, which can be affected by poor quality telephone lines. Modern digital connections are much better.

Review questions

These questions are to help you review the ideas covered in this chapter. If you have any difficulty with them, refer back to the text rather than look in the answers.

1. Why are graphics important in any business? Give at least three reasons.

2. List some of the limitations of a basic painting package like Windows Paintbrush. What features are missing from the package you normally use which would be very useful?

3. How do colour graphics packages represent colours when printing on a monochrome printer?

4. Give two benefits of using a clip art library.

5. In what ways could the following professionals use computer graphics?
   - Architect
   - Estate agent
   - Teacher
   - Journalist
   - Industrial designer

6. What method would you use to include a picture, created with your usual graphics package, in one of your word processed reports?

7. If a scanner is used to create a computer copy of a picture, what precautions need to be taken before including it in a document?

8. What type of printer would be the best kind to use if you needed to make a black and white transparency for a presentation?

9. Why are DTP packages required when so many of their functions can be carried out by word processors?

10. Give three advantages and two disadvantages of the use of computer based graphic design over conventional methods.

Exercises

If you have access to a computer with graphics software, you may like to try the following exercises to help you make use of some of its features. Try to customise the exercises for your own use rather than follow them precisely. Experiment as much as possible by trying different software features so that you become familiar with as much of the software as possible.

The assignments will require a little more work and can be used to demonstrate some of the skills you have acquired in the use of graphics when they are applied to specific problems.

1. The most useful features of drawing software are usually the shape drawing tools because they allow complex drawings to be created very easily. Overlaying shapes is the key to many clever drawings. Create an image for the front of an assignment as follows.
   (a) Select black as the foreground colour and white as the background colour, then draw a filled rectangle with rounded corners in the centre of the page. This should result in a black rectangle on screen.
   (b) Select white as the foreground colour and black as the background colour, then draw another filled rectangle with rounded corners on top of the previous one so that only the bottom and right side of the previous shape can be seen. These form a shadow for the top shape.
   (c) Change the foreground and background colours back to black and white respectively. Choose a suitable font from the text menu, size 18 point or larger, then enter the title of the report or assignment. If the text is not quite centred, use the selection box to highlight it, then move it into the required position. Add the date, your name and course code wherever seems best, to complete the page.
   (d) Print the page. It should be similar to that shown in Figure 9.10

2. Many paint packages use the Shift key to force the lines to be exactly vertical, horizontal or at 45°, rectangles to be squares, and ellipses to be circles. This can be used to make accurate drawings. Draw a shaded cube as follows:
   (a) Draw a square on the screen using the rectangle tool while holding the shift key.
   (b) Using the line tool, draw a short line at 45° from the top right-hand corner upwards and to the right.
   (c) Select the line carefully with the selection box and copy it. Then paste it onto the other corners at the top and right side of the square. Join the ends of these lines to complete the cube.
   (d) Check that there are no gaps in the sides of the cube, then fill the top with a light grey colour, and the right side with a darker grey colour. Print the finished drawing.

3. Draw a picture similar to the one shown in Figure 9.11. The basic techniques are exactly the same as those used in the previous exercises. Use the shape tools rather than freehand drawing and carefully select the foreground and background colours. Alternatively, all the shapes can be drawn first then filled with the required colour.

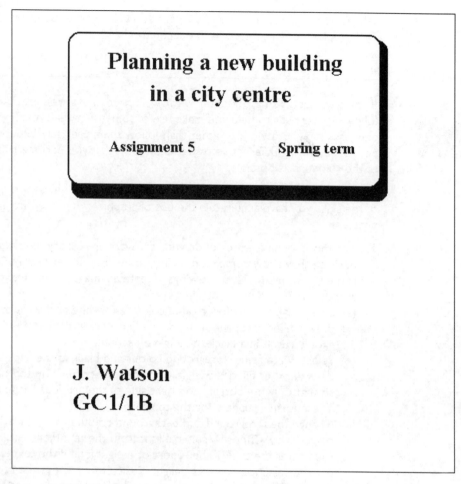

**Planning a new building
in a city centre**

Assignment 5   **Spring term**

**J. Watson
GC1/1B**

Figure 9.10 Example of an assignment front page

Figure 9.11 Simple drawing

4. Often you may need to illustrate what you see on a computer screen by providing a hard copy. The easiest way to do this is to produce a 'screen dump' then print it or import it as a picture into a word processed document. Some DOS-based systems may not allow screen dumps to be done without special software, but if you are a Windows user the process is very simple.

(a) Choose any Windows application and arrange the screen to contain the information you want to keep.

(b) Press the 'Prt Sc' or 'Print screen' key on the keyboard. This stores the contents of the screen on the Windows clipboard. You can use the clipboard viewer to check.

(c) Open a paint program such as Windows Paintbrush, and select 'Paste' from the 'Edit' menu. The image saved from the previous application should appear on the screen and this can then be edited or saved in the normal way. For example, bits of it may be cut out or changed in colour if required.

(d) When you are satisfied with the changes to the image, save it with a file name related to its contents and print a hard copy for reference.

5. Images can be imported into many types of document. Ensure that you have an image file on disk, then proceed as follows:

(a) Open a new document in your normal word processor, and write the title 'Example of a screen image' in the centre of the page. Now create a frame just below the title which will be large enough to hold the screen image saved from the previous exercise.

(b) Find the command to import the picture from the 'File' or 'Insert' menus. Import the file into the frame in the document, and save the document with a new file name. Change the frame size if necessary to accommodate the whole picture. Now add text below the image to describe the screen contents. You may need to be careful that the text does not get broken up and placed at the sides of the frame you have created, by choosing 'No wrap beside' in the 'Frame' menu. Save the completed document.

6. If you have access to a scanner, find a passport-sized photograph of yourself to scan into a simple identity card.

(a) Open your scanning software and set it up so that it will scan a small picture. You may need to preview a complete page with a desktop scanner, then select only a part of it for proper scanning. With a hand-held scanner one pass should be sufficient.

(b) Scan your picture, and check the quality on screen. If it is reasonable, save the image as a .BMP file, with a file name of your choice.

(c) If you wish, load the picture into your paint software and add your name below the image, then save and print it.

Assignment I starts on the next page

Assignment 1
Drawing an organisation chart

This assignment could provide evidence for the following Performance Criteria of the GNVQ Core Skills:

Element 2.1 PCs 1 to 4

Element 2.2 PCs 1, 2, 4, 5 and 6

Element 2.3 PCs 1 to 5

Element 2.4 PCs 1 to 4

Element 3.1 PCs 1 to 4

Element 3.2 PCs 1, 2, 4, 5 and 6

Element 3.3 PCs 1 to 6

Element 3.4 PCs 1 to 5

Introduction

The company where you work has just been reorganised and you have been asked to draw the new organisation chart to go into a report for the directors.
Your manager has left a rough outline of what is required but it needs to be tidied up. Each of the functions need to be enclosed in a box and they all have to be connected with lines to show levels of responsibility. The rough outline is illustrated in Figure 9.12.

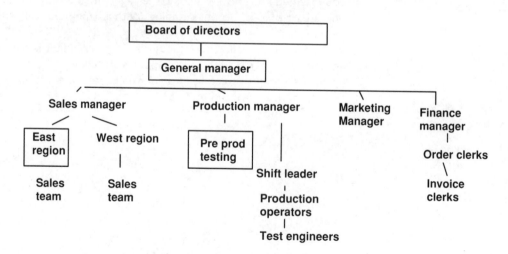

Figure 9.12 Rough organisation chart

Your task

1. The first task is to decide on the type of software to choose to do the drawing. Since it has to go into a report, it may be a good idea to use the facilities built into

a word processor. However, it may be quicker to try a graphics package. Write down the type of software you have chosen and your reason for doing so.

2. The chart in Figure 9.12 is very rough, so the first step is to draw it completely as a sketch. This will help you to estimate the size and layout better. Estimate how long it would take you to do the whole drawing on paper, then stick it into the report.

3. Use the drawing facilities of your computer to produce the chart required at the correct size for the page. Save the document regularly as you work, and choose suitable file names as you progress. Make sure you have a suitable backup. Make a note of any problems and try to find out their cause.

4. When the chart is complete, note the time taken to do it and compare this with the estimated time of the manual method.

5. Produce a neat printout of the drawing as part of a document and as a drawing centred on a page on its own.

Assignment 2
Scanning an image for a publicity handout

This assignment could provide evidence for the following Performance Criteria of the GNVQ Core Skills:

Element 2.1	PCs 1 to 4
Element 2.2	PCs 1, 2, 4, 5 and 6
Element 2.3	PCs 1 to 5
Element 3.1	PCs 1 to 4
Element 3.2	PCs 1, 2, 4, 5 and 6
Element 3.3	PCs 1 to 6

Introduction

A friend of yours is hoping to raise money for a local charity by cycling round a track for 12 hours non-stop. She has asked if you can help by designing a poster and a publicity leaflet. The leaflet will be a smaller version of the poster.

You decide to include a picture of a cyclist, but because they are quite difficult to draw, you want to scan one from a photograph.

Your task

1. First choose a suitable photograph, but be careful to avoid having to do too much alteration later.

2. Arrange to have access to a suitable scanner, of the desktop or the hand-held kind. You may need to ask for some help with the software at first, although most of it is easy to use after a little tuition.

3. Scan the picture into the computer's memory and check it carefully before saving it on disk. If the image is not very good, change some of the settings, such as the brightness or contrast and try again. Some software allows the image to be altered after it has been scanned, but it is always best to start with as good an image as possible.

   Select a suitable file name (one which you will be able to remember later) and note the file type. If you have a choice, choose a file type which can be read easily into your word processing software.

4. It may be necessary to change the picture in some way so that it is the right size or shape. Use the size and crop facilities in the software so that the picture is the required shape for the poster. If necessary, zoom into the image to make more delicate changes which improve the impression it creates.

5. Print out a copy of the picture by selecting a printer which will give you the quality of image you need. Use the 'Print preview' facility if possible.

6. If you are happy with the picture when it is printed, start your word processor and write the text for the poster. Create a frame in the place the picture is to go. It is more convenient to work on the poster without the image for as long as possible, since as soon as it is loaded, the smallest modifications are likely to take a long time.

7. Copy the picture into the frame created for it and check that it looks correct. It may be necessary to change its size or position slightly for the best effect. Save the file on disk with a suitable file name.

8. When you are happy with the results, print the complete poster onto A4 paper.

9. If the facility exists with your printer driver, print another version of the poster in landscape mode, reduced to 67% of the size of the previous version. This should then be about the right size for a handbill.

Collect your source material and the results of your work into a suitable folder. Include any intermediate work such as the pictures before cropping, etc.

Assignment 3
Using a clip art library

This assignment could provide evidence for the following Performance Criteria of the GNVQ Core Skills:

Element 2.1   PCs 1 to 4
Element 2.2   PCs 1, 2, 4, 5 and 6
Element 2.3   PCs 1 to 5
Element 3.1   PCs 1 to 4
Element 3.2   PCs 1, 2, 4, 5 and 6
Element 3.3   PCs 1 to 6

Introduction

You would like to buy a computer to help you with your studies, but cannot afford to buy a new one. You decide to advertise for one on the college notice board. To make a greater impact, you want to illustrate your notice with a picture taken from some clip art. You think there may be some included with the word processor software, or available on your computer network. The clip art must have an explanation of the specification needed beside it on the advertisement.

Your task

1. The first task is to find a suitable clip art picture of a computer to illustrate your advertisement. Since computers are fairly popular in most clip art libraries, you should not have too much difficulty in locating one. Try any clip art which comes with your word processor or DTP software. There may be more with any presentation software or in the large clip art libraries which come with some drawing packages.

2. When you have found something suitable, write down its file name and its directory.

3. Start your normal word processor or DTP package, and create a document for the advertisement. Set up an appropriate page layout and choose a font which will stand out. Save your choices as an 'Adverts' style. Save the document before the clip art is entered with a suitable file name, just in case you have any problems later.

4. Make a frame for the image in the required place and import it from the directory you noted by selecting its file name. Check that your word processor or DTP package supports the file type first.

5. When you are happy with the look of the final version, print a copy of the complete advertisement. Check that it looks the same as the version on the computer screen.

6. List any faults which occurred during the assignment in a way that would help others avoid them.

Collect separate copies of each of the items making up your notice, together with the combined results. Make notes on any special features of the word processing, DTP or graphics packages you have used to create the notice.

Assignment 4 starts on the next page

Assignment 4
Using a CAD package to create a simple drawing from a design brief, and analysing the results

This assignment could provide evidence for the following Performance Criteria of the GNVQ Core Skills:

Element 2.1	PCs 1 to 4
Element 2.2	PCs 1, 2, 4, 5 and 6
Element 2.3	PCs 1 to 5
Element 2.4	PCs 1 to 4
Element 3.1	PCs 1 to 4
Element 3.2	PCs 1, 2, 4, 5 and 6
Element 3.3	PCs 1 to 6
Element 3.4	PCs 1 to 5

Introduction

You have just received a design brief for an electromechanical device which your project team have been asked to draw. It contains some metal parts which must be drawn to scale. There is also a small electronic circuit board which has to be fastened inside.

No one is available to give you any advice on which computer software to use, so you have to pick some yourself.

Your task

1. The first task is to choose a suitable method of drawing the parts. First, produce a list of all the features you will need in drawing the parts. For example, will you need to show dimensions, draw in colour, draw in layers?

2. Produce a list of all the possible software packages available to you which include drawing facilities, and list their advantages and disadvantages. Some will be easy to use while others may be much more difficult and require a lot of training. This could be an important consideration.

3. On the basis of the features of each of the packages considered, choose one to use for the drawings. It may be necessary to choose more than one if all of the features you require are not all available in one application.

4. Create the drawings and file them with appropriate file names. Print two copies of each one. At the same time, write down any difficulties you had, either with the software or the equipment itself. For example, did the drawings come out exactly as expected, the right way round on the printer, the first time they were printed?

5. In the light of your experiences, would you choose to use the same software again for a similar task? Use one of the drawings to mark with some of the problem areas. For example, the text may have to be a fixed font or of a fixed size, the lines may not be the correct thickness or the dimensions may not be exactly correct.

APPENDIX A

Answers to questions

Chapter 1

Progress check page 10

1. (a) An architect would need a computer which had a lot of memory for the large programs used, and a high speed so that large drawings could be produced very quickly.

   (b) A travelling salesman would probably need a portable computer with battery powered operation. This may need to be connected to the office computer from time to time to transfer information.

2. (a) A garage owner may use a standard personal computer which would not need to be particularly fast. The main software used would probably include business accounting, customer billing and other customer records. It may also include order processing software so that spare parts could be ordered via the computer system.

   (b) The manager of a large company would probably need a computer which was reasonably fast, and which was connected to the main business computer via a direct link or a network. The important features required are the access to company information in a simple form, and the ability to use it to make business decisions. Software such as databases, spreadsheets, word processing and accounting software would usually be needed.

   (c) A graphic designer would need a very fast computer with plenty of memory. This is because programs which manipulate images tend to be quite slow since they have to handle large amounts of data. As well as the software to create and alter images, designers also need to write text, so a word processor would usually be needed.

   (d) A travel agent normally uses a computer to find out travel information from remote databases. These provide the latest booking advice as well as the flight and holiday availability. The computer itself does not need any special features other than the ability to be connected via a telephone line to another computer.

3. A computer operating system contains the programs which control the way in which the computer runs itself. For example, they control the operation of the keyboard, the display screen and the disk drives.

4. (a) Software
   (b) Hardware
   (c) Hardware
   (d) Software
   (e) Peripheral
   (f) Peripheral
   (g) Software
   (h) Peripheral
   (i) Software
   (j) Peripheral

5. The purpose of function keys depends upon the program operating at the time. They are special keys which can simplify the operation of many types of software by providing 'short-cuts' to certain operations.

Review questions page 22

1. The hotel manager would probably need to have access to the whole of the hotel booking system and all of the financial transactions. The computer package may have everything included in one piece of software or it may have separate modules. It is likely that financial planning would require the use of a spreadsheet and there may also be a need for some word processing software. The main peripheral apart from the keyboard and screen would be a good quality printer.

   The reception desk would need access to the booking system software including all of the billing information which may come from other computers in the hotel. A printer would be required to print bills on pre-printed stationery.

   The bar and restaurant would need computers mainly for billing purposes. They may be connected to the room allocation information from another computer so that customers could have their bills charged directly to their room number. They may need special printers to print bills on pre-printed stationery.

2. A hard disk is used to store large quantities of software. Most modern computers need a range of different programs and these are normally kept on a hard disk inside the machine. Not all computers need a hard disk. Some can work only with floppy disks but these are fairly rare. Others use a computer network instead of the hard disk to store their programs.

3. *Serial connection* is used for peripherals which either need information relatively slowly or are a long way away from the computer. They use only one pair of wires to pass data in each direction, although other wires are needed to synchronise the data.

   Parallel connections are needed for high speed peripherals. Data is passed over eight wires at the same time.

4. Networks allow computers to be connected to enormous quantities of information and computer programs. They allow printers, plotters and other peripherals to be shared. They permit electronic mail between users, and they make it easy to update software. They also make it easy to back up important work.

   Networks have the disadvantage that they require extra hardware and cable installation before they can work. Sometimes they can be unreliable and need regular maintenance.

5. If a computer is equipped with a modem, it is possible to connect it to the telephone network. Then, by dialling the right numbers and by using the correct passwords, it is possible to connect to computers all over the world.

6. *Dot matrix* printers are very cheap and can be used for almost any type of printing. They are particularly good for wide paper printouts of financial information or databases.

   Laser printers give the best black and white print quality so they are the most popular office printer.

   Ink jet printers are the most useful for printing colour transparencies or any other type of colour printing within a limited budget.

7. A scanner is used to transfer pictures or typed information into a computer.

The scanner is most often used for pictures so that this could be a great help in the production of a report. With optical character recognition software the scanner can also be used to save a lot of typing.

Chapter 2

Progress check page 39

1. Computers need an operating system so that they can operate themselves. Three of the functions an operating system performs are reading keystrokes from the keyboard, displaying them on the screen and sending data to the printer. In addition they respond to the mouse movement and, most importantly, they store and retrieve data from the computer disk storage system.

2. In MS-DOS file names can have only eight characters before a full stop and three after it. They cannot be any of the special reserved words which the operating system uses, such as COM or LPT, and they cannot contain spaces or some punctuation marks.

3. The first part of a file name is chosen by the user and can be anything. It is needed so that the file can be identified later. The second part of the file name may be chosen by the user but it may also be added by the computer in some cases. It is often used to indicate the type of file, such as a document, spreadsheet or image.

4. The tree-structured directory improves efficiency because it allows the computer to find the files it needs quickly. If the files are all stored together in one directory, the search process is shorter than if the files are scattered all over a large disk.

5. It has to be formatted. This can be done by running the formatting program on the computer with the new disk inserted in the disk drive.

6. To store all of the files related to a particular project or assignment for example.

7. In the MS-DOS operating system, use the 'Copy' command COPY C: REPORT.HDR A:. With Windows, use the File Manager program. Click on the file to be copied then drag it to the 'A: drive' icon.

8. Windows is a popular operating system because it is very easy to learn and most of the applications programs which operate with it behave in a similar way.

9. Certainly a word processor, a spreadsheet, a graphics package and probably a database. Other more specific applications may also be used, such as an accounting program or a computer aided design program.

10. A file attribute is a special characteristic which allows the file to be hidden, or which prevents it from being overwritten. It can also indicate that a file is a special system file or that it has not been backed up.

Progress check page 45

1. The first program the computer operates when it is switched on is the AUTOEXEC.BAT file. By altering the contents of this file the computer can be made to do anything the user requires at switch-on.

2. This depends upon whether or not the disk in drive A: has any operating system programs on it or not. If not, an error message will appear. Some computers may ignore drive A: altogether when they are first switched on.

3. Use the mouse dialog box in the Windows Control Panel.

4. Different preferences, the ability to use different screens and the need for different displays to be able to alter their colour schemes for the best

display. For example some colour schemes look much better on a mono-chrome display.

5. A printer driver converts the basic output of an applications program or operating system into the right form for the type of printer used.

7. A 'PostScript' printer is one which takes a certain type of coded instruction which enables it to print many types of graphics and many different fonts. Most 'PostScript' printers are laser printers.

Review questions page 49

1. There are no commands built into the operating system of MS-DOS to control the mouse.

2. File names can have up to eight characters, a full stop, then a three-character extension. There are certain punctuation marks which cannot be included, such as , . ; : ? ' and spaces. Reserved words, such as LPT, COM and CON, must not be used.

3. Windows is a graphical system which can be operated without having to remember any commands. Everything appears on the screen in the form of icons. All Windows software behaves in the same way so that once one applications program has been learned the others will operate in the same way. This results in greater user efficiency because it requires a shorter learning time and is easier to operate. Some operations are much faster in Windows than DOS.

5. Each printer needs to have its own printer driver loaded into the computer operating system. When this is done, each printer can be chosen to receive the printed output and it will be sent the right type of data.

6. Different directories are very useful if a number of projects are being studied at the same time. Each one can have its own directory and the files can therefore be kept tidy.

8. Check that the file name which the computer could not find had been typed correctly. If it has, check that the correct directory was being searched.

9. Computers break down at the most inconvenient moment, they can sometimes corrupt files for no apparent reason and sometimes fail to read disks properly. It is therefore a good idea to keep two copies of any files you need. If one computer corrupts your file or if you cannot retrieve it because of a fault you can use the backup copy in another computer and save a lot of time.

10. A password for a computer helps to keep the data on its hard disk secure. Alternatively, a password for a network system prevents any unauthorised access to sensitive information.

Chapter 3

Progress check page 66

1. Top, bottom, left and right margins, centring, indents and tabs.
3. (a) Words from one line are automatically placed on the next line by the word processor.
   (b) Line lengths are adjusted so that the right margin is straight.
   (c) The shape of the letters.
   (d) Moving the text up or down the screen so that the desired part can be seen.
5. When producing a multi-chapter document.
6. To print a document which will be bound, or for special effect.

Progress check page 72

1. Each word processor will be different but the main methods include bold, underlined and italic characters, changes in point size, font and colour (in some systems). Some other more unusual methods include changes in line and character spacing, double underlines, using spaces around text and the addition of borders or coloured backgrounds.

2. The speed of error correction and the ease with which text can be formatted and presented exactly as it will appear on a printer.

4. In a formula or as part of an equation.

5. Bold letters, underlining and centring, indentation and the use of tabs. Margins have also been set for the top, bottom, left and right of the page.

Progress check page 76

2. Style refers to the font, the font size, the justification and special characteristics of a paragraph.

3. Letters, memos, reports and faxes, to name but four.

4. The size of the text, the margins and the type of printer to be used to produce it.

6. Ensure that the words to be replaced are specified precisely and that you use the opportunity to check each one if possible.

7. The group of letters or other characters which the word processor looks for in the document when performing a search operation.

Review questions page 81

2. Business efficiency can be improved with a word processor by reducing the time taken to type any correspondence. This includes single letters but, more particularly, the same letter personalised for many different people. The word processor also makes it possible to create simple drawings, charts and pictures in documents that would have had to be assembled by 'cut and paste' methods in the past.

   Efficiency can be reduced if inappropriate equipment is employed, such as printers that need constant attention before they create good results. More time can be spent in trying to get a good copy than in typing a letter in the first place.

3. A word processor can be an advantage when writing a CV because the layout can be varied to ensure that it looks impressive. The content can also be varied as your experience changes or as you want to emphasise different points. Some companies ask for a hand-written letter of application because they think that they can tell a lot about a person from their handwriting.

4. Not all printers can produce all of the effects available in a word processing package. The highest quality is obtained with a laser printer, but you are unlikely to be able to have access to one that prints in colour.

5. Frames are used to contain elements of a document such as pictures, or tables that need to be positioned accurately on a page. They can improve the page layout because they can easily be moved to give a pleasing effect.

7. Ensure that the pictures are created by the word processor software itself or that they are in a file format which the word processor can accept.

Chapter 4

Progress check page 96

1. Tables are needed in word processors because they can simplify the production of all types of tabulated text, not just that which contains numbers. Often the best layout for information is in the form of a table.

4. Use the tab facility to line up the text and the numbers on the page. Left-justified tabs will normally be needed for the text, and right-justified or decimal tabs for the numbers.

Progress check page 107

1. Page layout, page numbering, indexing, spelling and grammar. They can also make the operation of producing an assignment much more efficient by making it easier to correct mistakes and by helping to organise the layout.
2. The best quality printing normally comes from a laser printer, although some ink jet printers are almost as good. If a dot matrix printer is used, the quality will be good, but not as good as the others since the size of the dots it creates are larger.
3. (a) Laser or ink jet.
   (b) Dot matrix.
   (c) Colour ink jet.
   (d) Laser.
   (e) Dot matrix.
   (f) Any type with the correct type of labels.
4. 300 dots per inch, although some modern lasers can achieve 600 dots per inch.
5. (b) and (c). A PostScript laser printer will not work directly from some programs if the correct printer drivers are not available.
6. To hold the page number. It may also be used for the document or chapter title.
7. Use the 'Page preview' facility of your word processor if it has one.
8. Alignment of the text is the biggest problem. Vertical alignment can be achieved by printing on exactly the right line number or by using text in frames. Horizontal alignment requires the correct use of tabs.
9. Outlining a document allows the main ideas to be organised before the main typing starts. It also allows a large document to be easily subdivided if several authors are involved.
11. The page numbers must be continuous. There are both automatic and manual methods which can be used to achieve this.
12. A file with the master document or template and another with the database of information to be inserted in it.

Review questions page 110

1. There are a number of disadvantages, including:
   • Different types have different features, which must be learned.
   • They cannot be used to print on paper that cannot go through a printer, for example folded forms.
   • They are generally very slow if graphics are included in a document.
   • Printing at angles is very difficult.
6. Create a personal dictionary.
7. Decide on the page layout, font size and type, indentation conventions for paragraphs, body text, headings, etc., headers, footers and other layout conventions. Then ensure that all the chapters follow these design rules.
8. It speeds up the typing process, improves the accuracy of documents and reduces retyping. Some word processors can allow documents to be sent by electronic mail.

Chapter 5

Progress check page 127

1. Electronic databases have greater storage capacity for a given size, more rapid retrieval and the ability to analyse data which manual systems do not have. Card index systems are simple to set up and do not require a computer, so they are relatively cheap.
2. (a) A record is one complete set of data relating to a single entry in the database.
   (b) A view is a selection of a number of fields from the database.
   (c) A field is part of a record which holds one item of data.
   (d) Data types are the kind of data that can be stored, such as numbers, characters, dates.
3. They are entitled to access personal information held about them on a database, although it may involve a fee being paid. If the information is incorrect, they have the right to have it corrected or erased.
4. (a) Decide on the descriptions of the data which needs to be kept.
   (b) Choose suitable field names and sizes together with the types of data to be stored.
   (c) Create the database using the chosen structure then enter the data.
5. The size of the computer disk to keep it on.
6. Ensuring that the data held is correct. It may be achieved by ensuring that checks are made on the values being entered. Sensitive data can be entered twice and double checked.
8. The width of the screen and the number of characters it can display along a line.
9. A report can display database information in a more convenient way with headings, sub-headings and totals of columns, etc.

Review questions page 136

1. The size of the field and the number of decimal places.
2. By selecting only the data which meets certain conditions, the database can be used to analyse the data it contains and provide answers to questions which would be otherwise very difficult to obtain.
3. To provide statistics for opinion polls and the views of a section of the country on recent political events.
4. *And* and *or* are logical operators. They are used to select data that meets more than one condition.
5. *Sorting* reorganises the records in a database. *Creating an index* allows the data to be displayed or listed in a chosen order very quickly without reorganising the records.
6. The order they were entered. If a secondary index exists, the order is determined by its sequence.
7. If a postcode is part of the last line of an address some space may be saved on disk. However, it will be very difficult to select records on the basis of the postcode unless it is held as a separate field.
8. Data can be analysed correctly only if all the entries are coded in the same way for the same answers.
9. A computer, a modem and a connection to a telephone line. In addition suitable software would be needed and the correct accounts with the data providers and the telephone company.

Chapter 6

Progress check page 148

1. A report presents fields from selected records in the database in a convenient format. It can group the records in various ways according to the users' requirements.

   A student database may provide reports such as
   - Lists of students by course
   - Lists of students by age
   - Total of students by department
   - Fees paid per student.

2. In commercial databases, the most common way to extract data is via a report. The database is usually too big to print all of the records so reports print only those which meet the selection criteria. Deciding the selection criteria and the layout of the resulting report is a very time consuming operation, so most software suppliers provide the most obvious reports for the customers as part of the package.

3. First link the report to a database or selected records from it, by opening the database. This is vital since the system can then present the available fields to be placed on the report template.

   Next, design the report template. This is achieved by placing the field names in the detail section of the report. Other fields, headings or text are then placed in the page, group or report header sections of the template.

   When the template has been designed, the report can be produced by executing the command that replaces the field names with the data from the database.

4. The *page header* appears on every page and can contain information such as the report title and the page number or date.

   The *detail section* contains the data extracted from the database in the selected fields.

   The *report summary* can contain totals for the columns that need to be added and other information relating to the report as a whole.

6. A word processor is generally used for mailing labels if the number of records in the database is relatively small and is kept mainly for the purpose of keeping addresses. It can therefore be quite quick and easy to produce a small number of labels.

   If the name and address are part of a much larger database, then it is better to use proper database software. This will make the full range of facilities available to the user, such as the creation of forms, reports, labels, indexes. However, for a simple name and address it·may be more complicated than necessary.

7. A laser printer or an ink jet printer.

8. Name badges, video labels, shipping labels, pricing labels, filing labels and address labels.

9. Ensure that the size of the labels and their spacing is exactly the same on the paper as the settings in the software. Also make sure that the first label prints in the correct place and that there is no slippage between labels on the same sheet.

Review questions page 159

1. Database information may be transferred to a word processor to include in a report or to merge with a form letter for a mail-merge operation.

3. Integrated IT packages such as Microsoft Works allow data to be transferred very easily between different applications such as the word processor, database, spreadsheet or graphics parts of the software. The data format is arranged to make the transfer straightforward. In addition, the transfers may be quicker since a change of package is not required.

   The disadvantage of the integrated package is that each part of the system may not be as powerful as the separate products. For example, the word processor in an integrated package may not include a grammar checker, and the charting facility of the spreadsheet may include only a limited set of charts.

4. A *flat database* holds all of its information in a single table. All the information for an entry is held in a single record. A *relational database* has a number of tables. Each one holds information on different aspects of the data entries.

5. A relational database is more efficient than a flat database because most data is held only once. The systems described by a relational system can be much more complex than simple databases. By joining the tables of a relational system in different ways, very complex queries can be executed which can may not have been anticipated when the database was designed.

7. A macro permits the operations of a database to be automated.

9. CD-ROMs can store much more data than any other portable system. Each one stores the equivalent of 450 floppy disks. Therefore they can be used for massive amounts of data, for sound, pictures and video. These applications are bound to increase.

11. A computer, a modem, a telephone line and some software are basic requirements. In addition you will need to know what number to call and may need to have a password ready.

12. Many types of data including text, sound, pictures and video, as well as computer programs.

13. A telephone charge (although this may only be a local charge), a connection charge (which depends upon the time of day), a data transfer charge if you wish to copy any blocks of information.

Chapter 7

Progress check page 177

1. The basic purpose of a spreadsheet is to help make complex calculations much easier, especially where there are many interrelated operations to do.

2. (a) The 'box' where the data is entered on a spreadsheet. It is where the rows and column meets.
   (b) The highlighted cell. It is where the data being entered appears.
   (c) A group of cells adjacent to each other.
   (d) A horizontal line of cells stretching across the spreadsheet.
   (e) A numerical relationship involving cell numbers and arithmetic operators.

3. • Use the cursor (arrow) keys to move along and down.
   • Use the mouse to move the active cell.
   • Use the 'Goto' function (F5), and enter D1266.

   The third method would be the quickest.

4. In cell C12 enter the formula =A17.

5. Numbers must line up so they are not misunderstood. Good layout means that the spreadsheet is easier to interpret.

For example, use the same number of decimal places in related numbers, choose appropriate column widths and use borders to highlight important information.

6. Because the letters are left justified, and the figures are right justified.

8. Complex calculations can be done much more quickly than they otherwise could. Small changes can be done almost instantaneously.

Review questions page 186

1. Reduce the column width, reduce the margins, reduce the font size or scale the whole spreadsheet.

2. To do more advanced calculations such as to 'Sum' numbers, to 'Round' up to the nearest whole number or to use 'Mod' to find the remainder after a calculation.

4. They are changed, unless a $ sign is placed before the cell reference row or column.

5. It is easier to understand the formulae, and easier to see what the spreadsheet is calculating, perhaps many months later.

6. To prevent important parts of the spreadsheet being changed, and ruining its operation.

7. Select the required 'print area' first, then select 'Print'.

Chapter 8

Progress check page 199

1. These vary but are likely to include DATE(), which gives the serial number of a specified date, NOW(), which gives the current date and time. DAY() converts a data serial number into the date.

3. One

4. (a) A bar chart, column chart or a pie chart for each question.
   (b) A line chart.
   (c) A column chart or a line chart.

5. When there are three quantities that all affect the results to be plotted. Sometimes three-dimensional charts can be used purely for added interest even with only one or two variables.

6. In one part of a spreadsheet with no spaces between cells and headings above each column.

Review questions page 207

1. Decide whether the main operation to be carried out is a set of calculations or a data storage and retrieval problem, or a written document. If the main operation is a complex set of calculations with a small data manipulation included, choose a spreadsheet. If most of the activity will involve data manipulation with only a few calculations, choose a database. If the main element is text processing, choose a word processor.

   In either case, before starting, make sure that the application chosen is capable of performing all of the functions required.

4. The spreadsheet may not accept the data directly from the spreadsheet, so it may have to be saved as a text file first. Some spreadsheets need special translation programs to allow this to take place. The document has to be set up properly before the data is included using TABS to fix the column widths.

7. (c).

9. A macro automates the operation of a spreadsheet. Macros can be used to combine data from several spreadsheets, format reports in a certain way, run other programs to provide extra features, etc.

10. Reduce the margins, change the column widths, reduce the font size, or use the built-in reduction feature that some spreadsheets include. Changing to landscape mode may also help in some cases.

Exercises page 208

1. Cell C2 contains `=IF(B2>A2,B2,A2)`
   Cell D2 contains `=SUM(A2:C2)`

3.

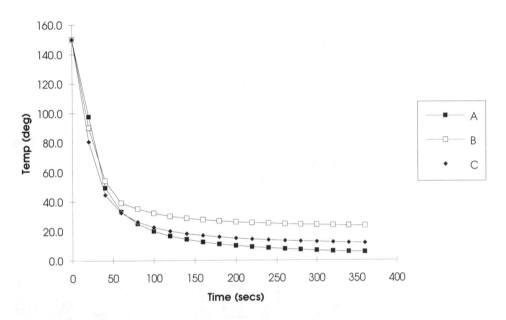

Figure A.1 Chart created from the data in Figure 8.16

7.

```
Region (r)
=OPEN("C:\EXCEL\LEEDS.XLS")
=SELECT("R1C1:R8C5")
=COPY()
=ACTIVATE("AREA.XLS")
=SELECT("R3C1")
=PASTE()
=ACTIVATE("LEEDS.XLS")
=FILE.CLOSE()
=OPEN("C:\EXCEL\YORK.XLS")
=SELECT("R1C1:R8C5")
=COPY()
=ACTIVATE("AREA.XLS")
=SELECT("R12C1")
=PASTE()
=ACTIVATE("YORK.XLS")
=FILE.CLOSE()
=VLINE(10)
=SELECT("R21C1")
=RETURN()
```

Figure A.2 Macro

Assignment 2 – Outline solution

THE CUSTOMER SURVEY
The survey results were obtained from a random sample of customers who had spent at least three hours in the theme park. Opinions from all members of a family were taken into consideration.

Each survey form was classified according to the time of year, and the results below represent the totals for one day in June.

Ride	Loved it	Liked it	OK	Disliked it	Hated it
Monster Looper	231	180	117	65	70
High Rapids	50	212	359	87	99
House of Horrors	38	75	191	226	164
Round and About	126	316	267	71	20

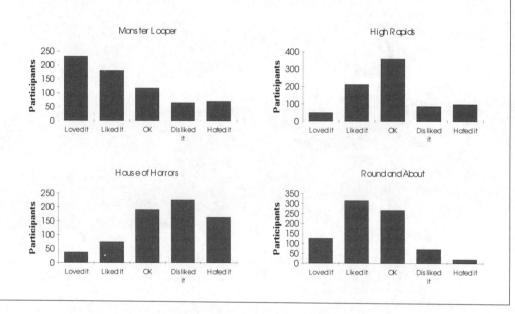

Figure A.3 Outline solution

Chapter 9

Progress check page 223

1. Advertisements, brochures, posters, logos, working drawings, staff bulletins.
2. High speed processing, large memory, mouse driven software.
3. Technical drawings, line drawings, photographs, clip art and, with modern computers, video.
4. Large storage capacity and relatively high data transfer speed.
5. They must be stored as digital images then compressed so they do not take up too much space.
6. *Vector graphics* store the drawing as a series of mathematically defined lines. Vector graphics are used mainly for computer aided design since calculations can easily be made on the drawing and the size of the files can be kept

as low as possible. This method also allows easy scaling and other more advanced design features such as rendering.

Bit mapped graphics store the drawing as a series of coloured dots. They are associated with the artistic use of graphics where the important features are the ability to manipulate colours and style.

7. A screen dump is a copy of the computer screen saved as a picture.
8. A high resolution picture has more pixels than a low resolution picture.

Progress check 231

3. Hand held scanners are much cheaper than desktop versions and are very easy to use. They can be used in some situations which may be difficult for other types, such as in scanning a picture from a thick book.
4. Because they have been devised by different people for different purposes, and have had to be updated as the technology has changed.
5. A colour ink jet printer.
6. By zooming in to the picture and correcting the drawing pixel by pixel.
7. To make it easy for users to line up different parts of their drawing.
8. Because most laser printers cannot print on wide paper or create NCR copies.
9. So that processing takes place faster.
10. Printer drivers contain the programs to make each type of printer work correctly when connected to the computer.

Review questions page 234

1. Graphics are important because they can create any image a business wishes to create. This can be part of the company logo or its 'house style'. Graphics are vital for advertising and they are also important for internal communications, such as reports.
2. There is a restricted range of colours available, limited line types and only basic drawing features. The resolution of the image is designed for the computer display, so it cannot provide good photographic quality when printed. Some features such as sizing and scaling are missing, as is the ability to rotate parts of the image.
3. They are represented by a series of dots in a fixed pattern to simulate the brightness of the colour.
4. Using a clip art library saves a lot of time in drawing pictures. The images are usually of very good quality and they create a very professional appearance.
5. *Architect*   to create working drawings.
    Estate agent   to produce house details, including photographs.
    Teacher   in presenting information as transparencies or handouts.
    Journalist   to create page layouts on screen for publication.
    Industrial designer   to create computer models of new products.
7. Make sure the file type created by the scanning software can be accepted by the word processor or desk top publishing software. Make sure the file is as small as possible.
8. Either a laser printer or an ink jet printer.
9. They can perform much more complex page layout than the basic features provided in a word processor. Anything which requires specialist layout, such as multiple overlapping images or shaded text, will need a DTP package to lay out the page correctly.
10. *Advantages*: Speed of processing, easy import of all types of images, special effects which are difficult to do by hand.

Disadvantages: Expensive software and hardware, and the tendency to be limited in imagination by what the computer can do.

Exercises page 235

2.

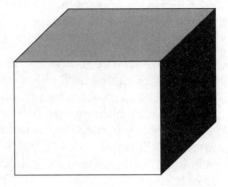

Figure A.4 The completed cube

GNVQ Core Skills Units – 1995

Information Technology Levels 2 and 3

Note: *indicates level 3 only

Elements 2.1 and 3.1: Prepare information

Performance criteria
1. **Select information** appropriate to the task.
2. **Enter information** into **software** in ways that will make it easy to edit.
3. Keep source **information** required for the task.
4. **Store input systematically** and make backup copies.
5.* **Configure software** to aid input of information

Range
Select: Information taken from existing sources, information developed during input.
Information: Text, graphics, numbers.
Enter: Inputting source information accurately, making immediate corrections to errors noticed on entry, putting right simple equipment faults, asking for help as appropriate.
Software: For text, for graphics, for numbers.
Store input systematically: Naming files sensibly to indicate the contents, locating files conveniently for subsequent use, creating and using directories to group related files: saving work before and after important changes, saving work when all the information has been input.
Configure software*: Creating style sheets for text input, creating spreadsheet templates, creating database structures

Elements 2.2 and 3.2: Process information

Performance criteria
1. **Find information** required for a task.
2. Use appropriate **software** to **edit information**.
3. Process numerical **information** by using **software** to **make calculations**.
4. **Reorganise information** as required for the task.
5. Save work at **appropriate intervals**.
6. **Combine information** from different sources, resolving differences in format.
7.* Create automated routines that aid efficient processing of **information**.

Range
Find: By looking in the right directory, by looking for files with a given name, by searching for information which meets specified criteria, *by accessing remote sources.
Information: Text, graphics, numbers.
Software: For text, for graphics, for numbers.
Edit: Amending, moving, reformatting, copying, deleting inserting.
Make calculations*: By creating totals in databases or spreadsheets, by using

formulas incorporating absolute and relative references to spreadsheet cells.

Reorganise: Sorting, restructuring stored information.

Save work: At regular intervals, before and after important changes, when processing is complete.

Appropriate intervals: Before and after important changes, when processing is complete.

Combine: Importing information of the same type, import information of a different type.

Elements 2.3 and 3.3: Present information

Performance criteria

1.* **Prepare information** for presentation.
2. Present **information** in different ways which best meet **requirements** of the task.
3. Use appropriate **software** to display **information**.
4. Use appropriate **software** to produce hard copy of **information**.
5. Present combined **information** in a consistent format.
6. Store **information** in files and make backup copies.

Range

Prepare*: Selecting the form and content of the information to match the requirements of the task, date-stamping and paginating documents, using named directories for associated display files, storing successive developments of information for presentation with version numbers and informative file names.

Information: Text, numbers, graphics.

Requirements: Fitness for purpose, matched to audience, clarity, accuracy, consistent format.

Software: For text, for graphics, for numbers.

Elements 2.4 and 3.4: Evaluate the use of information technology

Performance criteria

1. Explain and justify the reasons for using information technology.
2. **Compare** the **methods** used by the student and by others for preparing, processing and presenting information.
3.* **Evaluate** alternative **systems** for managing information.
4. Describe the software facilities used to meet the requirements of the task.
5. Explain the effects on users of **problems** that can occur when using information technology.
6. Explain the importance of **working safely** and in line with good working practices.

Range

Compare: In terms of speed, ease of use, effort, accuracy.

Methods: Manual, alternative ways of using information technology.

Evaluate*: Effectiveness, cost, effects on employment, benefits (to individuals, to organisations), disadvantages (to individuals, to organisations).

Systems: Manual, information technology.

Problems: Errors, equipment faults, loss of information.

Working safely: Safety of the user, safety of the equipment, safety of the information.

APPENDIX C

Elements and Performance Criteria (PCs) which can be covered by the assignments in the book

Elements		2.1 Prepare information				2.2 Process information						2.3 Present information					2.4 Evaluate the use of IT				
PCs		1	2	3	4	1	2	3	4	5	6	1	2	3	4	5	1	2	3	4	5
		3.1 Prepare information					3.2 Process information							3.3 Present information						3.4 Evaluate the use of IT		
Chapter	Assignment	1	2	3	4	5	1	2	3	4	5	6	7	1	2	3	4	5	6	1	2	3	4	5	6
1	1																			√		√			
1	2																								√
2	1				√																				
2	2																			√	√		√	√	
2	3																				√		√	√	
2	4	√	√	√	√	√	√	√		√	√		√										√	√	√
3	1	√	√	√	√		√	√		√	√	√		√	√	√	√		√		√				
3	2	√	√	√	√	√	√	√		√	√		√	√	√	√	√	√	√		√				
3	3	√	√	√	√	√	√	√		√	√		√	√	√	√	√	√			√				
4	1	√	√	√	√		√	√		√	√		√	√	√	√	√	√	√	√	√	√		√	√
4	2	√	√	√	√		√	√		√	√		√	√	√	√	√	√	√	√	√				
4	3	√	√	√	√		√	√		√	√		√	√	√	√	√	√	√	√	√	√		√	√
5	1	√	√	√	√	√	√	√		√	√		√	√	√	√	√	√	√	√	√	√		√	√
5	2	√	√	√	√	√	√	√		√	√		√	√	√	√	√		√	√	√	√		√	√
6	1	√	√	√	√	√	√	√	√	√	√		√	√	√	√	√		√	√	√	√		√	√
6	2	√	√	√	√	√	√	√		√	√		√	√	√	√	√		√	√	√	√		√	√
6	3	√	√	√	√		√	√		√	√	√		√	√	√	√	√	√	√	√	√		√	√
7	1	√	√	√	√	√	√	√	√	√	√		√	√	√	√	√		√						√
7	2	√	√	√	√	√	√	√	√	√	√		√	√	√	√	√		√		√	√			
8	1	√	√	√	√	√	√	√	√	√	√	√	√	√	√	√	√	√	√		√	√	√		
8	2	√	√	√	√	√	√	√	√	√	√	√	√	√	√	√	√	√	√	√	√	√			
8	3	√	√	√	√	√	√	√	√	√	√	√	√	√	√	√	√		√	√	√	√			
9	1	√	√	√	√	√	√	√		√	√	√		√	√	√	√	√	√	√	√	√	√	√	
9	2	√	√	√	√		√	√		√	√	√		√	√	√	√	√	√						
9	3	√	√	√	√		√	√		√	√	√		√	√	√	√	√	√						
9	4	√	√	√	√		√	√		√	√	√		√	√	√	√	√	√	√	√	√	√	√	

Index